MICHAEL
BOLTON

MICHAEL BOLTON

The Passion, Secrets, Soul & Truths

By Layne Seeloff, Elizabeth Seib,
Margaret Eaton & Joyce Logan

Lifetime Books, Inc.
Hollywood, Florida

Library of Congress Cataloging-in Publication Data

Michael Bolton : the passion, secrets, soul, and truths / Layne A. Seeloff . . . [et al.].

       p. cm.

   Includes index.

   Discography :

   Videography :

   ISBN 0-8119-0866-6 (paper)

    1. Bolton, Michael. 2. Singers--United States--Biography.

I. Seeloff, Layne A., 1958-

ML420.B683M53   1997

782.42164 ' 092--dc21   97-8559

[B]   CIP

                                         MN

Design by Vicki Heil
Front Cover Design by David Eaton
and Dennis Garrity

Photo Credits:

Pages 5 (right-hand side), 8, 22, 54 (right-hand side)—Bolton Family Photo; Page 101(bottom left)—Allan Carrano; Pages 2, 4, 6, 19 (left-hand side), 20 (right-hand side), 25, 29, 39, 40, 41, 42 (top),45, 46, 55 (top), 56 (left-hand side), 58 (right-hand side), 59, 60, 70, 89, 114—Phillip Eaton; Pages 15, 34 (top), 35, 36, 100, 104, 122—Margaret Eaton; Page 86 (right-hand side), 118—Finlan Family Photo; Page 82—Jim Finlan; Page 86 (bottom left)—Frost Family Photo; 88 (top right)—Hickman Family Photo; Page 87 (bottom)—Kincaid Family Photo; 87 (top)—Knapman Family Photo; Pages vii, xiii, 1, 3, 5 (top), 9, 13, 14, 16, 17, 19, 23, 24, 25 (top), 26, 27, 31, 34, 37, 42, 45, 47, 48, 49, 51, 53, 54 (left-hand side), 58 (left-hand side), 61, 62, 65, 68, 69, 72 (bottom left), 76, 83, 93, 95, 96, 98, 101 (bottom right), 105, 107, 108, 109, 110, 112, 113, 115, 119—Wayne Logan; Page 55 (bottom)—Paul Natkin/Photo Reserve, Inc.; Page 72 (bottom right)—Sharon Poteet; Page 88 (top left)—Reveulta Family Photo; Page 87 (bottom left)—Sears Portrait Studio; Pages 7, 56 (right-hand side), 99, 106, 111, 116, 120—Layne Seeloff; Page 12—Paul Seeloff; Page 88 (bottom right)—Elizabeth Seib; Page 20 (top)—Anita and Steve Shevett; Page 117—Nancy Shorter; Page 88 (bottom left)—St. Pierre Family Photo

Printed in Canada
10 9 8 7 6 5 4 3 2 1

Words of Praise
for Michael Bolton

"Michael Bolton is great!"

—Will Smith, Actor, *US Magazine*, July 1997

"Michael Bolton's commitment to his music is evident in the way he gives 100 percent to every performance. The enjoyment his audience derives from his music is a reflection of the joy Michael takes in performing it."

—Quincy Jones, Grammy-winning Singer

"That's Michael...He sings songs and you can't believe he's hitting those notes...He has a gift."

—Kenny G., Grammy-winning Singer

"He's one of the best singers to come along. He's earned the right to sing whatever he wants to sing."

—David Foster, Record Producer

"That I was afforded the opportunity to express my very real admiration for you as an artist possessed of incomparable skill, talent, imagination and transcendent passion, was an accident of fate."

—Steven Stills, Crosby, Stills & Nash

"I think that Michael Bolton is very similar to me in terms of being very fortunate that we've gotten this far through the success and God-given talent that we both have."

—Michael Jordan, World Champion NBA All-Star

"When someone has something to say, we should all listen...What you say through your music is powerful and life changing."

—Pat Riley, NBA World Champion Coach

"I admire your success in the world of entertainment as well as in your other roles as father, ballplayer, and humanitarian."

—Barry Bonds, 3-Time MVP, Major League Baseball

Contents

This book is dedicated to "The Man," Michael Bolton.

A Word from Michael's Mother

I'm so pleased to be part of any celebration of my son, Michael. As you can imagine, I'm very proud of my son — of all the years of hard work, waiting for the world to discover his talents. Michael always wanted his music to touch people, so I can barely describe my joy when he finally started seeing his dreams come true. When I think of all the lives his music has made happier, and the people that have been healed in some manner by his lyrics around the world, this mother's heart is full of pride.

Over the years, many of you have written me letters letting me know how much Michael and his music have meant to you. It never fails to warm my heart. You ask me about myself and my memories of Michael. I have so many wonderful memories I'd love to share with *all* of you — of young Michael playing his first guitar...hearing his strong voice for the first time...watching him perform in front of an audience. Precious moments like the births of my three lovely granddaughters — Isa, Holly and Taryn — whom I've watched grow into beautiful young women...seeing my son on television winning Grammy Awards!! Michael's been blessed with success after success, right up to having a song in a Disney movie!

I could go on and on, but I'll leave you with this: All the years of effort, patience, and perseverance that my son Michael has put in are for *you*. You make it all worthwhile. Your smiles, your tears, your love. They keep him going, keep him focused. And they make *me* so very happy. What more could a mother ask for?

—All my love and best wishes
Helen Bolotin

Foreword

We have spent several years conducting research for this book. Although libraries, record stores, newspapers, and government offices all played a big role in its production, the largest (and most enjoyable) part of the research was done in person, at various concerts and events throughout Northeast America.

Spending a great deal of our time in lines (ticket lines, concert lines, and softball game lines), we met many of Michael's fans, all eager to share their experiences and knowledge with us. Throughout this book are four story sections, detailing Michael Bolton-related events and escapades. Although some parts of the stories are our own first-hand experiences, we have incorporated the best of the tales we were told to produce a cohesive, complete modern-day fairy tale, from first introduction to Cinderella's Ball, detailing the tribulations along the way.

We believe it makes up the ultimate fan experience and hope you can share in the magic.

—Layne Seeloff, Elizabeth Seib, Margaret Eaton and Joyce Logan

Editor's Statement

Lifetime Books is so pleased to be a part of history, as we proudly present a wonderful photograph-intensive book on one of the world's most-gifted and top-selling musical artists, Michael Bolton.

Produced with the help of his greatest admirers, including the president of the official Michael Bolton Fan Club, this is the special collector's gift edition every fan will cherish for years.

According to *USA Today*, the typical Bolton fan is a 36-year-old female, white collar worker, living in a mid to large sized city. Half are married and 98% have high school diplomas. Basically, just about everyone can be a Bolton fan — and many are! This book was written from the perspective of what it's like to live the Bolton fan experience, offering readers an up close and inside perspective into the celebrity singer's career and personal life.

Lifetime Books has published over 1600 books in the past 50 years, including other interesting entertainment tomes such as DAVID JANSSEN: MY FUGITIVE, JEOPARDY! and ALL THE SECRETS OF MAGIC REVEALED. We feel MICHAEL BOLTON: Passion, Secrets, Soul and Truths offers fans an intimate look — with over 150 rare or never-before-published photographs.

We proudly recognize and honor the story-book career and accomplishments of a man who has sold over 30,000,000 albums and entertained people across the globe. Lifetime Books is certain Michael Bolton and his fans will enjoy this special tribute and we thank you for your support.

—**Brian Feinblum**
Senior Editor
Lifetime Books

Introduction

by Joyce Logan

During the late 1970's and early 80's, I was extremely fortunate to see Michael Bolton perform in most of the local clubs in the greater New Haven area. As far as I was concerned there was no greater talent than this man, and I wondered when someone would discover him so that the entire world could enjoy his music!

At that time, I was a promotions director for a rock radio station in New Haven, Connecticut, Michael's hometown. Because of my enthusiasm for Michael's new album in 1983 featuring the hit song, "Fool's Game," I was able to convince the station that I worked for to feature Michael in our Columbus Day Parade and call a segment of the parade "Hometown Hero"— which, as you Bolton fans already know, was a cut off his first self-titled album. The radio station went for it, but they insisted that I promote ALL the local bands in the greater New Haven area and to call it "Our Home Town Heroes." Well, I would have none of that because Michael was far superior...and he was the one with the MTV video at the time! So, I pondered awhile and called Michael's new manager, Louis Levin, and said, "You don't want Michael in a parade with a bunch of unknown singers using the title of his song as their banner, do you?" Of course, Louis said, "Absolutely not." This was the ammunition I needed! I went to the station manager and said, "Look, you're going to lose Bolton because his manager won't allow it, and I think we should really promote this guy and drop the other unknowns, as it's Michael that will be going far. He's the one we're playing on our station, not them." I won! It was a great parade, and Michael rode in the back of a convertible, waving to his fans as we blared out "Hometown Hero" through speakers attached to the station's van as it was driving behind us in the parade.

Early on, Michael and his family became like my own family to me. It was a time when we were still all struggling. I was divorced with two young sons and Michael was living in a duplex apartment in Milford, CT with his then-wife, Maureen, and their three young daughters. I have fond memories of those days. Maureen would invite me over frequently for dinner...and she usually had a pot of the best tasting vegetarian soup on the stove along with a treat in the oven. We'd sit talking for hours about our kids, a new recipe, fashion, etc., and then Michael would come home from the city (New York) via the late train after a long, long day of finalizing demo tapes. We would get into lengthy conversations about the music industry — with all it's glory and frustrations. They were good people and I felt at peace with them even though my own life felt like it was falling apart! I worked long hours at the radio station and even longer ones at home, as I was trying to keep a database for Michael, speak to his fans at night or on weekends, handwrite postcards to let his fans know where he'd be performing next, take care of my sons, and begin what is now one of the largest fan clubs in the world...The Michael Bolton Fan Club! This was all done on a "shoestring" budget and out of pure love and belief in the man and his music.

Michael and his family deserved the best out of life, and I was determined to help out in any way that I could. And they also supported me! When I didn't have enough money to put toys under the tree one Christmas, it was Michael that handed me a check, which he could barely afford to give, saying, "This is for your sons...buy them presents." When my washing machine broke down in my apartment complex for a few months, it was Maureen that insisted that I not only wash and dry my clothes at their place, but that we all have dinner...and she even cut my hair to save me money! She wasn't a hairdresser, but she had a steady hand and an eye for style and that was good enough for me. I would baby-sit their girls at times when Maureen was at work and Michael was in the city working on his music, and they would send me home with a "care package" of home-cooked goodies.

Things may have been tough for us back then, but love and friendship out-shined any problems. I always knew I could count on Michael and his family, and they could always count on me. I will treasure those memories forever. Thank you, Michael, for taking me along on your incredible journey through life.

Preface:
The Search for Michael Bolton

In recent years, it has become fashionable to blame fairy tales for many of the problems women are facing in their day-to-day lives. Our fondness for Cinderella, Sleeping Beauty, Prince Charming and all things magical has led to generations of women with unreal expectations of their mates, their lives, and themselves. Fairy tales have been blamed for the high divorce rate, the inability of women to get ahead in a "man's" world, and the general oppression of women's rights everywhere today. As modern women of the '90s, our group of women is aware of these theories, and absolutely positive that they had no bearing on our lives. We were all engaged in careers, happily married or happily single, juggling the over-full agendas of work, home, relationships, motherhood, and outside personal interests. Only in rare, fleeting moments did we even suspect that something could be missing. Unsure of what that something could be, we shrugged our unnamed yearnings off as weariness, nostalgia, or PMS. It has only been quite recently, in fact, that we could put a name to those yearnings at all. What we were missing was our fairy tale...and magic...and, yes, Prince Charming.

It began innocently enough. We were looking for a suitable venue for a "Ladies Night Out" and when a local date for a Michael Bolton concert was announced in the summer of 1992, we decided that was it. We did get to the mall a bit early to wait in line for tickets (5:00 a.m.!) but we rationalized that we wanted the best seats we could get for our first Bolton concert. We WERE first in line and a mere four and one-half hours later, we were in the parking lot with our tickets in hand, very pleased with ourselves.

We spent a minimum amount of time primping for the concert, our main concern being clothes baggy enough that we could smuggle a camera into the show. We did the "Park & Ride" thing, taking a subway into the city from the suburbs because none of us wanted to fight downtown traffic, and the ride in itself was a novel experience. We entered the auditorium excited (but not overly) and bought tour books and t-shirts with the rest of the crowd, before finally proceeding to our seats.

When we got there, we found that we had a total view of the activity backstage. Minutes later, the lights went down and Kathy Trocolli, Michael's opening act, took the stage. After the normal amount of time and the obligatory one encore, Ms. Trocolli left the stage and the houselights came on. Our excitement increased with the activity backstage as long-haired musicians mixed with long-haired stage hands and we feverishly turned pages in our tour books trying to sort out who was who. Then, a young man we identified as Michael's head of security casually jumped the railing in front of us and climbed the steps to sit down at our left and watch the show. And I, feeling the weight of the cold, hard little Polaroid camera inside my blouse (fitting snugly into the pocket my waistband created for it), watched in amazement as the girl in front of me unpacked and openly assembled a monster camera that would take two hands just to hold. (We have since discovered that Michael Bolton's official fan club actively solicits fans' concert photos, so our camera was not as big an issue as we had supposed.)

Then, suddenly, the lights went down, the band took the stage and music took the air. The voice and the spotlight hit at the same time, and we were left looking at THE MAN directly in front of us. He was amazing. We had all heard the songs on our radios and we had seen the Grammy performance with Kenny G. but we were totally unprepared for the charisma emanating from that man and that voice that night. He strode back and forth across the stage singing all his standards and giving us every bit of emotion that he had. He connected with the crowd in a hundred different ways, pulling us in and carrying us with him through his rockers, his ballads, and his inspirational call-to-arms. He joked, told stories, interacted with his band and generally made us feel like we were the only people in the room with him. We were so caught up in the magic of Michael Bolton that, as he left the stage for the final time from the steps directly in front of us, we felt exhaustion and elation, as if WE had just performed a two-hour, very active show. Before descending the stairs from the stage, he paused and raised his arm in a last wave to the crowd. Much to our embarrassment, we seasoned, hardened concert-goers who would never have believed we could behave in such a manner, raised our hands to wave good-bye without so much as a thought or a hesitation. We really believed he was waving at *us*.

Leaving the auditorium took time that night, none of us wanting it to be over. We even stopped to eat on the way home (an "After-Michael" ritual that would prove as habit forming as smoking after sex), mutually agreeing to hold on to and savor the experience just a little while longer, even though we all had to get up for work the next morning. Thoughts of our daily lives had no place here; we were caught up in the magic.

We had found our Prince Charming and the pull of him would prove addictive.

"If I can just do the best I can do and maintain a certain level of quality and integrity...*that's* the challenge...and just doing more of what you love to do, that's the challenge of life for me."

—Michael Bolton
Soul Provider:The Videos

A to Z
The Life of Michael Bolton

"A Love So Beautiful" — Written by Jeff Lynne and Roy Orbison Appeared on GREATEST HITS 1985-1995 (Columbia, 1995). Produced by Walter Afanasieff. Arranged by Walter Afanasieff and Michael Bolton. This song, the second single from Michael's Greatest Hits album, was recorded at Wally World, Passion Studios, and The Record Plant.

"A Love So Beautiful" — This strictly limited edition UK single import included the album version of the song "A Love So Beautiful" and two versions of "Can I Touch You...There?"—a classic club version and the Mokran version. A special bonus of 4-color postcards of Michael Bolton were also enclosed in the package.

A Night Under the Stars — This benefit concert hosted by Petula Clark was held in Los Angeles on June 25, 1995.

"A Time For Letting Go" — Written by Michael Bolton and Diane Warren.
> Appears on THE ONE THING (Columbia, 1993). Produced and arranged by Walter Afanasieff and Michael Bolton.

"A Very Special Christmas 2" — Released in 1994, this was the second Special Olympics Christmas Album. Michael sings "White Christmas" on this compilation and other performers on the album include Tom Petty & The Heartbreakers, Randy Travis, Luther Vandross, Frank Sinatra and Cyndi Lauper, Boys II Men, Jon Bon Jovi, Paul Young, Aretha Franklin, Ronnie Spector and Darlene Love, Run DMC, Extreme, Bonnie Raitt and Charles Brown, Tevin Campbell, Debbie Gibson, Vanessa Williams, Ann and Nancy Wilson, Sinead O'Connor, and Wilson Phillips.

Abbey Road Studios — Michael recorded portions of his aria album in this legendary studio in February, 1997.

Michael Bolton Spreading Christmas Cheer

Abdul, Paula — Michael Bolton and Paula Abdul have appeared on many of the same child-related benefit shows, such as Disney's "For Our Children: The Concert" and "CityKids All-Star Celebration."

Although they have been romantically linked by gossip columnists in the past, it has been reported that his earliest relationship with her was as her babysitter. "But that's a slight exaggeration," according to Michael. It seems that his keyboard player at the time was dating Paula's older sister and they had to hang out at the house because Paula was too young to be left alone.

More recently, Paula has the distinction of having presented Michael with three of his numerous music awards: his first Grammy in 1990, one of the two American Music Awards he won in 1992, and one of his two 1995 American Music Awards. She also did the choreography for Michael's "Wait On Love" video.

Ace of Diamonds — Michael's picture was on this playing card on the back cover of the BLACKJACK album.

Acting — Michael has said that he is interested in developing an acting career and is developing two movie scripts, a suspense legal thriller and a period piece about a singer. According to *In Style* magazine's December, 1996 issue, the latter script is titled, "The Voice," and stars Michael as an 18th century opera singer. Shooting began in May of 1997. The February 3, 1996 edition of *USA Today* included an article on Michael that reported he would consider cutting his hair for the right acting role and Michael jokingly told Jay Leno on one of his Tonight Show appearances that he may do a "combination of Seagal and Dangerfield."

Adams, Catte — Catte joined Michael's back-up singers in 1995 as a replacement for Pat Hawke, who was on maternity leave having twins. Catte sings middle harmony and has quite a list of musical credits to her name. Catte has toured with several different (and diverse) musicians, beginning in 1984 with Liberace, continuing through the '80s and '90s with Chaka Kahn, Jermaine Jackson, Go West, and Natalie Cole, before winding up, as we know, with Michael. She has recorded with many different musicians and appears on the soundtracks of three feature films (Blank Check, Swan Princess, and Fletch Lives). Since winning the $100,000 prize on *Star Search*, it sometimes seems that Catte can "do it all," from writing and publishing songs to producing for other artists, from singing jingles for nine large advertising campaigns to appearing as guest artist for Johnny Carson and Arsenio Hall. Catte is certainly a talented addition to Michael's band.

"Addicted to Fame" — Prime time TV special hosted by Maria Shriver detailing the trials and tribulations of being in the public eye. A segment on Michael Bolton Gold Club member Donna Wong was done showing clips of Donna preparing for, and attending, a softball game and concert. Michael was shown at the game, and both backstage and performing at the concert. An interview segment with him was also featured, during which he said, "...it can really be a great thing when people feel positively about you..."

Address — Mail has been known to make it to Michael addressed simply: THE Michael Bolton (P.O. officials, you must know where he lives).

Advocacy Day — March 14-15, 1995 in Washington, D.C. Michael and Mary Chapin Carpenter hosted a breakfast to kick off the two-day rally in support of the future funding of the National Endowment of the Arts. Also attending were Tony Bennett, Garth Brooks, and Kenny G. An afternoon rally was held on the Capitol steps.

Afanasieff, Walter — A producer and collaborator with Michael, Walter first showed up on the SOUL PROVIDER album, co-producing and playing keyboards, bass and drums on "How Can We Be Lovers" and "When I'm Back On My Feet Again." He has since produced TIME, LOVE AND TENDERNESS; THE ONE THING; four tracks of TIMELESS: THE CLASSICS; six tracks of MICHAEL BOLTON'S GREATEST HITS 1985-1995 with Michael and others, and six tracks from THIS IS THE TIME. He also collaborated on the songs, "Soul of My Soul," "Never Get Enough of Your Love," "Missing You Now," "Save Me," and "Love is the Power." Walter was interviewed briefly for the THIS IS MICHAEL BOLTON TV special and videotape.

Agassi, Andre — Andre has been rated the number 1 tennis player in the world. Having been a friend of Michael's for a number of years, Andre participated in the First Annual Tennis, Softball, and Black Tie Fundraiser for the Michael Bolton Foundation and cohosted the Third Annual event for the Foundation. Before he cut his hair, he appeared as a guest on *The Jay Leno Show* one of the same nights as Michael and after a commercial break, Jay welcomed viewers back to the "Hair Club for Men show." Andre is now married to Brooke Shields (who was once romantically linked to Michael Bolton).

"Ain't Got Nothing If You Ain't Got Love" — Written by Michael Bolton and Robert John "Mutt" Lange. Appeared on THE ONE THING (Columbia, 1993). Produced by Robert John "Mutt" Lange and Michael Bolton. This song was recorded at Out Of Pocket Productions, Ltd. in Surrey, England.

"Airwaves" — Written by Michael Bolotin and Bruce Kulick.

Appeared on BLACKJACK - WORLD'S APART (Polydor, 1980).

Produced by Eddy Offord.

Alex Award — In 1995, the Michael Bolton hot line was nominated for, and won, an Alex Award, named after Alexander Graham Bell. The phone line won in the category of "Excellence In Entertainment."

Allen, Woody — Michael, a self-professed movie addict, has a special preference for Woody Allen films. He got to meet Woody at the Knicks/Bulls playoff game in 1993 and Michael said, "We shook hands and it was one of the few times that I've been actually speechless."

Alliance of Artists and Recording Companies — Michael was one of the first performers to join this group, which was created by the Recording Industry Association of America (RIAA) to collect artist digital home taping royalties.

"All The World Loves M&Ms" — A version of this commercial jingle was done by Michael early in his career.

Amazing Journey — "I'm really blessed in so many ways 'cause I've had the chance to take this amazing journey. Like everyone else, my life has been shaped by challenge and disappointment. What I've learned is when you trust your instincts and follow your heart, your dreams do come true." —*Michael Bolton*

Dreams Can Come True . . .

American Cinema Awards Foundation — This Foundation hosted a party honoring "ALL MY CHILDREN" soap opera diva Susan Lucci in the summer of 1996 and Michael Bolton attended as a guest. Photos of Michael posing with Ms. Lucci and actress Tonja Walker appeared in several tabloid magazines.

American Music Awards — To date, Michael has won 6 American Music Awards. In 1992, Michael won FAVORITE MALE ARTIST and FAVORITE ALBUM in the Pop/Rock Category for his TIME, LOVE & TENDERNESS album. In 1993, Michael won FAVORITE POP/ROCK MALE ARTIST and FAVORITE ADULT CONTEMPORARY ARTIST. He performed the songs "To Love Somebody" and "Drift Away" on the televised awards show. In 1994, Michael performed "Said I Loved You...But I Lied" on the show, but did not win an award. He did, however, win again in 1995 for BEST POP/ROCK MALE and BEST MALE CONTEMPORARY ARTIST.

American Music Hall Writer's Special — Aired on CBS during August, 1989, this show gave us Michael performing a duet with Jeffrey Osborne on "You've Lost That Lovin' Feeling" and solo on "Yesterday".

Amusement Parks — Michael enjoys amusement parks and especially "thrill rides." The higher, faster, and scarier, the better.

"An American Reunion" — This promotional compilation album was released by Warner and Sony Music in 1993. One of the tracks features Michael singing, "When I'm Back On My Feet Again."

Anterior Cruciate Ligament — The body part Michael tore at a Winter 1993 Cystic Fibrosis Skiing Fundraiser, resulting in surgery and the need to wear a knee brace for tennis matches and Bolton Bomber games for the 1993 and 1994 seasons.

"Any Man's Country" — Written by Michael Bolton and Jonathon Cain. This song, written for the Sylvester Stallone movie, "Over The Top," didn't make it into the final screen edition.

Arcadia Ballroom — A 1970's New Haven club frequently played by Michael.

Artichokes — One of Michael's favorite foods.

Artist Relations Office — Set up by Michael's fan club to act as a liaison between the man and his fans, this office is managed by Judine McGinley and usually handles questions or problems dealing with tour dates and venues. (See address listing at the back of this book.)

"Artistry of Michael Bolotin"— 1993 re-release of selected tracks from Michael's first two RCA albums. The songs were: *Rocky Mountain Way; Take Me As I Am; Time Is On My Side; Dancing In The Street; Your Love; These Eyes; You're No Good; If I Had Your Love; It's Just A Feeling; Lost In The City*. (See individual song listings for writer and producer information.)

ASCAP Music Awards — Michael won ASCAP (American Society of Composers, Authors, and Publishers) Writer/Publisher awards in 1989 for "That's What Love Is All About" and "I Found Someone." He won a Publishers Award again in 1991 for "How Am I Supposed To Live Without You."

"Ave Maria" — Written by Franz Schubert (Op. 52 No. 6). Appeared on THIS IS THE TIME - THE CHRISTMAS ALBUM (Columbia, 1996).
    Produced by Walter Afanasieff and Michael Bolton.
    Placido Domingo's Vocals produced by Grace Row.
    Placido Domingo performed this song as a duet with Michael for this album.

Average Michael Bolton Fan — As profiled in the September 28, 1993 edition of *USA Today*, the average fan is a 36-year old female white collar worker living in a mid- to large-sized city having an annual income of over $30,000. 90% are high school graduates and 49% are married. Like all averages, very few of us meet the profile dead-on but it's nice to know that our education levels beat the national average.

Babyface — Michael has been working on songs with this hit performer and it is rumored that the 1997 studio album may be a collaboration between the two of them.

"Back In My Arms Again" — Written by B. Holland, L. Dozier, and E. Holland. Appeared on MICHAEL BOLTON (Columbia, 1983).
    Produced by Gerry Block and Michael Bolton.
    Aldo Nova plays a guitar solo for this track.

BACK TO SCHOOL — A movie starring Rodney Dangerfield. Michael's song, "Everybody's Crazy" is used in it.

Backstage Perks — We've often heard stories of the demands of performers for their favorite foods and drinks to be backstage at concerts. And why not? Being on the road is demanding and grueling and if a few of your favorite foods make it less stressful, what's the harm? Well, Michael has a list of items that he requests backstage but they are not what we normally expect from rock stars. Michael's list includes Berry Zinger tea, Cherry 7-Up and Raspberry Ginger Ale, and peanut M&Ms.

"Bah Bah Bah" — Written by Michael Bolotin. Appeared as a single released by Joy (Epic Records, 1968). Produced by Ken Cooper.
    Because Michael was under-age when this song was recorded, his mother had to co-sign the contract with Epic Records. (Although Michael was only fifteen when this song was recorded, he already had the voice of a mature singer.) The "B" side of the single was "It's For You," written by Lennon and McCartney. This was Michael's first single and he has said that not only was his name spelled incorrectly as M. Bolotkin on the song's writing credits, but that it was the "wrong version of the wrong song." It was the first song that Michael actually got paid for and became a minor success in Connecticut wherever it received airplay but was relatively unheard in the rest of the country.

Balcony — During his 1994 concert tour, Michael used a balcony and crystal chandelier as props for his "opera solo" on stage.

Ballpark Uniforms — This company, based in Australia, is the official supplier of Bolton Bomber's uniforms.

Baker, Jeanne — She was the first "Fan's Corner" honoree in the premier edition of *Bolton Behind the Scenes* for creating and donating bears for Michael to autograph and give to children during the annual TOYS FOR TOTS campaign.

Band, The — Above, with Michael, included:
> *Tommy (Mugs) Cain* - drums
> *Chris Camozzi* - lead guitar
> *Schuyler Deale* - bass guitar
> *Joey Melotti* - keyboards and back-up vocals
> *Steve Scales* - percussion
> *Joe Turano* - keyboard, sax, and back-up vocals
> *Pat Hawk* (who recently gave birth to twins), *Vann Johnson, Janis Liebhart*, and since 1995, *Catte Adams* — Background vocals

Barbieri, Paula — Paula was featured in the "Completely" video after which she was incorrectly romantically linked to Michael by the tabloids. Her status as O.J. Simpson's long-time girlfriend gained national attention with the murders of Nicole Brown Simpson and Ronald Goldman.

Barry Bonds' Super Stars Game — Jackie Robinson Memorial Stadium was the setting for a November 6, 1994 benefit softball game between the Bolton Bombers and Barry Bonds' Super Stars. The Super Stars lost, 29-17. The game was part of a fundraising weekend to benefit both Barry Bonds' and Michael Bolton's Foundations and included the softball game, a silent memorabilia auction, and a black tie gala. The weekend raised over $1.4 million. Joe DiMaggio made an appearance and the Super Stars team included Frank Thomas, Jeff Bagwell, Scott Erickson, Ken Griffey, Jr., Ozzie Smith, Joe Morgan, Matt Williams, Bobby Bonilla, and Bip Roberts.

Barefoot — Michael appears this way in the GREATEST HITS 1985- 1995 promos.

Barr, Mary — Mary's official title with Fan Emporium is Information Exchange Manager, but she is the person responsible for keeping up the messages on the fan phone line regarding Michael's concerts, softball games, and personal appearances.

Barrier, Dottie — Dottie is the Print Coordinator for Fan Emporium, Inc.

Baseball Caps — Michael has a large collection of these, many given to him by his fans. According to his mom, when Michael was playing Little League (at right, circa 1960), he wouldn't take his cap off at all; he even slept in it.

Basketball — One of Michael's favorite sports. He has done charity basketball games, including one where 6,000 people attended to benefit a Ronald McDonald House.

Bazooka Gun — Michael jokingly says he greets his daughters' dates with one of these.

Beatles — Michael has said, "I remember when I was 12 and growing up in a small town in Connecticut, I wanted to be one of the Beatles and have all the girls chasing me. I wanted cars. I wanted to be famous." Ask and you shall receive, Michael.

"Behind Closed Doors" with Joan Lunden — This primetime special aired October 17, 1995 and included an interview with Michael at his home studio in Connecticut. Michael chatted comfortably with Joan, even detailing some of the "disguises" he uses to avoid recognition. Old concert clips and footage from the 1995 Black Tie Gala were also shown.

Belize — This Central American country is where the video for "Can I Touch You...There?" was filmed. Michael described this video as "a jungle fantasy in which Apocalypse Now meets African Queen with Casablanca" and said he sang the song about eighty times while making the video.

Bennett, Tony — Michael has said that Tony Bennett is his role model. When they both appeared on same Oprah Winfrey show, Michael did a Wayne and Garth impersonation from the movie WAYNE'S WORLD, bowing to Tony, saying, "I'm not worthy, I'm not worthy."

Best Male Singer — Michael was voted this in the 1992 US magazine reader poll.

Big Daddy — The nickname given to Dave Reitzas, an engineer on MICHAEL BOLTON GREATEST HITS 1985-1995.

"Bill" — How President Clinton has requested that Michael Bolton address him.

Billboard Music Awards — Michael opened the 1993 awards show with "Said I Loved You...But I Lied." On December 6, 1995, Michael again performed on the awards show, this time singing a medley consisting of "Said I Loved You...But I Lied," "When A Man Loves A Woman," "Can I Touch You...There?" and "Time, Love and Tenderness" (backed by the Harlem Boys Choir).

"Billboard's Top Ten of 1992 — Michael was voted #2 album artist (behind Garth Brooks).

"Blackjack" — Blackjack was Michael's rock n' roll band, formed in the autumn of 1978. The quartet consisted of Sandy Gennaro on drums, Bruce Kulick on guitar, Jimmy Haslip on bass, and Michael Bolotin on vocals. The band was signed to Polydor Records and released two albums, BLACKJACK in 1979 and WORLDS APART in 1980. (Note: In light of Michael's later success, Polydor repackaged the two Blackjack albums as a double set, called it "BLACKJACK," and re-released it in 1992).

"Blackjack" — Michael's first album with the band, Blackjack, was released on June 18, 1979 by Polydor Records. It was recorded in Massachusetts, New York, and Florida and was produced by Tom Dowd. The album was a special tribute to the memory of Peter Gennaro. It is no longer available through record outlets.

The songs were:
1. *Love Me Tonight*
2. *Heart Of Stone*
3. *The Night Has Me Calling For You*
4. *Southern Ballad (If This Means Losing You)*
5. *Fallin'*
6. *Without Your Love*
7. *Countin' On You*
8. *I'm Aware Of Your Love*
9. *For You*
10. *Heart Of Mine*

(See individual song listings for writer and producer information.)

"Blackjack" — In 1992, Polydor re-released Michael's two Blackjack albums as a double-album set simply titled *Blackjack*. This album is no longer available at record outlets.

Blake, Rebecca — Rebecca directed the "Said I Loved You...But I Lied" and "Completely" videos. We think she knows exactly how women want to see Michael portrayed and should handle the job ALWAYS.

Bloomfield, Mike — Michael has said, "I learned guitar by studying Mike Bloomfield and Eric Clapton."

Blue-Turquoise — Michael's favorite color.

"Blume in Love" — This was a 1973 movie starring Susan Anspach, George Segal, and Kris Kristofferson. Acting as an extra in this movie, Michael is shown sitting in the welfare office reading a book. (Note: His hair is much darker in the movie than it is now.)

BMI — Among other things, BMI is a music licensing organization that monitors how often songs are played. Since 1990 they have presented Michael with several awards and honors:
1990 — "How Am I Supposed To Live Without You" was awarded the Most Performed Song Award. Michael received Writer and Publisher Awards for that song and "Soul Provider."
1991 — "How Am I Supposed To Live Without You" was BMI's song of the year and Michael received a "Million-Airs" award for over one million broadcasts of it. He also received Writer and Publisher Awards for "How Can We Be Lovers." See listing in back.

B'nai B'rith — B'nai B'rith is the oldest and largest American Jewish service organization. In 1990, their Music and Performing Arts Division presented Michael with a Creative Achievement Award.

Bolotin — The surname Michael was born with, pronounced Buh-LO-tin.

Bolotin, George — George Bolotin (Michael's father) was the son of Russian immigrants. A New Haven Democratic Ward chairman, he was a driving force behind Michael, first in his sports activities (cheering Michael on the baseball field) and later in his career ("You're gonna be big, big, big"). Speaking about his father, Michael says, "My father taught me to always keep going forward, keep forward movement happening. Perserverance. That thought has always stayed with me. You have to love what you do to be good at it. It's like my father used to say: 'Keep punching, Mike.'" George passed away in 1981 before he could see just how true his prediction would be.

Bolotin, Helen — Helen, Michael's mother, was the first musical influence in Michael's life. She plays keyboards, sings, and writes songs. (Michael has said her songs notably included, "You Kids Are Killing Me," and "You

Michael's mother, Helen, signing autographs.

Oughta Have Kids Like You When You Grow Up.") Helen's progressive mothering techniques ("I believed in live and let live") met with raised eyebrows and community disapproval but her support of Michael in all of his efforts has been instrumental in shaping the artist and the man.

She has been referred to as Michael's number one fan and can be found front and center in his concert audience whenever possible. (She was seated there with Michael's daughters at the concert at Yale University in April, 1994 when Michael gave a personal and emotional introduction about generations and their connections before singing "Soul of My Soul.").

Michael recently moved his mother into a new condominium that she says is "just beautiful" and he says that she has found several perks to being the mother of Michael Bolton, such as giving interviews (he cringes, "I never know what she's going to say.") to keeping the bars open after-hours (a statement made in a little story that he told on Jay Leno one night, which necessitated an explanation on a later appearance after his mom received phone calls from her friends ribbing her about it).

Bolotin, Maureen (McGuire) — Maureen was working in a record store when she first met Michael Bolotin and several years later, in 1975, they married. Their marriage produced three daughters before it dissolved in divorce in 1990. According to Dennis Mardell, of the band Rival, Maureen is the one who gave Michael his first frizzy perm in the early years of their marriage.

7

Bolotin, Sandra — Sandra (pictured at right with Michael and Helen, Atlantic City, 1961) is Michael's older sister (by two years) and she is employed as a social worker.

Bolotkin — The way that Michael's name was mispelled on the label of the "Bah Bah Bah" single.

Bolton Bad Boys — Formed in 1990, this was the original name of the Bolton Bombers.

Bolton Beat, The — First published in 1989 with a circulation of two hundred by Fan Emporium, *The Bolton Beat* was Michael's Official Fan Club newsletter. It carried stories, photos, games, and an information network. In 1994, with the advent of the *Michael Bolton Gold Club* and his magazine, *Bolton Behind the Scenes*, it was announced that the original fan club and *The Bolton Beat* were being phased out. However, they were both reinstated in the Spring of 1995 by popular demand. The newsletter now includes a Pen Pal Exchange. Currently, Michael has two fan clubs, a newsletter and a quarterly magazine devoted to him. Back issues (at $3.00 per issue) are available from Fan Emporium. You must send a self-addressed business-sized envelope bearing 64 cents postage for each issue. (See address section at back of book for more information.)

Bolton Behind the Scenes — The premier issue of this quarterly magazine appeared in 1994. It features a two-page pull-out poster of Michael in the center of every issue. Articles include interviews with band members, What's New with Michael Bolton, and Michael's Mailbag where Michael answers questions from the fans. There are two features called Scrapbook (which highlights fan's photos of Michael) and Backstage (which gives us professional pictures of Michael and a look behind the scenes at shows and events.) This is Michael's official magazine and is published by Fan Emporium, Inc. The Editor is Joyce Logan and Assistant Editors are Vicki Lovett and Judine McGinley. Michael Bolton is listed as a Contributing Editor. Back issues of *Bolton Behind The Scenes* are available from Fan Emporium at a cost of $8.50 for U.S. and Canadian orders and $10.00 for international orders. (A portion of the subscription fee goes to the Michael Bolton Foundation. See address listings at the back of the book for more information.)

Bolton Bombers — For the 1991-92 tour, Bolton's Bad Boys became the Bolton Bombers. They have been referred to as the premier softball team in the world and as of September 7, 1994, their record was 122 wins - 10 losses. The Bombers frequently "sandwich concerts between ballgames" when on tour, trying to play 60 games a year. Their games raise money for local charities and (since 1993) The Michael Bolton Foundation. Line-ups in past years have included Michael, Louis Levin, Mugs Cain, Chris Camozzi, Schuyler Deale, and Joe Turano. Bombers' games are always entertaining and part of the fun stems from the nicknames of the team members. Bombers' nicknames sometimes have a way of changing from game to game. A sampling of past nicknames follows:

#4 - Jerry "Meet My Cousins" Mele
#7 - Michael "The Bomber" Bolton
#8 - Johnny "The Kid" Dodd
#9 - Richie "The Ripper" Vaughn
#11 - Bucky "Get Back On The Bus" Ford
#12 - Phil "New Ball" Higgins
#15 - Gary "Big Stick" Whitefield
#18 - Bobby "The Stinger" Olah
#22 - Tim "No Relation" Bolton
#23 - Doug "Free Agent" Flynn
#25 - Dan "The Sarge" Schuck
#57 - Louis "The Judge" Levin (Louis' nickname at the Field of Dreams was "Flip 'Em Again")
#81 - Flip "Not Flip 'Em Again" Mize
- Kim "The Killer" Turner
- Dennis "The Menace" Rodriguez
- "Shoeless" Joey Melotti
- Dave "The Coach" Carroll

(Additional Bombers participating in the Fourth Annual Michael Bolton Foundation Celebrity Softball Game in Connecticut were #1- Jerry Lembo, #18- Rich Pinsky, #30A- Rebecca Sligh, and #30- Donnie Sligh, Rebecca's father.)

Bolton Collector's Journal — This spiral-bound plastic-covered journal contains almost 50 pages of photocopied newspaper and magazine articles on Michael Bolton, plus a discography and videography, notes for collectors, and a song list featuring background vocals, duets, and feature songs from Michael. Two editions (1993 and 1994) have been sold through Fan Emporium, but the first edition is no longer available. Fans are requested to send any articles and photos from newspapers and magazines to the Editor, Vicki Lovett, for inclusion in possible updates of the journal. (Note: A special "Contest for all Bolton Collectors and News Hounds" has been instituted. Send your articles and information addressed to "Bolton News Contest" and include a 3x5 card with your name and address. Drawings will be held for special prizes. For the address, see listing at the back of this book.)

Bolton Music — This is the company that runs Michael's personal and professional business, including Passion Studios.

Bolton, Orrin — Orrin is four years older than his brother Michael and he was the person who "...played those classic records while little brother was listening." Orrin plays drums and guitar, and together he and Michael would make music for anybody who would listen. He was a member of "George's Boys" and one of Michael's first managers. Michael sang "That's What Love Is All About" at Orrin's 1989 wedding and they still remain close, with Orrin working in Michael's Westport studios. In December, 1995, Orrin appeared (and sang) on an Oprah Winfrey show that featured Michael. Orrin and his wife, Gillis, have two children, a son and a daughter.

Bolton Photos — Although many concert venues do not allow cameras at their shows, Fan Emporium has requested copies of fan's photos of Michael Bolton for inclusion in their magazine and newsletter on a regular basis. (Obviously, Michael doesn't mind candid photos being taken by his fans.) If you have any photos you'd like to share, you can send them to Joyce Logan at the address found in the back of this book. Please send copies and written permission to reprint them in a Fan Emporium publication.

Bolton Rules! — Leather-clad rockers (mainly male) would jab the air with their fists and shout this at Michael's heavy metal concerts in the early eighties.

Boots — Michael wears Justin brand boots.

Boss — This is what approximately 60 people call Michael Bolton when he's on tour.

Bowling — In September, 1989, the fan club newsletter listed this as one of Michael's hobbies.

Michael caught strutting his stuff!

Boxer Shorts — Fan Emporium offered a pair of Black Cotton-Flannel Boxer Shorts embroidered with a white MB for sale in their Michael Bolton Collectibles Christmas flyer in 1996.

Brander, Joel — One of Michael's friends since childhood, Joel (center) suffered from Acute Myelogenous Leukemia and died on February 5, 1992. He set up "THIS CLOSE for Cancer Research, Inc" before his death and his widow, Julie, is the current President of the organization. Michael Bolton is the National Chairman and performs at the annual fund-raiser.

"Breakaway" — Written by Michael Bolotin and Bruce Kulick.
Appeared on WORLDS APART (Polydor, 1980).
Produced by Eddy Offord.

"The Bridge Is Broken" — This song ended the live show, "Pavarotti and Friends - Concert for Bosnia" in Modena, Italy, 1995. It was sung onstage by the entire ensemble, but does not appear on either the videotape or CD released from the concert.

"Bridges of Madison County" — This book, written by Robert James Waller, was highly recommended by Michael Bolton in the first issue of *Bolton Behind the Scenes*.

Briley, Martin — This songwriter collaborated with Michael Bolton on "Hot Love" and "Take A Look At My Face."

"Bring It On Home To Me" — Written by Sam Cooke
    Appeared on TIMELESS-THE CLASSICS
      (Columbia, 1992).
    Also appeared on THINKING OF YOU
      (Sony Music, 1996).
    Produced and arranged by David Foster and
      Michael Bolton.
    Rhythm arranged by David Foster and
      Michael Bolton.
    Orchestra arranged and conducted by Johnny Mandel
    Recorded in part at Passion Studio, CT.

Brodsky, Joel — Joel is listed as the photographer on the WORLDS APART album by Blackjack.

Brooks, Bobby — A special acknowledgement to him appears in both of Michael's tour books saying, "...but you were also my friend.

Your memory is forever in my soul." Bobby Brooks, Michael's Creative Artists Agency agent, died tragically in a helicopter crash that also claimed the life of Stevie Ray Vaughn.

Brooks, Garth — Michael Bolton appears in Garth's video for the song, "We Shall Be Free." During the video, Michael says, "Racism is easy to define. It's a form of ignorance." The video appears on GARTH BROOKS VIDEO VOLUME 2, released in 1996.

Brown Suede Coat — Michael Bolton wore this coat to sing the National Anthem at the World Series, he wore it in his video "Said I Loved You... But I Lied," and at numerous personal and television appearances. It appears to be a favorite of his and, we have to admit, we like it, too.

Budweiser — Michael Bolton sang a commercial jingle for them in the '80's.

Buffalo Memorial Auditorium — 8:00 p.m., August 19, 1992. Kathy Trocolli was Michael's opening act for this concert. This show was Michael's last appearance on his 1992 tour and the authors' first Michael Bolton concert experience. (See "The Search for Michael Bolton" for more information.)

Burr, Gary — Gary is the top Nashville songwriter that co-wrote the song "This Is The Time" with Michael Bolton.

Buses, 5400 — As part of the 1995 Awareness Campaign, Michael was named National Bus Chairman by the National Committee for the Prevention of Child Abuse. His picture, with the saying, "It shouldn't hurt to be a child" was on the side of 5400 buses.

"By The Time This Night Is Over" —Written by Michael Bolton, Diane Warren, and Andrew Goldmark. Appeared on BREATHLESS by Kenny G. (Arista).

This song is sung by Peabo Bryson on the album but the demo that Michael made of it has the distinction of being the first song recorded in Passion Studios, Connecticut.

 Cain, Jonathan — This songwriter-musician was a member of the rock group, Journey, and later was a member of the group, Bad English. He has collaborated with Michael on the songs "Wait On Love," "The Hunger," and "You're All That I Need." Jonathan is the brother of Michael's drummer, Mugs Cain, and worked on Michael's album, THE HUNGER, producing the song "(Sittin' On) The Dock of The Bay."

Cain, Tommy "Mugs" — Mugs first met Michael Bolton when Michael was writing songs with Mugs' brother, Jonathan. Currently the drummer for Michael's band, Mugs has been a part of the group since "THE HUNGER" tour. He has also appeared in many of Michael's videos, beginning with "(Sittin' On) The Dock Of The Bay." Mugs enjoys touring, saying he likes it "when people are having fun" and relaxes by working out and golfing with Chris Camozzi.

A talented musician, he has performing and writing credits on both THE TERMINATOR and IF LOOKS

COULD KILL movie soundtracks. When not on tour with Michael, he works with The Rail Birds, a band consisting of Schuyler Deale, Brett Walker (singer-songwriter) and himself. They have released an album in Europe that is expected to be available through Fan Emporium soon.

Mugs, whose birthday is October 7, is a native of Chicago and presently lives in California with his wife, Tyra, and their two daughters.

Call For Reunion — On January 17, 1993, Quincy Jones produced the CALL FOR REUNION pre-inaugural concert in honor of President-elect Clinton. The concert took place on the steps of the Lincoln Memorial and featured a vast diversity of performers. Michael performed Sam Cooke's "A Change Is Gonna Come."

"Call My Name" — Written by Michael Bolton and M. Radice.
> Appeared on EVERYBODY'S CRAZY
> (Columbia, 1985).

This song was the "B" side of the "(Sittin' On) The Dock Of The Bay" single. It was also released by Night Ranger on the album, DAWN PATROL, MCA Records, 1982.

Camozzi, Chris — Having joined Michael on his 1990 SOUL PROVIDER tour, Chris currently plays lead guitar with the band. Before he became a bandmember, Chris was a well-known session musician and had played lead guitar on a television performance for Mariah Carey.

Having played guitar since the age of seven, Chris, a California boy since birth, has a home in the desert equipped with its own recording studio where he writes and records solo instrumentals that he describes as "New Age Jazz." In the summer of 1996, Chris released his debut solo album on the Higher Octave Music label. Entitled "Windows Of My Soul," the album consisted of a collection of guitar instrumentals, and the first two hundred albums ordered through Fan Emporium were accompanied by a limited edition black and white autographed photo of Chris.

"Can't Hold On, Can't Let Go" — Written by Michael Bolton.
> Appeared on MICHAEL BOLTON
> (Columbia, 1983).
> Produced by Gerry Block and Michael Bolton.
> Aldo Nova played synthesizer on this song.

"Can I Touch You...There?" — Written by Michael Bolton and Robert John "Mutt" Lange.
> Appears on MICHAEL BOLTON GREATEST HITS
> 1985-1995 (Columbia, 1995).
> Produced by Robert John "Mutt" Lange.

This song was recorded at Passion Studios and was the first single released from the GREATEST HITS album. Michael says, "the song is about intimacy, not sex," although he did admit the video was "hot and steamy" in his personal message on the 900-number. (The video appears on Michael's videotape, DECADE.) Hitmaker called this song "the best Michael Bolton ever."

Michael recut his vocals for a dance club mix with Frankie Knuckles on the sound board and engineer/musician John Poppo.

"Can't Turn It Off" — Written by Michael Bolton and Mark Mangold.
> Appeared on EVERYBODY'S CRAZY
> (Columbia, 1985).
> Produced by Neil Kernon and Michael Bolton.

Cappuccino — Along with coffee, Michael says this is probably the "worst thing" he puts into his body. It also appears that a beautiful fake cup of cappuccino is involved in one of the many practical jokes Michael likes to play. Upon offering the unwary guest a cup of cappuccino, Michael substitutes the fake for the real thing and then "stumbles" when he brings it to them, prompting most recipients to jump back in fear of being covered in the steaming brew.

Captain — This is the title Michael held on his school baseball team.

Cara, Irene — Recorded "Give Me Love" by Michael Bolton and Patrick Henderson. She also recorded Michael Bolton's "Don't Wanna Let Go," "Lock Me Up," and "Now That It's Over."

Carey, Mariah — Mariah sang the duet, "We're Not Making Love Anymore" with Michael at a convention for Record Retailers in Los Angeles. He attended her million dollar wedding to Tommy Mottola in 1994.

Caricature — This seems to be an extremely popular method of illustrating articles on Michael Bolton.

Carillo — Michael sang background vocals on "Under the Gun" for their 1979 album, STREET OF DREAMS, released by Atlantic Records.

Carrey, Jim — When Jim Carrey appeared on the off-beat Fox Network comedy show, IN LIVING COLOR, one of the skits featured him doing a characterization of Michael Bolton in concert. His singing became so vehement that his head exploded and fans in the audience fought over the flying pieces of his hair.

"Carrie" — Written by Michael Bolton.
  Appeared on MICHAEL BOLTON
    (Columbia, 1983).
  Produced by Gerry Block and Michael Bolton.

Carroll, Dave — This softball legend became Michael's personal softball trainer and is featured in the "MICHAEL BOLTON'S WINNING SOFTBALL: HIT HARDER, PLAY SMARTER" videotape.

CBS This Morning — A network morning news show that featured a segment on Michael Bolton during Michael's THE ONE THING promotion. The segment showed CBS correspondent Mark McEwen playing a game of pool with Michael at Michael's home. Mark interviewed Michael during the game and lost "big," while Michael spoke about his new album. (Note: Michael's pool room has interesting wall coverings. During the interview you can see framed *People* and *US* magazines with his picture on the cover, a photograph of Michael at the Grammys, a photo of Andre Agassi at Wimbledon, a picture of Michael with Kenny G. and his wife, and a framed Barry Bonds jersey autographed by the team.)

Celebrations — Although Michael frequently appears at celebrations around the world for charities, honors, and industry awards, he also regularly appears at smaller, more personal celebrations "in absentia." Fan gatherings the world over add Michael — his music and his likeness — to their guest list.

Celebrity Tennis Classic, Softball Game and Black Tie Gala — This annual event is the main fundraiser for the Michael Bolton Foundation and is traditionally held in October. The Old Greenwich area of Connecticut was the site of the first four events. Originally a weekend-long event consisting of a Bolton Bombers softball game, celebrity tennis matches, and a black tie dinner featuring both live and silent auctions, the event became a one-day event in 1996 when the tennis matches were discontinued. Michael and his band headline the entertainment, which generally includes at least one known comic and another musical guest. In 1995, The Michael Bolton Foundation awarded "The Michael Bolton Lifetime Achievement Awards" to acknowledge people who have made a major difference in the lives of women and children at risk.

Centerstage — This informal VH1 concert appearance was taped and first shown on Valentine's Day, 1993. Michael was casually dressed and unshaven. Together, he and his band played all their hits.

Michael was joined onstage by Percy Sledge for a duet on "When A Man Loves A Woman". Michael also spoke between songs and at one point, impersonated Rodney Dangerfield.

Chapel Alley Associates — According to an advertisement in a New Haven newspaper, Michael gave voice lessons here in 1980.

Charities — Michael is deeply involved in helping children realize their potential and actively donates his time and money to many charities whose goals he believes in.

Some of the many organizations he has been associated with are: THIS CLOSE for Cancer Research, The National Committee for the Prevention of Child Abuse, Pediatric Aids Foundation, The Cystic Fibrosis Foundation, The City of Hope, The T.J. Martell Foundation, The United Negro College Fund, Ronald McDonald Charities, The Starlight Foundation, the Harlem School of the Arts, and, of course, his own Michael Bolton Foundation.

Charlie Rose Show, The — Apparently, Michael's daughter, Isa, is a big fan of this talk show and it's host. Michael made an appearance and even took home an autograph for her.

Michael at Rockefeller Center — Christmas Time

Charles, Ray — Ray was one of Michael's first musical influences. Michael relates, "Ray Charles definitely had a tremendous initial impact on me." He also counts singing a duet with Ray Charles as one of the highest points of his career. (For more information on the duet, see the listing RAY CHARLES - 50 Years In Music.)

Cher — Michael co-wrote three songs (and produced two of them) on Cher's 1988 self-titled album. One of those songs, "I Found Someone" (co-written with Mark Mangold) became a hit for her. When she went back into the studio to make her 1989 album, "HEART OF STONE," she wanted Michael to go, too, as her producer. He wrote and produced three more songs for that album and her album notes thanked "Michael 'How's My Hair?' Bolton" for his help. Michael also sang backup for her song, "Emotional Fire" and in the fall of 1995, they both appeared on the Swedish *Save The Children* telethon.

Child, Desmond — This songwriter has frequently collaborated with Michael Bolton. Some examples of their work together include: "How Can We Be Lovers," "Love Cuts Deep," "New Love," "Forever Isn't Long Enough," "In The Arms Of Love," and "The One Thing." Desmond was one of the songwriters who traveled to Russia during Glasnost in October, 1987. He released a solo album, DISCIPLINE (Elektra) in 1991.

Children — Michael has said, "It's more important that the support is there no matter how they do." He's also said, "No matter what happens, we have to remember that these are children. A plant or a tree when it's first put in the ground needs a lot of protection until it can handle whatever the world exposes it to. Our children need the same kind of nurturing. We have to protect them from the worst side of ourselves."

Chimpanzees — At first, Michael compared most music critics to this animal, but later retracted his statement, saying that chimpanzees are a higher life form.

China Club, The — This was a Manhattan club that featured Michael Bolton in the 1980's.

Choice Seats — 200 of these are put aside at all Michael Bolton concerts for Gold Club members only.

Christmas at Rockefeller Center — This televised special, aired live on December 3, 1996, featured Michael Bolton singing "Santa Claus Is Coming To Town" while Ekaterina Gordeeva skated. Later, Michael and Ekaterina had the honor of flipping the switch on the Rockefeller Center Christmas Tree.

"The Christmas Song" — Written by Mel Torme and Robert Wells.
    Appeared on THIS IS THE TIME —
        THE CHRISTMAS ALBUM (Columbia, 1996).
    Produced by Johnny Mandel and Michael Bolton.
    Orchestra Arranged and Conducted by Johnny
       Mandel.

Circus Magazine —In the June 30, 1985 edition of this magazine, the words to Michael's song, "Everybody's Crazy" appeared with a short biography and one picture.

CityKids All Star Celebration — This benefit special, which marked the 10th anniversary of the CityKids Foundation, took place on October 13, 1995 in New York City. CityKids Foundation is a non-profit organization dedicated to fostering communication and leadership among young people. This show, hosted by Demi Moore, featured performances by Michael Bolton and Paula Abdul, among others. A television special taped at the show was aired on April 20, 1996 and showed Michael singing Marvin Gaye's hit, "What's Going On" backed by the CityKids Repertory Company.

Clapton, Eric — Michael has said that he learned to play guitar by studying Eric Clapton and Mike Bloomfield.

Coaching — Although Michael is generally found playing softball, he has been known to coach his team at third base, also. Michael loves the game and has acquired quite a bit of knowledge, too, which led to a slight problem while dad Michael was coaching third base for one of his daughters softball games. He apparently had a difference of opinion about the game with his daughter's coach, which led to an argument that ended when Michael was asked to leave the field and wound up watching the end of the game from the stands.

Coke Classic and Diet Coke — Michael Bolton was "The Voice" for them in the mid-80s, and sang the jingle behind Michael Jordan in a 1990 commercial for Coke Classic.

Collective Sigh — This is what Canadian reviewer Nick Krewen says Michael Bolton's fans give when they see him "clutching a cute cuddl-wee widdle toy" given him by a fan. He also reflects that this sight and the ensuing sigh tests the gag reflex of music critics.

Collinet, Susan — Susan is the TV Coordinator for Fan Emporium, Inc.

Collyer, David Sorin — A dedication to David, Michael's longtime friend, mentor, and vocal coach, appears on the THIS IS THE TIME album. David Sorin Collyer was 81 when he died in 1996.

Cologne — Michael does not wear cologne.

Columbus Day Parade, New Haven, 1983

Columbus Day Parade — A Columbus Day Parade was held in the city of New Haven, Connecticut in October of 1983. Michael had released the album, MICHAEL BOLTON, which featured the song, "Hometown Hero." Joyce Logan, who was at the time working as a promotions director at WPLR radio arranged for Michael to appear in the parade as a real life 'Hometown Hero' with his album playing on the sound system behind him.

"Completely" — Written by Diane Warren.
    Appeared on THE ONE THING album
      (Columbia, 1993).
    Produced by David Foster and Michael Bolton.
    Arranged by David Foster.
    Orchestra arranged by David Foster and
      Jeremy Lubbock.
This was the second single released from Michael's THE ONE THING album, and the B side of the single was a live version of "That's What Love Is All About" recorded at Wembley Arena, England. According to Michael, "Completely" is not just about romantic love, but about a way of life. Anything you love and want to do, you must give yourself to completely, heart and soul. The video of this song appears on Michael's videotape, DECADE.

Connecticut Artist Awards — The first Annual Connecticut Artist Awards was held October 17, 1995 in the Palace Theatre in Stamford, Connecticut. Along with Gene Wilder, Claire Bloom, and others, Michael received a Distinguished Achievement Award. Christopher Plummer was awarded the Lifetime Achievement Award.

Contact Lenses-Blue — We know, we thought they were, too. Apparently, though, the beautiful blue eyes that first appeared on the cover of THE ONE THING album were truly Michael's own. The eye change was due to the photographer's enhancement of color. It seems that Michael's eyes have that well-known hazel trait of changing when it suits them. (If blue gets into the color mix, it reflects the blue that is in Michael's eyes and if there arc grccn hues, his eyes appear green.) Sony Music liked the look and went with it for the album cover.

Control Freak — Michael is a self-confessed control freak.

Michael Takes His Softball Game Very Seriously

"Countin' On You" — Written by Michael Bolotin and Bruce Kulick.

> Appeared on BLACKJACK (Polydor, 1979).
> Produced by Tom Dowd.

Country Music Association Awards — Michael caused eyebrows to rise and tongues to wag when he appeared (and sang) at the 30th Annual Awards show on October 2, 1996. Michael performed the duet "This Is The Time" with country star Wynonna Judd and although he co-wrote the song with a top country songwriter (Gary Burr) and sang it with one of country music's top female performers, there was still quite an outcry over a "POP" singer appearing on the CMAs.

USA Today's Country Music Critic, David Zimmerman wrote about "...a duet between Wynonna Judd and Michael Bolton(!), which some here equate with the work of the devil." Responding to the critics, Wynonna was quoted as saying, "the duet looks good on my resume," and Michael said, "I feel fortunate to be invited into this (country) world." (Special Note for the fashion conscious: Michael appeared in BLACK LEATHER PANTS!)

Covers of Classics — Michael's many covers of classics throughout his career has led to a great deal of trouble with the music critics over the years. Nonetheless, Michael continues pleasing both himself and his fans with his renditions of old favorites. According to a radio interview, Michael believes that covering a classic is "...not about doing a classic better—it's about doing a classic justice."

Cramming — This is the method most often applied by Michael Bolton when it becomes necessary for him to learn something new. For instance, when the opera projects required him to learn Italian, he loaded his jeep with cassettes and took up "power-driving," just driving for hours with the cassettes (and himself) singing and speaking at full volume.

Creative Artists Agency — This agency was listed in the first two tour books as being Michael's booking agency. They were also listed as a California mailing address for Michael Bolton.

Crush, The — The credits of this 1993 movie listed Michael Bolton as the Production Designer. No, it wasn't OUR Michael Bolton.

 Dances With Wolves — An American epic movie starring Kevin Costner. Michael, an avid movie watcher, loved this film.

"Dancing In The Street" — Written by W. Stevenson, M. Gayle, and I. Hunter.

> Appeared on EVERY DAY OF MY LIFE (RCA, 1976).
> Also appeared on THE ARTISTRY OF MICHAEL BOLOTIN (RCA, 1993).
> Produced by Jack Richardson for Nimbus 9 Productions.

Dangerfield, Rodney — Michael Bolton can, and does, do a Rodney Dangerfield impersonation so good that Buddy Hackett thought he was a professional impersonator after Michael did a walk-on appearance on Jay Leno's show. Rodney was a special celebrity guest at the 3rd Annual "This Close" for Cancer Research benefit and, after seeing Michael's Dangerfield impersonation, said, "He does me better than I do." Michael's song, "Everybody's Crazy," was featured in Rodney's movie, "Back to School" and Michael has a cameo role in the Dangerfield movie, "Meet Wally Sparks." In a press release for Michael's EVERYBODY'S CRAZY album, Rodney is quoted as saying, "What's normal? Normal is what you think people are until you get to know them."

Michael With Rodney Dangerfield

Davis, Mick — Co-wrote the screenplay for Michael's up-coming movie, *L'Voce*, with Michael Bolton.

Davis, Rob — The dedication on the Blackjack album, WORLDS APART, includes a special thanks to Rob Davis, "whose patience, dedication and abilities have made this album a reality."

Deale, Schuyler — Schuyler is Michael's bass player and his infectious smile and guitar skills are real crowd pleasers at Bolton concerts. Born in Long Island, New York in 1960, Schuyler grew up in Long Beach, first discovering his talent for music in 1969 with the bass-playing uncle of a close friend. At the age of 14, Schuyler owned his first bass guitar and found himself playing in a band called Primo. Primo opened for the legendary New York band, Good Rats, and eventually Schuyler was drafted into that band. It was during his two-year stint as a Good Rat that he met Bruce Kulick (who had been a guitar player for Blackjack) and when Bruce went into the studio with Michael in 1985 to record EVERYBODY'S CRAZY, he took Schuyler with him.

Schuyler went on to play with a large roster of artists, including Julian Lennon, Angela Bofill, Heart, and Billy Joel. After touring with Billy Joel, he received a phone call from Louis Levin asking if he "was available." It was then that he became a member of Michael's band, rehearsing and touring on the TIME, LOVE & TENDERNESS tour. He has been with them ever since. Besides playing bass for Michael, Schuyler has also played softball with the Bolton Bombers.

DECADE 1985-1995 — This videotape, released in 1995 by Columbia Music Video, features nine of Michael's videos separated by short interview segments. The videos are: *Soul Provider; How Am I Supposed to Live Without You; How Can We Be Lovers* (a live performance from Center Stage); *Georgia On My Mind; Time, Love & Tenderness;*

Joe DiMaggio and Michael

When a Man Loves a Woman (a live performance from CenterStage, featuring Percy Sledge); *Said I Loved You...But I Lied; Completely* (Adult Version); *Can I Touch You...There?*
The International Collection includes six more videos.

Demons, The — Michael sang background vocals on their 1977 promo record, released on Mercury Records (Stock No. SRMI-1164).

"Desperate Heart" — Written by Michael Bolton and R. Goodrum. Appeared on EVERYBODY'S CRAZY (Columbia, 1985). Jefferson Starship later recorded this song. A press release for this song called it "a[n] observation of the hopeless denial of a relationship ending."

Diamond, Keith — This late songwriter collaborated with Michael on "Gina," which appeared on THE HUNGER album. Keith also co-produced much of this album.

Diamond Stud — Michael wears a diamond stud earring in his left ear.

DiMaggio, Joe — Joe DiMaggio (also known as the Yankee Clipper) is one of Michael's baseball heroes. Michael first met him on January 17, 1993 at a charity ballgame for Habitat for Humanity in Florida to benefit Dade County after the hurricane disaster. Since their first meeting, Michael has played on Joe DiMaggio's team in his All Stars Legend Game in Florida and Joe threw out the first pitch at the Bomber's softball game as part of the Michael Bolton Foundation's Third Annual Celebrity Tennis Classic, Softball Game, and Black Tie Weekend. Michael also appeared at the Joe DiMaggio

Classic event in February, 1997 and played softball the next day in the All Stars Game. Michael's awe of this baseball great and regard for his father's memory was apparent when he said, "What a story to be able to tell my father that Joe DiMaggio and I just sat down and talked for an hour." (See also JOE DIMAGGIO'S ALL-STARS LEGENDS GAME.)

Dion, Celine — She was one of Michael's opening acts for his 1994 tour. Celine later demonstrated her appreciation of Michael Bolton by thanking him publicly for his help and support during concerts on her own solo 1996 tour.

Divine Light Mission — This was a Hindu-based cult dedicated to promoting Guru Maharaj Ji whose followers were called "Premies." They employed four techniques of meditation. Michael and his wife were members in the '70s.

"(Sittin' On) The Dock Of The Bay" — Written by Otis Redding and S. Cropper.
>   Appeared on THE HUNGER (Columbia, 1987).
>   Also appeared on GREATEST HITS 1985-1995
>   (Columbia, 1996) and THINKING OF YOU
>   (Sony Music Special Products, 1996).
>   Produced by Jonathan Cain for Cain
>   Street Productions.

This was the second single from THE HUNGER album and the B side of the single was "Call My Name." Besides producing this song, Jonathan Cain played keyboards and fellow "Journey" men Neal Schon, Randy Jackson, and Mike Baird also appeared. James Ingram does background vocals. This song led to Michael's being asked to perform on the "Showtime At The Apollo" show and in January of 1988, Michael received a letter from Zelma Redding, Otis' widow, saying that Michael's version was her favorite version since her husband's. The video for this song appears on Michael's videotape, SOUL & PASSION.

Domich, Rich — Rich was co-announcer with Tom Gross at the Bolton Bombers Celebrity Softball Game for the Michael Bolton Foundation in Connecticut, 1996. Rich works for Phoenix Communications, the company that produced Michael's softball video

Donations — Michael has been very generous with both his time and money for needy charities around the country. He is especially generous when the charities are related to children and their needs. An example was the $25,000 donation that he gave to the Harlem School of the Arts in February, 1993. (His donation was matched by his record label, Columbia Records.)

"Don't Make Me Wait For Love" — Written by Glass, Afanasieff, and Walden.
>   Appeared on KENNY G LIVE (Arista, 1989).
>   Michael sang this song in a live appearance with Kenny G. for the album.

"Don't Tell Me It's Over" — Written by Michael Bolton and J. Mullaney.
>   Appeared on EVERYBODY'S CRAZY
>   (Columbia, 1985).
>   Produced by Neil Kernon and Michael Bolton.

Dorothy Chandler Pavillion — Michael Bolton performed at a benefit for the United Negro College Fund here on June 26, 1993.

Downs, Kim — Kim is currently Vice President of Bolton Music but she started out as a fan. She became "phone buddies" with Joyce Logan through the fan club and was invited to Connecticut to meet Michael. The rest is history and she's been working with him for several years.

Dr. Bolton — Michael was awarded a Doctor of Fine Arts Degree by the University of Connecticut on May 20, 1995. He is now officially entitled to be called, "Dr. Bolton."

"Dreaming Dreams" — Written by Michael Bolton This song is unpublished and unrecorded. Mention of it was made by Michael in the fan club newsletter, *The Bolton Beat*, volume 2, in response to a question from a fan.

"Dream While You Can" — Written by Michael Bolotin.
>   Appeared on MICHAEL BOLOTIN (RCA, 1975).
>   Also appeared on MICHAEL BOLOTIN:
>   THE EARLY YEARS (RCA, 1991).
>   Produced by Joe Cy.
>   Wayne Perkins plays slide guitar and Dave Sanborn plays alto sax on this track.

"Drift Away" — Written by M. Williams.
Appeared on TIMELESS: THE CLASSICS (Columbia, 1992). Produced by Walter Afanasieff and Michael Bolton. Background vocals sung by PH1 Choir and Pat, Vann, and Janice. The lead vocals were recorded at Passion Studios, CT.

Dylan, Bob — This famous singer/songwriter collaborated with Michael Bolton on "Steel Bars." Michael told the story of their meeting to Michael Angeli (from *Esquire* magazine) and said Dylan proposed lyrics like, "I could not bear what would materialize, but you, so ready to etherealize." Michael also relates this story at concerts in his introduction to the song and ends it with a pretty good impersonation of Dylan. He has said that "Steel Bars" was written the fastest of all his songs and that he would like to collaborate with Dylan again.

Eggplant Parmesan — One of Michael's favorite dishes, sliced *very* thin.

Egotrips, Inc. — Michael Bolton's tour trucking company. We really like the name of this company.

Eichner, Mickey, Joe McEwen, and Al Teller – The liner notes of THE HUNGER album gives Michael's "deepest gratitude" to them "who showed their faith and belief." These three people are the Columbia executives who kept talking about "the next album" and talked Michael into recording his ballads himself. Michael's fans owe them thanks, too.

11:30 AM — The time of day that Michael claimed he gets up "most days" when he appeared on Rosie O'Donnell's talk show. She had introduced him by saying, "Here's Michael 'I'm so happy to be up in the morning' Bolton," and continued to gently tease him about it throughout the interview. (See O'Donnell, Rosie listing for more information.)

ELVIS ARON PRESLEY: THE TRIBUTE — A live tribute concert was held on October 8, 1994 and telecast on Pay-Per-View tv. Many different performers did their renditions of Elvis Presley classics and Michael was one of them. He sang and danced to "Jailhouse Rock" dressed in a black pin-striped double-breasted suit with a black shirt and white tie. With his hair tucked up into a hat, he looked every bit the gangster. The legendary Carl Perkins accompanied him on guitar. An album, "NOW OR NEVER — A TRIBUTE TO ELVIS" was later released from the show.

Emote — The Funk & Wagnalls Standard Desk Dictionary (Volume 1) defines this as "to exhibit an exaggerated emotion, as in acting." For an alternative definition, see Michael's videotape, DECADE 1985-1995.

Entertainment Tonight — This is an evening entertainment news show that has featured numerous segments on Michael Bolton, covering such subjects as his concerts, his baseball games, his charity events, and the making of his videos. In February, 1996, they did a segment on a Victoria's Secret Valentine's Runway show in New York City that featured backstage interviews with (and footage of) the models. Michael was interviewed after the fashion show and, although he tried to give thoughtful insight into what he had just seen, the only truly coherent thought that came out was, "Wow."

Erler, Glen — This photographer was responsible for the SOUL PROVIDER album cover photo.

ESPN and ESPN2 — ESPN, the all-sports cable station, televised a Tribute to Richard Petty on July 4, 1992 that featured Michael singing the song, "One More Time," from the movie SING. Also, selected Bolton Bombers games were telecast on ESPN2 during the summer and fall of 1995 and summer of 1997.

ESPY Awards — At the Awards presentation in 1995, Michael Bolton and Kim Alexis presented the Baseball Player of the Year Award to Jeff Bagwell, Jr.

Essence Awards — On May 12, 1995, Michael appeared at the 25th Anniversary of the Essence Awards, singing "Rock Me" with the legendary B.B. King. Michael said

Going to the Well . . .

19

Michael, Jeff Bagwell, Jr. and Kim Alexis at the 1995 ESPY Awards

that he was very nervous backstage before the show and B.B. told him to calm down. Michael replied, "That's easy for you to say. You don't have to play guitar with B.B. King." Michael also appeared for the finale, playing guitar again on "Let The Good Times Roll." The show was taped and televised on June 13, 1995.

European Tour Featuring Kenny G — This tour took place from April 21 to May 2, 1993 and included concerts in Switzerland, Germany, Holland, France, Sweden, Norway, Denmark, Scotland, and Great Britain. This time around, Michael was the head-liner.

Evert, Chris — This professional tennis player appeared at, and played in, matches at the first two Michael Bolton Foundation Celebrity Tennis Classics, Softball Games, and Black Tie Gala weekends. She also hosted the "Chris Evert Pro-Celebrity Tennis Classic" in Boca Raton, Florida in 1994. The match partnered Michael Bolton with Tracey Austin against Chris Evert and President George Bush and was televised in it's entirety on ESPN in October, 1994. The participants all wore microphones and the comments and chatter were as entertaining as the tennis. The Evert-Bush team won the match, but the real winners were Chris' Foundation, beneficiaries of the proceeds.

EVERY DAY OF MY LIFE — This album, Michael's second on the RCA label, was produced by Jack Richardson and released in 1976. It was recorded in Toronto, Canada. Featured musicians are Patrick Henderson, Jan Mullaney, Billy Elworthy, Gary Ferraro, Jay Michaels, and Papa John Creach. The songs were:

1. *You Make Me Feel Like Loving You*
2. *You're No Better Than A Common Thief*
3. *Every Day Of My Life*
4. *You Mean More To Me*
5. *Singin' The Blues*
6. *You've Got The Love I Need*
7. *If I Had Your Love*
8. *These Eyes*
9. *Rocky Mountain Way*
10. *Dancing In The Street*

(See individual song listings for writer and producer information.)

"Every Day Of My Life" — Written by Henderson and Hillman. Appeared on EVERY DAY OF MY LIFE (RCA, 1976). Produced by Jack Richardson

EVERYBODY'S CRAZY —This album, produced by Neil Kernon and Michael Bolton was released by Columbia in 1985. Michael's manager, Louis Levin, was the executive producer. Bruce Kulick, who had been an original member of Blackjack, played guitar with Michael and Schuyler Deale. The record was dedicated to the memory of

Wally Meyrowitz and special thanks included Bob Seger & The Silver Bullet Band, as well as Irene Cara. The album also features Michael's version of "Desperate Heart," which was later covered by Jefferson Starship. The album tracks are:

1. *Save Our Love*
2. *Everybody's Crazy*
3. *Can't Turn It Off*
4. *Call My Name*
5. *Don't Tell Me It's Over*
6. *Everytime*
7. *Desperate Heart*
8. *Start Breaking My Heart*
9. *You Don't Want Me Bad Enough*

(See individual song listings for writer and producer information.)

"Everybody's Crazy" — Written by Michael Bolton.
> Appeared on EVERYBODY'S CRAZY
> > (Columbia, 1985).
> Also appeared in the movie, BACK TO SCHOOL.
> This song was Michael's second video and according to a press release, it is partially autobiographical. Although widely interpreted as a party song, it actually depicts "kids who are having a hard time dealing with everyone else in the world— because they can't quite deal with themselves." In the video, his band is shown performing in front of large screens upon which scenes of real-life craziness are being shown. (Sort of an "America's Craziest Home Videos" kind of show.) Schuyler Deale plays bass for Michael on this song.

"Everybody Needs A Reason" — Written by Michael Bolotin.
> Appeared on MICHAEL BOLOTIN (RCA, 1975).
> Also appeared on MICHAEL BOLOTIN: THE
> > EARLY YEARS (RCA, 1991).
> Produced by Joe Cy and Michael Bolotin.
> Strings for this song were arranged and conducted by John Abbott.

"Everytime" — Written by Michael Bolton and Mark Mangold.
> Appeared on EVERYBODY'S CRAZY (Columbia, 1985).
> Produced by Neil Kernon and Michael Bolton.

Evian Water — One of Michael's favorite drinks.

Evolution — Michael has said that THE GREATEST HITS 1985-1995 demonstrates the evolution of his music in this way: With THE HUNGER, he was finding his strength; with SOUL PROVIDER, he was locking in on his direction; with TIME, LOVE & TENDERNESS, he hit a Bull's Eye, with THE CLASSICS, he took a brief departure back to his early influences; and with THE ONE THING, he turned and reached for new directions.

Extra — This evening entertainment show has featured several segments on Michael Bolton. One of the segments, titled CHANCE OF A LIFETIME, which aired on December 14, 1995, gave information about the LIFETIME CABLE-sponsored contest to win an interactive concert by Michael Bolton. (See LIFETIME CABLE CONTEST OF A LIFETIME listing for more information.) Another notable clip was titled HAIR TODAY, GONE TOMORROW which aired in February, 1996 and told about the possibility of Michael cutting his hair for acting roles. The segment included computer-enhanced projections of Michael Bolton in different hairstyles-Elvis, Beatles, and Coolio. This is entertainment?

 Fairness in Musical Licensing Act of 1995 — In an advertisement sponsored by the Songwriters and Music Publishers of BMI which appeared in *Billboard* on December 2, 1995, Michael Bolton spoke out against this Act. Under a heading that read, "Don't Take The Property of America's Songwriters!" a picture of Michael appeared with the quote, "Songwriting royalties put food on the table for years before my first hit as a recording artist. That's a pretty typical story in our business. Don't let them stifle the next generation of songwriters."

Falana, James — He is the designer of The Michael Bolton Foundation Logo. James is also the Creative Director of both the Michale Bolton Foundation and Bolton Music.

"Fallin'" — Written by Michael Bolotin and Bruce Kulick. Appeared on BLACKJACK (Polydor, 1979). Produced by Tom Dowd.

Family Vacations — This item is an important part of the Bolton agenda and a long-time tradition in Michael's family, beginning with childhood vacations in places like Washington, D.C. and Atlantic City, N.J. through to today's vacations in Aspen. CO, and assorted tropical islands.

21

Michael, Sandra and Orrin in Washington, D.C.

Fan Emporium, Inc. — Fan Emporium was started in October, 1984 by Joyce Logan and has grown into the thriving business it is today. It is responsible for all facets of Michael Bolton's fan club: the newsletters, memorabilia, artist liaison, magazines, and hotlines. Today this spreading business has offices operating in Georgia, London, and Tokyo, besides the home office in Branford, Connecticut. (See address listings at the back of the book for postal and e-mail addresses.)

Fan Mail — Michael says, "Music is a really powerful, powerful thing. It really affects people's lives. People lean on it; they hold on to certain records to get them through the toughest times of their life. You don't realize that until you read the fan mail."

Favorite Baseball Teams — Michael's are the San Francisco Giants and the New York Yankees.

Febbraio, Tommy — Michael's close friend and key event organizer for the Michael Bolton Foundation Annual Black Tie Gala.

February 26 — Michael Bolton's birthday. (Per the December 7, 1992 *People Magazine* article, his birth year is 1953.)

Feinstein, David — Michael's business manager.

Field of Dream Awards — This was a gala 200-star salute honoring Anthony Quinn, Maureen O'Hara, Sid Caesar, David Foster, Kenny "Babyface" Edmonds, Joe DiMaggio, and Don Ienner, as well as the Major League Baseball Players Choice Awards. It was held on November 6, 1994 and was co-hosted by Michael Bolton and Barry Bonds to benefit both the Michael Bolton Foundation and the Bonds Family Foundation. Tickets to the gala were $2,500 each or $50,000 for a table. The event also included a softball game between the Bolton Bombers and Barry Bonds with Major League players that was taped and later televised by ESPN.

50/50 Split — The proceeds from Bolton Bombers games are split between a local charity and The Michael Bolton Foundation this way.

"Fighting For My Life" — Written by Michael Bolton.
    Appeared on MICHAEL BOLTON
        (Columbia, 1983).
    Produced by Gerry Block and Michael Bolton.

First Kiss — first girl that Michael Bolton ever kissed was reportedly Dorian Shapiro of Connecticut.

Flack, Roberta — Along with Michael Bolton, she presented the 1995 American Music Award for the Pop/Rock New Artist. (Michael had a bit of a problem getting the envelope open.)

Floor-Length Wool Trenchcoat — Michael donated this coat to the 2nd Annual Project Overcoat Celebrity Coat Auction to benefit children with aids. An advertisement for the phone-in auction appeared in the 11/7-11/13/92 issue of TV GUIDE.

"Fool's Game" — Written by Michael Bolton, Mark Mangold, and Craig Brooks.
    Appeared on MICHAEL BOLTON
        (Columbia, 1983).
    Produced by Gerry Block and Michael Bolton.
    Michael plays guitar solo on this track and Mark Mangold plays synthesizer. Background vocals are done by Michael, Mark Mangold, and Craig Brooks. This song was Michael's first video and then it became one of MTV's most requested videos. Bobby "T" Torello appears in the video playing drums and Bruce Kulick (of Blackjack) plays guitar.

For Our Children: The Concert — This special benefit concert was filmed in Disneyland in November, 1992 and first telecast on the Disney Channel in February, 1993. The concert and a CD/video package (released February 16, 1993 on Disney's Spotlight Artist Series) was to raise money for the Pediatric Aids Foundation. Performers included Sheila E., Paula Abdul, Kriss Kross,

Salt-N-Pepa, Woody Harrelson, and Michael Bolton. Michael sang "You Are My Sunshine."

"For You" — Written by Michael Bolotin. Appeared on BLACKJACK (Polydor, 1979). Produced by Tom Dowd.

"Forever" — Written by Michael Bolton and Paul Stanley. Although this song has appeared on two KISS albums, Michael has never recorded it.

"Forever Eyes" — This song, written by Michael Bolton and Bob Halligan, Jr., ONLY appears as the B side of the "How Am I Supposed To Live Without You" single, released in 1989 by Columbia Records.

"Forever Isn't Long Enough" — Written by Michael Bolton, Diane Warren, and Desmond Child.
    Appeared on TIME, LOVE & TENDERNESS (Columbia, 1991).
    Produced by Walter Afanasieff and Michael Bolton.
    Walter plays keyboards, Hammond B-3 Organ, Synthesizers, Synth Bass, drums, and percussion. Background vocals include Joe Turano and Desmond Child.

Formal Education — Michael says his formal education was stopped at the age of 15, when he was "drafted into the world of music."

Forrest Gump — When asked in an interview what he does to relax, Michael replied, "It's difficult to tell the machine to slow down. It's like Forrest Gump running into the locker room after the touchdown."

Forward Face — Michael Bolton performed at the April 21, 1994 Forward Face Spring Benefit for children around the world with craniofacial conditions.

Michael at the Forward Face Spring Benefit, 1994

Foster, David — Grammy Award winning composer who was co-producer of TIMELESS-THE CLASSICS and THE ONE THING albums. He produced "In The Arms Of Love" with Michael Bolton, and produced and arranged "Bring It On Home To Me," "Completely," "White Christmas," "Yesterday," and "You Send Me." He also played keyboards on "Completely."

Fourth Annual Salute to the American Songwriter —Michael performed four songs at this VH1 televised show from the Wiltern Theater in Los Angeles.

Free Range Chickens — On April 20, 1991, *Saturday Night Live* did a spoof of "musicians for causes" songs featuring Michael joining the cast of SNL made up as various rock stars. At one point during the skit, Victoria Jackson sang solo and her throat visibly and exaggeratedly contorted itself with her efforts. Michael, watching her, had a hard time keeping a straight face, stumbled over his part, and had to swallow hard to continue.

Friedland, Richard (Ribs) — Michael has said that this man (a manager of a local band in New Haven) launched his career in the '60s. In 1970, Richard ran a vegetarian restaurant in Los Angeles and had Michael make demos that he could play for his record company clientele. Some producers heard them and Michael started to record with Pentagram Records.

Frione, Donna — Donna is the artist responsible for the cover art on the MICHAEL BOLOTIN album.

"From Now On" — Written by Michael Bolton and E. Kaz. Appeared on SOUL PROVIDER (Columbia, 1989). Produced by Michael Bolton for MBO. Productions, Inc.
    Suzie Benson sang this duet with Michael.

 Gaye, Marvin — One of Michael's earliest musical influences, Michael sang Marvin's hit, "What's Going On" at the CityKids All Star Celebration in New York City, October 13, 1995.

George's Boys — Fairly well-known New Haven group in the '60s. Michael was the lead singer and his brother Orrin played drums.

"Georgia On My Mind" — Written by H. Carmichael and S. Gorrell.
    Appeared on SOUL PROVIDER (Columbia, 1989).

Also appeared on GREATEST HITS 1985-1995 (Columbia, 1995) and THINKING OF YOU (Sony Music Special Products, 1996).

Produced by Michael Bolton and Susan Hamilton.

Schuyler Deale played bass on this song and it won Michael his second Grammy nomination. It didn't, however, win him a Grammy. When asked why he recorded this song, Michael replied, "Every instinct was telling me I should record this song at this time." The "Georgia On My Mind" video appears on Michael's SOUL & PASSION and DECADE 1985-1995 videotapes.

German Shepherd — Michael's favorite pet.

"Gimme Some Lovin' " — Michael performed this song live in Orlando, Florida on May 14, 1988. A former member of his band, Blackjack, played guitar for this song and Mugs Cain was on drums. Michael also performed this song on his "The Hunger" tour and while opening for Heart.

"Gina" — Written by Michael Bolton, B. Halligan, Jr. and K. Diamond. Appeared on THE HUNGER (Columbia, 1987). Produced by the late Keith Diamond, who also played bass, drums, and keyboards on the track.

"Say It's Forever . . ."

"Give It A Shot" — "Go ahead and really give it a shot. And nobody can make you do that except yourself." —Michael Bolton on the importance of trying to reach your dreams.

"Give Me A Reason" — Written by Michael Bolotin. Appeared on MICHAEL BOLOTIN (RCA, 1975). Also appeared on MICHAEL BOLOTIN-THE EARLY YEARS (RCA, 1991). Produced by Joe Cy and recorded January 20, 1975.

GLASNOST — Michael traveled to Moscow in October, 1988 to collaborate on the writing and performing of this album made up of American and Russian songwriters and performers.

"Go The Distance" — Michael performed and recorded this song for Walt Disney Records. Written by Alan Menken and David Zippel, this was the first single released from the soundtrack to Disney's 35th full-length animated feature, HERCULES. Michael is also featured in the song's music video.

Goldberg, Whoopi — Whoopi introduced Michael Bolton on the televised special to celebrate President Clinton's first year in office. In her intro, Whoopi chided Michael for "not showing up at rehearsal." Michael sang "Said I Loved You...But I Lied."

Golden Phone Award, 1994 — This California award was given to Michael's 900-number for excellence in fundraising. (This is like the Grammy for the interactive phone service, being an industry award judged on quality, clarity, creativity, and designs of print ads.) Some other finalists were: Nickelodeon, Michael Jackson, ESPN, and the Coca-Cola Company. 1994 was the last year this award was given; in 1995, it became the Alex Award. (See Alex Award listing for more information.)

Goldmark, Andrew — Songwriter who collaborated with Michael Bolton on "Save Me," "Soul Provider," and "Love Is A Wonderful Thing."

Good Morning America — A morning network news show that has done several segments on Michael. In the autumn of 1993, Michael did an interview with Joan Lunden at his Westport, Connecticut home as promotion for THE ONE THING album. During the interview he said, "The ultimate romantic is part of who I am." Several months later, on December 15, Michael was again a guest on the show, this time speaking about Child Abuse Prevention. He told the story of how he got actively involved in the prevention of child abuse through a request on behalf of an abused teenager who later committed suicide.

Goodrum, Randy — This songwriter collaborated with Michael on the song "Desperate Heart."

Gordeeva, Ektarina — This world famous figure skater performed twice during the 1996 Christmas at Rockefeller Center Special. The last performance was accompanied by Michael singing, "Santa Claus is Coming to Town."

Grammy Awards — As of 1996, Michael had won two of the four Grammy's that he had been nominated for. *(At right, Joyce Logan and Michael hold one of Michael's Grammy Awards.)* He received his first nomination in 1990 for BEST POP VOCAL-MALE, nominated for the song, "How Am I Supposed To Live Without You." He performed that song with Kenny G. on the televised award show and went home with his first Grammy.

In 1991, Michael was nominated for "Georgia On My Mind" but didn't win.

In 1992, Michael was again nominated for BEST POP VOCAL-MALE for "When A Man Loves A Woman" and again performed his nominating song on the show. Once more, he won, but through an oversight, neglected to mention Percy Sledge in his acceptance speech. The critics were merciless, booing him backstage as he accepted his award. Happy and excited, Michael was genuinely shocked at their reaction and this was the beginning of the open war between them.

Michael did not receive any nominations in 1993 and 1994, but in 1995 he was nominated for BEST POP VOCAL-MALE, this time for "Said I Loved You...But I Lied." He lost to Elton John and, because the award was given out before the televised show, did not attend the ceremony, saying, "I decided that if it wasn't important enough for them to air, it wasn't important enough for me to be there."

GRAMMY'S GREATEST MOMENTS, Vol. II — This videotape contains the Michael Bolton/Kenny G. performance of "How Am I Supposed To Live Without You" from the 1990 Grammy Awards show. (This performance was the first time that the authors had ever seen the face that went

with the voice.) This video was released by A*Vision Entertainment (a division of Atlantic Records) in 1994.

Great American Music Hall — This performance hall was located at 138 Whalley Avenue, New Haven and was owned by Bobby Lucabello. Blackjack (with Michael Bolotin) made an appearance there in 1980. It's predecessor was the Arcadia Ballroom.

GREATEST HITS 1985 - 1995, Special Edition — This album, released by Columbia in 1995, consisted of twelve of Michael's greatest hits and five new album tracks. A special Australian tour souvenir edition was also released and could be purchased state-side through Fan Emporium. The souvenir edition included a bonus live CD recorded at Sony Studios in New York City on December 14, 1995. The CD tracks are:
1. *Soul Provider*
2. *(Sittin' On) The Dock of The Bay*
3. *How Am I Supposed To Live Without You*
4. *How Can We Be Lovers*
5. *When I'm Back On My Feet Again*
6. *Georgia On My Mind*
7. *Time, Love And Tenderness*
8. *When A Man Loves A Woman*
9. *Missing You Now*
10. *Steel Bars*
11. *Said I Loved You...But I Lied*
12. *Lean On Me*
13. *Can I Touch You...There?*
14. *I Promise You*
15. *I Found Someone*
16. *A Love So Beautiful*
17. *This River*

Bonus CD Tracks from the Souvenir Edition:
1. *How Am I Supposed To Live Without You*
2. *Soul Provider/Missing You Now*
3. *When I'm Back On My Feet Again*
4. *Said I Loved You...But I Lied*
5. *I Pagliacci*
(See individual song listings for writer and producer information.)

Greene, Michael — This president of NARAS is the Grammy official who wrote Michael a consoling letter after the critics/Bolton debacle following Michael's 1992 Grammy win. Michael framed Mr. Greene's letter and hung it in his home office as a reminder.

Grooming — Nancy Sprague was responsible for this on the cover notes of THE ONE THING album. We're not sure what the job entails, but we'd like to volunteer for it in the future.

Gross, Tom — Tom is the host of one of the most successful resort cable TV shows in the country. He has been the announcer at over 200 ski races and annually announces and emcees at both the Robert F. Kennedy Memorial Gulf Tournament in Hyannisport, Massachusetts and the American Airlines Celebrity Golf Event in San Diego, California.

Tom has appeared as announcer at the first four Michael Bolton Foundation Weekend Softball games, and kept up an interesting and amusing courtside patter at the three MBF Weekend Tennis Matches. He has also co-announced the MBF Gala Celebrity Auction with American Airlines' Jack Williams.

Tom heads a photographic design poster company, Legends Production, and has donated his time to help raise more than $10 million for organizations involved with Human Rights, Cystic Fibrosis, Women and Children At Risk, Education, Cancer, Birth Defects, and Adoption.

Tom is always an enjoyable addition to the MBF Weekend, and we certainly hope he is a part of it in the future.

Guitar — Michael's first guitar was a Kay, bought for him by his mother when he was about 12 years old.

Gunn, Michael — Michael Gunn is a former Vice President of Marketing for American Airlines. On October 8, 1995, the Michael Bolton Foundation presented him with a Lifetime Achievement Award for his humanitarian efforts, extensive work and lifelong dedication on behalf of women and children. The award presentation took place at the Michael Bolton Foundation's Third Annual Black Tie Gala.

Gym — Michael has stated that the hotels he frequents while traveling must have one of these.

Michael Bolton's Massive Willow

Hair — To date, Michael's long, curly locks have been his trademark feature, whether blonde, brunette, or any of various shades in-between. Michael likened it to a "massive willow growing out of [his] head" and said that he hadn't had more than the ends trimmed since 1966. It has been rumored that he may cut his hair to get an acting role, much to the consternation of many fans.

Hall, Arsenio — Michael appeared on Arsenio's very popular talk show in January of 1990 during his promotional tour for SOUL PROVIDER. Michael, having just been nominated for his Grammy for "How Am I Supposed To Live Without You," talked about Laura Branigan's version of the song and working with Cher during the interview portion of his appearance. He also performed the songs, "How Am I Supposed To Live Without You," and "How Can We Be Lovers."

Halligan, Bob, Jr. — This songwriter collaborated with Michael on "Gina," "Forever Eyes," and others.

Hamilton Clock Factory Building — During the '70s, Michael held rehearsals in a large, second floor space of this building located in the center of New Haven.

Hard Copy — This entertainment news show has featured a segment on Michael titled "Secrets of Seduction." They referred to him as the "sexiest singer to hit the stage since Tom Jones."(?!) Short people-on-the-street interviews were shown asking what they thought of Michael Bolton. Some cited his raspy voice and smooth moves, while one referred to his look as having "got that Lion King thing going there."

"Hard Enough Getting Over You" — Written by Michael Bolton and Doug James. Appeared on Cher's self-title album, CHER, released by Geffen Records in 1987. Michael sang back-up on this song.

Harlem Boys Choir — Michael has used this choir frequently as back up singers at his appearances. They appeared at the Michael Bolton Foundation Second Annual Black Tie Gala, the 1995 Billboard Awards, and were on the Phil Donahue Show with Michael. They are also recipients of one of the grants from the Michael Bolton Foundation.

Harlem School of the Arts — Michael and Columbia Records donated $50,000 from the sales of TIMELESS-THE CLASSICS to this New York City school and they are one of the recipients of grants from the Michael Bolton Foundation.

Michael Performs with the Harlem Boys Choir

Hatcher, Teri — She was featured in the "Missing You" video and had been romantically linked with Michael. She co-starred in the TV series, "LOIS & CLARK" as Lois Lane.

"Have Yourself a Merry Little Christmas" —
Written by Ralph Blane and Hugh Martin.
    Appeared on THIS IS THE TIME -
       THE CHRISTMAS ALBUM (Columbia, 1996).

Produced by Johnny Mandel and Michael Bolton. Orchestra arranged and conducted by Johnny Mandel.

Hawk, Pat — Pat joined Michael as a back-up singer for the SOUL PROVIDER tour in 1990 singing middle harmony. She had previously sung with the Righteous Brothers and was featured in the DIRTY DANCING tour. (She sang "The Time of My Life" with Bill Medley.) She has also toured with the Pet Shop Boys. In March, 1993, Pat married Alan Deremo, and in 1995 was replaced by Catte Adams in Michael's group while Pat was on maternity leave having twins. The babies, a boy named Hagen and a girl named Emily, were born on Halloween, 1995, ten weeks premature. A picture of them appeared in the Summer 1996 edition of the *Bolton Beat*, along with a note from Pat saying she had made the very difficult decision NOT to go back on tour, but to stay with her babies for the early years. Everyone is doing well and we wish them all the best.

Hazel — The color of Michael Bolton's eyes (except on the covers of THE ONE THING and MICHAEL BOLTON'S GREATEST HITS 1985-1995 albums where they appear to be extremely blue.) Michael's elementary school teacher, Mrs. T.C. of Palm Beach, Florida, said, "I didn't know it was him until I saw those hazel eyes. I'll never forget them," according to the June 17, 1993 edition of *USA Today*.

"He's looking at me!" — This caption appeared on a photo that was sent in to *Bolton Beat* by fans but it is also an exclamation that can be heard all over the audience at every Michael Bolton concert. Michael has the gift of making everyone believe he is truly looking at (and seeing) them.

Heart — Michael toured with them while promoting THE HUNGER album in the summer of 1988.

HEARTS OF GOLD-THE POP COLLECTION — This album, released on Foundation Records in 1991, benefits the T.J. Martell Foundation for Leukemia, Cancer and AIDS Research. The 17-track collection consists of various artists (from Paula Abdul to Rod Stewart to Sinead O'Connor) performing one song each. Michael sings, "How Am I Supposed To Live Without You."

"Heart of Mine" — Written by Michael Bolotin and Bruce Kulick.
    Appeared on BLACKJACK (Polydor, 1979).
    Produced by Tom Dowd.

"Heart of Stone" — Written by Michael Bolotin and Bruce Kulick.

    Appeared on BLACKJACK (Polydor, 1979).

    Produced by Tom Dowd.

    Cher sang this song on her album, HEART OF STONE (Geffen Records, 1989).

Henderson, Patrick — This songwriter began collaborating with Michael in 1976, writing the song, "You've Got The Love I Need." Then, in 1983, they wrote three songs to get Michael a record deal but when Henderson's publishing company said they could place the songs, Michael needed cash and gave his approval. One of the songs, "Still Thinking of You," had been recorded seven times by 1986. Some of the other songs Patrick co-wrote with Michael are: "Talkin' 'Bout My Baby," "Give Me Love," and "I Almost Believed You," which appears on Michael's self-titled 1983 album.

Hendon Fellowship Fund — This fund supplements the educational programs of Yale's residential colleges by arranging chances for the students to meet with representatives of the government, the arts, the professions, and the business world. They sponsored Michael Bolton's concert at Yale in April of 1994 and, as part of the fellowship, presented him with an award in the fall of that year where he had a chance to meet and speak to the students.

"Hercules" — Michael recorded a song for this Disney released in June, 1997.

Hibbs, Bruce Alan — Photographer responsible for the picture of Michael that appears on the back of the MICHAEL BOLOTIN album.

Hideaway — This book, written by Dean R. Koontz, mentions Michael on page 56. This is the second mention of Michael Bolton in a Dean Koontz book. Looks like he's a fan, too.

High School Graduation of L.A.'s Foster Children — Michael Bolton performed "When I'm Back On My Feet Again" with Patti LaBelle at this event in 1991.

"History of Rock & Roll (Sounds of Soul)" — Michael appeared with Ray Charles in a short clip appearing on this 1995 television special.

HITS — This album, comprised of songs by various artists and released by Pioneer Records in 1990, included four Michael Bolton songs: "How Am I Supposed To Live Without You," "How Can We Be Lovers," "When I'm Back On My Feet Again," and "Georgia On My Mind." In 1991, Pioneer Records released a follow-up version and included two more of Michael's hits, "When A Man Loves A Woman," and "Time, Love, and Tenderness."

"Hold On, I'm Coming" — Written by I. Hayes and D. Porter.

    Appeared on TIMELESS-THE CLASSICS (Columbia, 1992).

    Produced by Walter Afanasieff and Michael Bolton.

    Horn Arrangement by Greg Adams and Walter Afanasieff.

    This song features the Tower of Power Horn Section.

Holden, Stephen — Stephen was an A&R man at RCA Records from 1974 to 1976 and he was responsible for signing Michael to that label in 1974. According to TIME, LOVE & TENDERNESS (written by Lee Randall, published by Simon & Schuster, 1993), he was "enraptured by (Michael's) version of an original ballad, 'Dream While You Can,' that...seemed to float mystically out of the huge speakers..." Mr. Holden is presently a reviewer for *The N.Y. Times*.

Holly — Michael's middle daughter, currently living with her father in Connecticut. Her birthday is July 7.

HOLLYWOOD SOUNDTRACKS — This album, released by Blockbuster Music, include Michael's "Once In A Lifetime" among its hits.

Homecoming Concert — Michael celebrated his victorious return with a concert at the New Haven Coliseum on December 19, 1991.

"Hometown Hero" — Written by Michael Bolton and Scott Zito.

    Appeared on MICHAEL BOLTON (Columbia, 1983).

    Produced by Gerry Block and Michael Bolton.

    Mike Spoerndle of Toad's Place in New Haven, Connecticut was reportedly the inspiration for this song.

"Hot Corner, The" — At Bomber's games, it's third base, one of the two positions normally played by Michael Bolton. (Michael's other field position is first base.)

"Hot Love" — Written by Michael Bolton and Martin Briley.

> Appears on THE HUNGER (Columbia, 1987).
> Produced by the late Keith Diamond.

The late Keith Diamond also played drums, bass, keyboards, and fairlight for this track.

HOT NO. 1 HITS — Compilation record done in 1992 by Foundation Records to benefit the T.J. Martell Foundation for Leukemia, Cancer and Aids Research. Michael sings, "When A Man Loves A Woman." Other artists appearing on the disc are George Michael and Elton John, Janet Jackson, Marky Mark and the Funky Bunch, Vanessa Williams, Boyz II Men, Roxett, Jon Bon Jovi, Wilson Phillips, New Kids On The Block, C+C Music Company, and Gloria Estefan.

Hot Shots! Part Deux The 1993 movie starring Charlie Sheen and Lloyd Bridges. Michael is given a tongue-in-check song listing in the credits for this comedy hit movie.

Houghton, Jim — Photographer who was responsible for the photos on the BLACKJACK album cover.

"How Am I Supposed To Live Without You" — Written by Michael Bolton and Doug James.

> Appeared on SOUL PROVIDER (Columbia, 1989).
> Also appeared on GREATEST HITS 1985-1995 (Columbia, 1995) and THINKING OF YOU (Sony Music Special Productions, 1996).
> Produced by Michael Omartian for Rhema Productions.

Laura Brunigan had a hit with this song in the early '80s and then Michael had a #1 hit on the Billboard Adult Contemporary and Pop Charts for three weeks in January, 1990. He called it his "first major hit as an artist." It won a BMI Most Performed Song Award in 1990, while Michael received Writer/Publisher awards. Also in 1990, it was nominated for a Grammy and won.

In 1991, Michael was given a MillionAirs award for over one million broadcasts of this song. It also received BMI's Song of the Year award and an ASCAP publisher award that year. The "B" side of the single is "Forever Eyes."

The video for "How Am I Supposed To Live Without You" appears on Michael's SOUL & PASSION, SOUL PROVIDER-THE VIDEOS, and DECADE 1985-1995 videotapes.

"How Can We Be Lovers" — Written by Michael Bolton, Diane Warren and Desmond Child.

> Appeared on SOUL PROVIDER (Columbia, 1989).
> Also appeared on GREATEST HITS 1985-1995 (Columbia, 1995).
> Produced by Desmond Child and Michael Bolton.

Walter Afanasieff did additonal production, and played keyboards and percussion for this track. Michael received a 1991 BMI Writer and Publisher award for this song. The video appears on Michael's SOUL PROVIDER and SOUL & PASSION videotapes.

"How to Get a Record Deal" — This 67-minute video features various recording artists (including Michael Bolton) giving advice about the recording industry and how to get involved in it.

Hubrich, Karen — Karen, born in London, England, has been Michael's cook since 1994. Several of her favorite recipes have appeared in *Bolton Behind The Scenes*. Karen and her husband, Michael, have two sons, Josh and Lucas.

HUNGER, THE — This album was released on Columbia, 1987. Produced by the late Keith Diamond, Jonathan Cain, and Susan Hamilton. Neal Schon, Randy Jackson, and Mike Baird (all from the band  Journey) appeared on this record with their bandmate, Jonathan Cain. Other special guests include James Ingram, David Glen Eigley, and Eric Martin. Singles released from this album were: "That's What Love Is All About," "(Sittin' On) The Dock Of The Bay," "Wait On Love," "Walk Away," and "Gina." With the exception of "Dock Of The Bay," every song on the album was co-written by Michael Bolton. Album tracks are:

1. *Hot Love*
2. *Wait On Love*
3. *The Dock Of The Bay*
4. *Gina*
5. *That's What Love Is All About*
6. *The Hunger*
7. *You're All That I Need*

8. *Take A Look At My Face*
9. *Walk Away*
(For additional information, see individual song listings.)

"Hunger, The" — Written by Michael Bolton and Jonathan Cain.

Title track of THE HUNGER (Columbia, 1987).
Produced by Jonathan Cain for Cain St. Productions.
Also, Jonathan played keyboards while his brother, Mugs Cain, played drums for this song.

Husk — The special quality Michael has said his voice had even in his early teenage years.

Hyatt Regency-Old Greenwich — This beautiful hotel, which features a 4-story atrium at its heart, has been the base for the first four annual Michael Bolton Foundation Weekends.

Hyperion — This is the division of Disney Books that is publishing Michael's book, *Secret of the Lost Kingdom*, scheduled for release in 1997. This children's book is set in a medieval fantasy world and tells the story of a young prince. The prince has been disillusioned with the political realities in his realm and sets out on a journey to find himself. There are also reportedly plans to turn the book into an animated or live action feature film.

"I Almost Believed You" — Written by Michael Bolton and Patrick Henderson. Appeared on MICHAEL BOLTON (Columbia, 1983). Produced by Gerry Block and Michael Bolton. George Clinton and Doug Katsaros play synthesizers on this track.

"I Found Someone" — Written by Michael Bolton and Mark Mangold.

Appeared on GREATEST HITS 1985-1995 (Columbia, 1995).
Produced and arranged by Walter Afanasieff and Michael Bolton.
Recorded at WallyWorld and Passion Studios.
Cher originally recorded this song for her self-titled album on Geffen Records in 1987. It was produced by Michael Bolton for MBO Productions, Inc. and Michael sang back-up for her. Michael received a 1989 ASCAP Writer/Producer award for this song, and until the release of the GREATEST HITS album, had only performed it in concerts.

"I Promise You" — Written by Michael Bolton and Robert John "Mutt" Lange.

Appeared on GREATEST HITS 1985-1995 (Columbia, 1995).
Produced by Robert John "Mutt" Lange and Michael Bolton at Passion Studios, Connecticut.
We believe this song will soon be THE wedding song of the '90s.

"If I Had Your Love" — Written by Michael Bolotin.

Appeared on EVERY DAY OF MY LIFE (RCA, 1976).
Also appeared on MICHAEL BOLOTIN-THE EARLY YEARS (RCA, 1991) and on THE ARTISTRY OF MICHAEL BOLOTIN (RCA, 1993).
Produced by Jack Richardson for Nimbus 9 Productions
This song was recorded on February 13, 1976.

"I'm Aware Of Your Love" — Written by Michael Bolotin and Bruce Kulick.

Appeared on BLACKJACK (Polydor, 1979).
Produced by Tom Dowd.

"I'm Not Made Of Steel" — Written by Michael Bolton, Diane Warren, and Robert John Lange.

Appeared on THE ONE THING (Columbia, 1993).
Also appeared on THINKING OF YOU (Sony Productions, 1996).
Produced by Robert John "Mutt" Lange and Michael Bolton.
This song was recorded at Out of Pocket Productions Ltd. Studios in Surrey, England. Mutt Lange is credited with background vocals. Michael also sang it on a Jay Leno show appearance. Michael described the meaning song as "it's about...realizing that no one is made of steel."

In Style **Magazine** — Michael was featured in a six-page article with many photos in the December, 1996 issue of this magazine.

"In The Arms Of Love" — Written by Michael Bolton, Diane Warren, and Desmond Child.

Appeared on THE ONE THING (Columbia, 1993).
Produced by David Foster and Michael Bolton.
Orchestra arranged and conducted by Jeremy Lubbock.

The Inner Circle

Inmates, The — This band was one of Michael's earliest groups. He played with them between the ages of 12 and 14. Michael has also said in interviews that he began singing at about the age of eight and began playing guitar at 12.

Inner Circle, The — Also called the Winning Team, this elite group consists of David Feinstein, Robert Epstein, Joel Weinstein, and Louis Levin.

Inside Sports — The April, 1996 issue of this magazine featured a one page article titled, "Just A Short Hop From Father To Son." This article has the distinction of being credited to Michael Bolton.

Inspiration — Michael says that "...it is a powerful, internal, uplifting feeling that makes singing and writing an effortless and ultimately desirable experience." He says he has found inspiration in all areas of his life.

International Achievement In The Arts Awards — The first annual awards presentation was hosted by Rob-

ert Wagner at the Dominion Theatre In London on December 18, 1994 to benefit the Great Ormond Street Children's Hospital Fund. The Dinner-dance and charity auction was held at the London Hilton following the awards presentation.

On December 2, 1995, the second annual presentation to benefit the Michael Bolton Foundation was held at the City Center in New York City. Again hosted by Robert Wagner, the presentation was followed by a dinner-dance and charity auction at the New York Hilton & Towers. Michael Bolton serves on the Board of Directors for this award.

Iron Curtain — As a part of Glasnost, Michael Bolton and fellow songwriters Barry Mann, Diane Warren, Desmond Child, Cyndi Lauper, Holly Knight, Brenda Russell, Frannie Golde, Tom Kelly, and Billy Steinberg went behind the Iron Curtain to Russia in October, 1987 to collaborate with Russian songwriters.

Isa — Isa is Michael's oldest daughter. Her birthday is August 3.

Islands (Hot Ones) — Michael's ideal vacation spots.

Italian — Many of Michael's favorite foods are Italian, including pasta, eggplant parmesan, and pizza.

"It's All Comin' Back To You" — Written by Michael Bolotin.
> Appeared on MICHAEL BOLOTIN (RCA, 1975).
> Produced by Joe Cy and Michael Bolotin.

"It's Just A Feeling"— Written by Michael Bolotin.
> Appeared on MICHAEL BOLOTIN (RCA, 1975).
> Also appeared on THE ARTISTRY OF MICHAEL BOLOTIN (RCA, 1993).
> Produced by Joe Cy and Michael Bolotin.

"It's Only My Heart" — Written by Michael Bolton and Diane Warren.
> Appears on SOUL PROVIDER (Columbia, 1989).
> Also appears on THINKING OF YOU (Sony Productions, 1996).
> Produced by Michael Omartian for Rhema Productions.
> Background vocals are credited to Richard Marx and Joe Turano, while Michael Omartian plays keyboards and drums.

Jackson, Teresa — Teresa is the Consulting Artist/Illustrator for Fan Emporium, Inc. and it's publications.

James, Doug — This songwriter has collaborated with Michael Bolton, most notably on the song, "How Am I Supposed To Live Without You."

January 20, 1993 — Michael Bolton attended Bill Clinton's inauguration with Kenny G.

Jeans — Michael wears several brands of jeans and his stage jeans are kept in a huge locked wardrobe closet, rendering that bit of information unavailable.

Jerry Lewis' 25th Anniversary Telethon — Michael Bolton appeared, spoke and sang the National Anthem at a softball game for Bolton's Bad Boys that was aired during the telethon in September, 1988.

JESUS CHRIST SUPERSTAR — The CD and video called "Grammy's Living Legends" features Michael on stage backed by a robed choir, singing this song.

Jewish Youth Center — On the radio program, The Michael Bolton Story, Michael said that he was eleven years old the first time he sang in public and that his 3-man band first played at a Jewish Youth Center on a make-shift stage formed from ping-pong tables.

Joe DiMaggio's All-Stars Legend Game — This ballgame was held the last weekend of February, 1995 in Ft. Lauderdale, Florida to benefit Joe DiMaggio's Children's Hospital. Michael played on Joe's team.

Johnson, Vann — Vann joined Michael's band on his 1991 tour as a back-up singer singing low harmony. She frequently duets with Michael on "We're Not Making Love Anymore."

Jordan, Michael — On July 25, 1993, the Bolton Bombers met Michael Jordan's Airforce Squad at Comiskey Park in Chicago. Michael Jordan's team was managed by none other than Bo Jackson and included Magic Johnson, Daniel and William Baldwin, Tom Selleck, Mark Harmon, Hammer, Evander Holyfield, Chris Chelias, and Ahmad Rashad.

Nevertheless, the Bombers were victorious by a final score of 7 to 1. A winner's trophy was awarded and, holding the trophy aloft, Michael Bolton is quoted as having joked, "If Michael Jordan wants to see this, I'll send him pictures."

Joy — This New Haven band was originally known as "The Nomads" and was very big with "Yalies" in the '60s. In 1968, Michael traveled to Berkley, California with them and got a recording contract with Epic Records, a division of Columbia.

Because Michael was underage, his mother had to co-sign the contract for him. They produced a single, "Bah Bah Bah" written by M. Bolotkin (aka Michael Bolton.)

"Joy To The World" — Traditional carol in public domain.
> Appeared on THIS IS THE TIME-THE CHRISTMAS ALBUM (Columbia, 1996).
> Produced by Walter Afanasieff and Michael Bolton.
> Arranged by Walter Afanasieff , Mariah Carey and Michael Bolton.

Judd, Ashley — This actress, best known for her role on the television show, "Sisters," had been romantically linked to Michael Bolton.

Judd, Wynonna — This country music star appeared and sang the duet, "This Is The Time" with Michael on the 1996 Country Music Awards show. She also recorded the duet with Michael for his THIS IS THE TIME : THE CHRISTMAS ALBUM release.

In a recent Sony Music online info release, Michael says, "I've always appreciated Wynonna as a vocal artist. She doesn't conform to anybody's concept of what she should or shouldn't do. She's just herself. We became friends and the next thing I knew, we were working on this song."

 Karate — Michael's 1989 fan club newsletter lists Karate as one of Michael's favorite activities. Specifically, it is shotokan karate that Michael practices. He studied shotokan karate for about 10 years in New Haven, Connecticut. Shotokan is the traditional Japanese karate which places importance on throwing the whole body into its techniques, enabling even a small person to deliver an effective punch or kick.

On October 14, 1995, Michael Bolton co-sponsored a martial arts competition with Paul Newman's Hole In The Wall Gang. It was held on the campus of Yale University. See the listings for Kids For Life Benefit or Paul Newman's Hole In The Wall Gang for more information

Karaoke — are several Michael Bolton karaoke CDs available from record stores. This could be just the ice-breaker your next party will need. See your local record distributor for more information.

Kaz, Eric — Songwriter who collaborated with Michael on the songs, "That's What Love Is All About" and "From Now On."

Kennedy, David — David is the photographer responsible for the picture on the MICHAEL BOLTON album cover.

Kenny G. — Michael Bolton opened for Kenny on a tour that began July 25, 1990. Typically, Kenny would join Michael during his 45-minute set for a duet on "Georgia On My Mind" and then Michael would rejoin Kenny during his show for a "How Am I Supposed To Live Without You" finale. It was on this tour that Michael began doing "Georgia" from the audience, a treat that he continues on tour today.

Michael and Kenny perform "Don't Make Me Wait For Love" (written by Michael Bolton) on the KENNY G LIVE album. From April 21 to May 2, 1993, Kenny joined Michael on his European Tour. Michael has described Kenny G. as one of the few people he will make the time to "hang with."

Kentucky Colonel — Michael is an official Kentucky Colonel, an award presented by the governor of Kentucky for contributions made throughout the world..

Kids For Life Benefit — Sponsored by United Studios for Self Defense (for The Hole In The Wall Gang Camp) and the Michael Bolton Foundation, this martial arts competition took place at Yale's Payne Whitney Gymnasium on December 14, 1995. Michael made a special guest appearance.

Knicks vs. Bulls — Michael sang the National Anthem at one of their 1992 Playoff games.

"Knock On Wood" — Written by E. Floyd and S. Cropper.
> Appeared on TIMELESS-THE CLASSICS
>   (Columbia, 1992).
> Produced by Walter Afanasieff and Michael Bolton.
> Horn arrangements by Greg Adams and
>   Walter Afanasieff.
> The Tower of Power Horn Section appears on this song.

Koop, C. Everett, M.D., Sc. D. — On October 8, 1995, the Michael Bolton Foundation presented this former Surgeon General with a Lifetime Achievement Award at their third annual Black Tie Gala. The award was presented to him for his humanitarian efforts, extensive work and lifelong dedication on behalf of women and children.

Koplik, Jim — Jim is the president of Metropolitan Entertainment. On October 8, 1995, he was presented with a Lifetime Achievement Award by the Michael Bolton Foundation. The award was presented to him at their third annual Black Tie Gala for his humanitarian efforts, extensive work and lifelong dedication on behalf of women and children.

Koz, Dave — This saxophone player (left) and his band were one of the openers for Michael on his 1994 concert tour. (We caught his set twice in three days and he quite literally blew us away.)

Kristofferson, Kris — He acted as one of the emcees for the Elvis Presley Tribute Show on pay-per-view and, after watching Michael's rendition of "Jailhouse Rock" and the crowd's extremely enthusiastic response to it, joked, "I think the kid's got a future."

Kulick, Bruce — Bruce was one of the original members of Blackjack with Michael Bolton, recording and touring with them in the early 1980's. He played guitar for the band, a role he was to repeat for Michael on his first Columbia album, MICHAEL BOLTON. After leaving Blackjack, Bruce became a member of the heavy metal band, KISS.

Kumnick, Andrena — Andrena is the Executive Assistant at the Michael Bolton Foundation and, if you have ever had reason to call the Foundation, hers is generally the voice at the other end of the line. We think Andrena is a sweetheart. She's always been extremely helpful with any of our questions and needs for the Michael Bolton Foundation Gala weekend.

Lake, Riki — During the Christmas season, 1995, Riki Lake invited two Michael Bolton Gold Club members, Glynis Drago and Jodi Ward, onto her show to receive a make-over. Michael made a special appearance to surprise his two fans by singing "White Christmas" to them on stage. As an added Christmas surprise, they each received a kiss from Michael!

Landau, Michael — Michael Landau has been a frequent sessions guitar player for Michael Bolton since SOUL PROVIDER.

Lange, R.J. "Mutt" — This songwriter collaborated with Michael on "Said I Loved You...But I Lied," "I'm Not Made Of Steel," "Ain't Got Nothin' If You Ain't Got Love," and "Can I Touch You...There?" Michael has said, "Having Mutt in the studio is like having a personal trainer pushing you to the ultimate limits. ...nothing but the best is good enough for the Mutt Man!" Michael said he refers to Mutt as the "Steven Spielberg of music" because he is a great producer who is also an incredible songwriter. Mr. Lange is married to country star Shania Twain.

Lead Guitar — Michael learned to play guitar when he was eleven years old and he played lead guitar in his groups in the '70s. (He also plays some keyboards.) Although Michael doesn't play much guitar at his concerts, concentrating instead on his singing, he showed his guitar prowess on the 1995 Essence Awards playing guitar with B.B. King. (Note: Michael was rocking!)

Michael Bolton Rocking on Lead Guitar

"Lean On Me" — Written by Bill Withers.
Appeared on THE ONE THING (Columbia, 1993). Produced by Walter Afanasieff and Michael Bolton. Arranged by Walter Afanasieff and Joey Melotti. Michael performed this song at the PreInaugaral Gala for President Clinton on January 19, 1993.

"Least Truthful Self-Review" — The February 19, 1993 issue of *Entertainment Weekly* magazine called Michael's TIMELESS-THE CLASSICS, "a Grammy nomination that slipped through the cracks."

34

Left Knee Twitch — Michael said this occurred uncontrollably during rehearsals with Luciano Pavarotti for his 1995 Benefit for the Children of Bosnia show.

Leno, Jay — Michael's first appearance with Jay was in November, 1989 on the Tonight Show, while touring for THE HUNGER album. Jay has hosted guest Michael Bolton on the Tonight Show frequently since March of 1990 when Jay was still guest-hosting for Johnny Carson. The appearance took place shortly after Michael won the Grammy for "How Am I Supposed To Live Without You," and Jay drew Michael out on the shock of winning and the "slow motion walk down the aisle" to get the award. Accompanied by Walter Afanasieff on the piano, Michael sang his award-winning song.

Since then, Michael has made promotional appearances on his show for TIMELESS-THE CLASSICS (singing "Since I Fell For You" and "To Love Somebody") and THE ONE THING (singing "I'm Not Made Of Steel" and "Said I Loved You...But I Lied.") He appeared on the show after his Asian Tour in 1994 and even did a walk-on one night, doing impersonations of Rodney Dangerfield.

During a personally favored appearance, Michael went out behind the studio to "hit a few softballs" with Jay. He didn't know that he'd been set up (the pitchers were professional women fast-pitch players) and had difficulty connecting with the first few pitches ("I'd hit it if I could SEE it") but finally got a good hit and supposedly knocked the satellite feed out of alignment. After some clowning with various cable shows, Michael appeared on screen again, on top of Jay's shoulders, adjusting the dish.

In August of 1995, Michael premiered his song "Can I Touch You...There?" on Jay's show and during discussion of Michael's operatic appearance with Luciano Pavarotti, Jay remarked that Michael and Pavarotti must look like the number 10 standing next to each other on stage. All in all, his appearances on Jay's shows are entertaining and fun. Leno seems to have a talent for getting some real emotions and laughs from Michael.

Letterman, David — Michael first appeared on David Letterman's "Late Show" in 1988 singing "Dock Of The Bay" backed by Letterman's house band and Ross Vallery. Then, on December 12, 1995, he made a second appearance singing "Can I Touch You...There?" On April 11, 1996, Michael appeared again, this time with Luciano Pavarotti, to sing "Nessun Dorma." Pavarotti introduced the song by saying it would be a "two tenor opera tonight." (Note to David Letterman—Watch an instant replay, Dave. Michael brings it on home.)

Levin, Louis —  Louis is Michael's manager and the man responsible for turning Michael Bolotin into Michael Bolton in 1982. As a junior partner in a management firm, he talked them into buying Michael's management contract. He then negotiated a two-part deal with Columbia Records The rest is history.

Besides being his manager, Louis is also a close friend and pitches for the Bolton Bombers. (It's Louis who can be seen playing ball with Michael and the children in the "Completely" video.) Although Louis was injured in a softball accident at 1996's Michael Bolton Foundation Celebrity Softball Game, Michael says Louis is doing much better and is "already figuring out the design of some kind of helmet to pitch and continue playing softball with the Bolton Bombers." Michael adds that Louis "plans on playing next year." Louis (or Luigi, as his picture in the back of the 1994 tourbook is labeled) attends many public appearances with Michael and is Secretary/Director of The Michael Bolton Foundation.

Lewis Hine Distinguished Service Award — This prestigious award was given to Michael in February, 1994 by the National Child Labor Committee in honor of his steadfast dedication to bettering the lives of children and youths. (Hillary Rodham Clinton was the 1993 Lewis Hine Award recipient.)

Lieber-Krebs — This is the management firm that Louis Levin was a junior partner with in 1982 when signing Michael Bolton. Michael sang jingles for them when he needed cash in the '70s.

Liebhart, Janis — Janis joined Michael's band for the 1991 tour, singing high harmony background vocals. According to Pat Hawk, Janis had "the right voice, the right personality, and the right size to fit the costume." She had previously toured with the Righteous Brothers and the Moody Blues.

Besides singing, Janis is also an accomplished composer, having composed songs (and sung vocals) for both Jim Henson's MUPPET BABIES and Disney's SONGS FROM UNDER THE SEA albums. Janis has also done voice-overs and commercials in the Los Angeles area and says *Scrabble* is a favorite backstage activity.

Lifetime Applauds the Fight Against Breast Cancer —Michael performed "A Love So Beautiful" at this Lifetime Cable station benefit show in 1995, saying he had three of the best reasons in the world to be there—his three daughters. Also appearing on the show were Meatloaf, Celine Dion, Jane Curtin, and others.

Lifetime's Concert of a Lifetime Contest — This contest, sponsored by Columbia Records and Lifetime Cable, awarded ten lucky winners (from the more than 25,000 entrants) their own "private" interactive concert with Michael Bolton. They received a satellite dish, special entertainment center, and special phone hook-up so that they could converse with Michael. On December 14, 1995, a concert done at a Sony Studio in New York City was beamed into their homes.

Lion — This is Michael's favorite wild animal.

Little Anthony & the Imperials — They were musical guests at the third annual Michael Bolton Foundation Black Tie Gala on October 8, 1995 in Connecticut.

Little Sisters of Assumption — This charity organization in East Harlem, NY, has been a recipient of aid from The Michael Bolton Foundation. They were featured on the video clip shown on Michael's VH1 Honors Award presentation segment.

Logan, Joyce — A friend of Michael's since the late 70s, Michael sang the "first dance" at her November 7, 1986 wedding to Wayne Logan. Joyce launched the first incarnation of Michael's fan club in 1983. Although it has grown considerably since it's inception, she still oversees the entire operation today.

Joyce is the editor of *Bolton Behind the Scenes* and *The Bolton Beat*. She and her husband, Wayne, reside in Connecticut with their two sons, Jeffrey and Timothy.

Logan, Wayne — Wayne, an award-winning professional photographer based in Connecticut, is the official Staff Photographer for *Bolton Behind the Scenes* and can often be found front and center, clicking away at special events for Michael. With his comfortable, friendly demeanor and his concentrated desire to "get the picture right," Wayne could have been used as a study guide by Clint Eastwood in his preparation for his "Bridges of Madison County" role.

Lorito, Phil — Operating under the aegis of MBO Artists, Inc./Artists One in Farmingdale, New York, Phil was reportedly Michael's "career consultant" in the late 70s.

"Lost In The City" — Written by Wayne Perkins.
Appeared on MICHAEL BOLOTIN (RCA, 1975).
Also appeared on THE ARTISTRY OF
    MICHAEL BOLOTIN (RCA, 1993).
Produced by Joe Cy and Michael Bolotin.
Besides Michael's vocals, the only other musician appearing on this song is Wayne Perkins playing acoustic and electric guitars.

Louisville Slugger — This is the type of softball bat that Michael Bolton (left) uses and this company sponsors Michael's team, the Bolton Bombers.

"Love Cuts Deep" — Written by Michael Bolton, Diane Warren, and Desmond Child.
Appears on SOUL PROVIDER (Columbia, 1989). Produced by Peter Bunetta and Rick Chudacoff.

"Love Is A Wonderful Thing" — Written by Michael Bolton and Andrew Goldmark.
Appears on TIME, LOVE & TENDERNESS
    (Columbia, 1991).
Produced and arranged by Walter Afanasieff and
    Michael Bolton.
Walter also played keyboards, Hammond B-3 organ, Synth Bass, synthesizers, drums, and percussion on this cut. This song was number 1 on the Billboard Charts for four weeks. When Michael performs this song in concert, he "shoots" the audience with his right index finger on the final "thing" before the fadeout. This video appears on Michael's SOUL & PASSION videotape.

"Love Is Hard To Find" — Written by Michael Bolotin and Bruce Kulick.
Appeared on WORLDS APART (Polydor, 1980).
Produced by Eddy Offord.

"Love Is The Power" — Written by Michael Bolton, Diane Warren, and Walter Afanasieff.
Appears on THIS IS THE TIME—
    THE CHRISTMAS ALBUM (Columbia, 1996).
Produced by Walter Afanasieff and Michael Bolton.

This song, the first single released from Michael's Christmas album, was recorded at WallyWorld Studios and Passion Studios. A special demo CD single was given to the attendees at the Fourth Annual Michael Bolton Foundation Black Tie Gala and included two different versions of the song.

"Love Me Tonight" — Written by Michael Bolotin, Bruce Kulick, and Robert Kulick.
> Appeared on BLACKJACK (Polydor, 1979).
> Produced by Tom Dowd.
> This song was released as a single from the album.

Lovett, Vicki — Vicki, formerly a nurse, is now the editor of *The Bolton Collector's Journal* and the Assistant Editor of *Bolton Behind the Scenes*. Vicki is also the Artist Relations Co-ordinator for Fan Emporium, Inc., the Letter Writing Campaign Manager, and the Collectors Exchange Manager.

Luciano Pavarotti & Friends Together For the Children of Bosnia — 14,000 attended this fourth benefit show in Modena, Italy, on September 12, 1995. Princess Di was the guest of honor. Michael performed three songs at the show: "Can I Touch You...There?," "Vesti la Giubba" (with Pavarotti), and "Nessun Dorma" (with Pavarotti and friends.) The 60-piece L'Orchestra Filamonica di Torino, conducted by Michael Kamen and/ or Marco Armiliato, accompanied the operatic pieces. (The story goes that operatic orchestras are notoriously hard to impress, but that after Michael's rehearsal, they were so overwhelmed they gave him a standing ova-

tion.) The show was taped and released on videocassette by LONDON, the Decca Record Co., in April, 1996. (Note: On the video, Italian rapper Jovanotti sings the first line of "Nessun Dorma," but on the CD, it is clearly Michael's voice that you hear.) This concert was also released on CD and cassette.

Lucky Charm — Michael says that his hair is the closest thing to a lucky charm that he has.

Lucky Number — Although he has a lucky number, Michael is too superstitious to tell what it is.

Lunden, Joan — Joan has been the Mistress of Ceremonies for the first three Michael Bolton Foundation Black Tie Galas and frequently interviews Michael for television. Michael also appeared on her BEHIND CLOSED DOORS primetime special and narrated "An Intimate Portrait—Joan Lunden" for Lifetime Cable

 M.I.T. — This is Internet shorthand for "Michael Induced Trance." Frequently used in chatrooms and messages dealing with Michael Bolton M.I.T.s are most often induced by hearing the voice, seeing the face in unexpected places, and, of course, in-person experiences.

Macaroni and Cheese — This dish (with frozen broccoli) was reportedly a main menu staple for Michael and family after the breakup of Blackjack in the early 80s.

Michael Bolton and Joan Lunden Behind Closed Doors Special, 1995

Macho Guys — In the July, 1992 issue of *US Magazine*, Michael is quoted as saying, "Macho guys might feel threatened by me."

Madison Square Garden — Michael celebrated with a New Year's Eve show in Madison Square Garden on December 31, 1992.

Mandel, Howie — Howie's tv special, "HOWIE SPENT OUR SUMMER," featured a segment that showed Michael visiting the comedian backstage at one of his shows. Michael thanked him for the tickets, telling him his show was "really neat." Howie was obviously less than impressed, repeating Michael's words in an aside to the camera. (We're sure it was a set-up and that Michael was "dressed" for the occasion.)

Mangold, Mark — This songwriter collaborated with Michael on the songs "Save Our Love," "Can't Turn It Off," "Everytime," and "I Found Someone." He also played keyboards for Michael's EVERYBODY'S CRAZY album.

Mann, Barry — This songwriter collaborated with Michael and Cynthia Weil on the song "Stand Up For Love."

Mantle, Mickey — Mickey Mantle is one of Michael's baseball heros and like Michael, Mickey wasn't always treated kindly by the critics. Michael keeps a framed 1950 article on his home office wall for inspiration wherein yet another short-sighted critic questions the talents of another idol, Mickey Mantle. (It is Mickey's baseball jersey number, #7, that Michael proudly wears on the back of his own jersey.)

Maples, Marla — Marla had been romantically linked with Michael Bolton and later married Donald Trump. It was reported that Marla kept a diary detailing her liasions with Michael, and the diary later came up missing, giving the Donald a few very bad moments.

Mardi Gras — Michael Bolton was the Grand Marshall of the Endymion Mardi Gras Parade in New Orleans in 1991. In Greek mythology, Endymion was a youth of exceptional beauty who sleeps eternally. When Selene, the Goddess of the Moon, fell in love with him, she put him to sleep forever so that she could have him to herself.

Marinara Sauce — One of Michael's favorite dishes that his mother prepares for him. According to her, "He liked anything with red sauce. Once it had red sauce, it was okay."

Marino, Dan — This Miami Dolphins quarterback hosted a softball game between the Bolton Bombers and the Dan Marino All-Stars in Florida in 1994. The game was to benefit the Dan Marino Foundation and the Michael Bolton Foundation.

Martin Luther King, Jr./C.O.R.E. (Congress of Racial Equality) Award — This award for "outstanding achievement" was presented to Michael in January, 1996, in recognition of his tireless efforts promoting civil rights for all people.

Martini and Underhill: Leap of Faith — This television special celebrating the twenty years of partnership of Canadian Figure Skaters Paul Martini and Barbara Underhill was televised on February 2, 1997. One of the segments featured a very moving and emotional skate by them to Michael Bolton's version of the song, "Yesterday."

"Maybe It's The Power Of Love" — Written by Michael Bolotin.
> Appeared on WORLDS APART (Polydor, 1980).
> Produced by Eddy Offord.

McDonald, Michael — Michael McDonald was one of the musical guests at the third annual Michael Bolton Foundation Black Tie Gala in Connecticut on October 8, 1995.

McEwen, Mark — This *CBS This Morning* correspondent played softball at the Third Annual Michael Bolton Foundation Celebrity Tennis Classic, Softball Game, and Black Tie Gala. He, his wife, and adorable baby daughter attended the other events, also. For more information, see listing for *CBS This Morning*.

McGinley, Judine — Judine, who is a professional writer, started out as a Fan Club Chapter President in Florida and now she runs Michael's Artist Relations Office and is an Assistant Editor for *Bolton Behind the Scenes*.

Meadows Music Theatre — Michael's concert performance marked the formal opening of this performing arts theatre in Hartford, Connecticut on July 14, 1995. Singing in temperatures of almost 100 degrees must have been difficult, but Michael and his concert opener, Sophie B. Hawkins, didn't seem to have much problem.

Meet Wally Sparks — Michael has a cameo role (playing himself) in this Rodney Dangerfield movie that was released in February, 1997.

Melotti, Joey — Joey, the musical director for the band, also plays keyboards and sings back-up for Michael. Joey was born in New Haven, Connecticut and learned to play the accordion at the age of five. When he was eleven, he played piano.

Joey first joined Michael in 1983 when Michael was opening for Bob Seger.

Mercedes 500SL — The name of the luxury car that Michael Bolton is shown driving in the "Missing You" video.

Metal Mania — This album, released by Columbia Records in 1985, consisted of various artists performing heavy metal music. Michael Bolton sings "Fool's Game" on this album.

Michael — Michael is a Hebrew name meaning "like unto the Lord."

Front Cover: Michael Bolotin

MICHAEL BOLOTIN — This album was released by RCA in 1975. It was produced by Joe Cy and co-produced by Michael Bolotin. The songs were:
1. *Your Love*
2. *Give Me A Reason*
3. *Dream While You Can*
4. *Tell Me How You Feel*
5. *It's All Comin' Back To You*
6. *It's Just A Feelin'*

7. *Everybody Needs A Reason*
8. *You're No Good*
9. *Time Is On My Side*
10. *Take Me As I Am*
11. *Lost In The City*

(See individual song listings for writer and producer information.)

Michael Bolotin: The Early Years — This album is a 1991 RCA reissue which contains 12 tracks from Michael's first two RCA albums. Producers listed on the album are Jack Richardson, Joe Cy, and Michael Bolotin. The tracks are:
1. *Lost In The City* (recorded 1/30/75)
2. *Everybody Needs A Reason* (recorded 12/18/74)
3. *Your Love* (recorded 12/18/74)
4. *It's Just A Feeling* (recorded 12/18/74)
5. *Dream While You Can* (recorded 1/20/75)
6. *Take Me As I Am* (recorded 12/19/74)
7. *These Eyes* (recorded 2/14/76)
8. *You Mean More To Me* (recorded 2/11/76)
9. *If I Had Your Love* (recorded 2/13/76)
10. *Give Me A Reason* (recorded 1/20/75)
11. *Tell Me How You Feel* (recorded 12/18/74)
12. *Time Is On My Side* (recorded 1/20/75)

(See individual song listings for writer and producer information.)

MICHAEL BOLTON —This album, released by Columbia in 1983, was dedicated to the memory of Michael's father, George Bolton. Produced by Gerry Block and Michael Bolton, the songs were:
1. *Fool's Game*
2. *She Did The Same Thing*
3. *Hometown Hero*
4. *Can't Hold On, Can't Let Go*
5. *Fighting For My Life*
6. *Paradise*
7. *Back In My Arms Again*
8. *Carrie*
9. *I Almost Believed You*

Michael Bolton & Kenny G. Day — VH1 named August 15, 1990 Michael Bolton & Kenny G. Day, showing videos and interview clips all day long.

Michael Bolton Bulletin Board — If you use America On-Line computer information service, you may want to go to the Music Message Center, enter Rock Artists A-H, and scroll to Michael Bolton to get the latest information.

Michael Bolton Calling Card — These special edition pre-paid long distance phone cards were available in three denominations—$20, $50, and $200. The $20 version was an unsigned card good for twenty minutes of long distance calls. The $50 edition featured an automated signature on the face of the card and was good for fifty long-distance minutes. The $200 card was personally signed by Michael Bolton and allowed you two hundred minutes of long-distance calling. (A portion of the proceeds is donated to the Michael Bolton Foundation with every call you make.) The cards can be reactivated by additional payment when your time is running out.

The $50 Michael Bolton Calling Card

Michael Bolton Day — New Haven, Connecticut (Michael's home town), declared March 20, 1990 Michael Bolton Day in their city.

Michael Bolton Fan Club — His fan club was established in 1983 by Joyce Logan and grew rapidly. In Autumn, 1993, *USA Today* did an article on the fan club and said it had more than 12,000 members. A *USA Today Weekend Magazine* article on February 4, 1996 updated that figure, saying there were 22,000 dues-paying members and 60,000 names on their mailing list. Enrollment in the original fan club would get the enrollee photos, newsletters, a pin, a fact sheet and merchandise information. A portion of the dues was donated to THIS CLOSE for Cancer Research.

When the Michael Bolton Gold Club was introduced in early 1994, it was intended that the original fan club be phased out as annual memberships ended but, due to overwhelming fan requests, it was announced in March, 1995 that the fan club would be continued in addition to the Gold Club. For your annual dues, you would receive two black and white 8x10 photos, one color 8x10 photo, a square, signed Michael Bolton photo pin imprinted "Official Fan Club Member," Michael's latest Facts and Figures booklet, a photo membership card, and *Bolton Beat* newsletters. The first 500 enrollees also received copies of the VH1 Video For Your Ears cassette. (For address and membership information, see listing at the back of this book.)

Michael Bolton Foundation Lifetime Achievement Award — This award was created by the Foundation in 1995 to honor individuals for their humanitarian efforts, extensive work, and lifelong dedication on behalf of women and children. The first three awards were given to Michael Gunn, Jim Koplik, and C. Everett Koop, M.D., Sc.D. at the Third Annual Michael Bolton Foundation Black Tie Gala.

Michael Bolton Gold Club — The Gold Club was established in 1994 and membership dues include a lifetime membership, a Gold Club card, bumper sticker, photos, a Gold Club pin, Michael's current bio, discounts on merchandise offers, and special ticketing opportunities for concert tickets. Also, quarterly drawings are held from Gold Club members for signed Michael Bolton memorabilia. A portion of the membership dues are donated to the Michael Bolton Foundation. (For address and membership information, see the listing at the back of the book.)

MICHAEL BOLTON GREATEST HITS 1985-1995

— Released on September 15, 1995 by Columbia Records, this album gives us twelve of Michael's greatest hits and five new songs. The GREATEST HITS was remastered by Vlado Meller at Sony Music Studio Operations. The cover of the album features a stark, black and white photo of Michael Bolton, the only coloring being the bright deep blue of one of his eyes. Besides the usual thanks to his family, management, and crew, Michael thanks Dr. Pepper. Album cuts are as follows:

1. *That's What Love Is All About*
2. *(Sittin' On) The Dock of the Bay*
3. *Soul Provider*
4. *How Am I Supposed to Live Without You*
5. *How Can We Be Lovers*
6. *When I'm Back On My Feet Again*
7. *Georgia On My Mind*
8. *Time, Love and Tenderness*
9. *When A Man Loves A Woman*
10. *Missing You Now*
11. *Steel Bars*
12. *Said I Loved You...But I Lied*
13. *Can I Touch You...There?*
14. *I Promise You*
15. *I Found Someone*
16. *A Love So Beautiful*
17. *This River*

(See individual songlistings for writer and producer information.)

Michael started his promotional tour for this album with an appearance on Live with Regis and Kathie Lee on September 19, 1995. On their show, he announced that he would be doing an album signing at HMV Records in New York City from Noon to 1:30, then fly to Los Angeles to sign autographs at Sam Goody's at 7:30 that evening.

Michael Bolton Music Screeners — This computer program, released by Sony Music in 1995, is for use on Windows-based personal computers. It is based on the "Said I Loved You...But I

Lied" video and consists of six different screensaver settings and two Michael Bolton computer games. The graphics are high quality; you really do have the video playing on your computer.

Michael Bolton Music Special, The — This radio special, hosted by Leeza Gibbons from Hollywood, was aired in early 1993 on the Entertainment Radio Network. It featured interview segments and Michael's music. The show was produced by Glen Gordon.

Michael Bolton 1997 Calendar — This exclusive calendar was included in the purchase of THIS IS THE TIME at select stores. The calendar is CD-sized unbound double-sided cards, each month showing a beautiful full-color photo of Michael. It came in it's own plastic CD case which, when opened, can be used to display the calendar.

Michael Bolton Story, The — This radio special, distributed by UNISTAR Radio Programming, was distributed for airplay July 13- 15, 1990. The program featured interviews with Michael, a short segment with Paul Stanley (of KISS) on his collaboration with Michael, and fifteen of Michael's songs.

Michael Bolton - The Lover — Michael is an extremely caring, sensitive lover as shown by the following quotes from the man himself: "I am a hopeless romantic, a very passionate person." "I think romance and sexuality are two different things, though they connect." "I believe in courtship big time, as something on-going." "For me, it's flowers, unexpected flowers, roses all the time." "...there are surprises and you've got to keep them coming." And finally, a quote from handwriting analyst Michael Watts - "When he does fall in love, [he] will be incredibly passionate, highly romantic, and overwhelmingly intense. He will...demonstrate a very powerful sexual appetite."

Michael Bolton—Time, Love & Tenderness — Lee Randall wrote this book, a biographical account of Michael's career, which was published by Simon & Schuster in 1993.

Michael Bolton's Annual Celebrity Challenge — The Bolton Bombers play George Teague's All-Stars team in Appleton, Wisconsin to benefit The Rebecca Fund and the Michael Bolton

Foundation. In the 1995 game, which was televised on ESPN 2, the Bombers beat the All-Stars by a score of 35-17.

Michael Bolton's Winning Softball: Hit Harder, Play Smarter - This instructional softball videotape was released in 1993 by Columbia Music Video. Produced

and directed by Verne Mattson, this video features Dave Carroll giving instructions and tips on how to play softball better. Some of the segments show Michael demonstrating the instructions. The tape also includes interviews with Michael, Michael singing the National Anthem at the World Series Game in Toronto, and a video of "Love Is A Wonderful Thing" with softball highlights and game action. ENTER-TAINMENT WEEKLY rated this tape the Top Sports Video of the Week on February 4, 1994.

Michael's First Love — According to Michael, "Before I had my first serious relationship, before I was married, long before I had children, there was a love for music," and "Music is the air I breathe, (it's) how I express myself."

Michael's Middle Name — Michael doesn't have one. If you find that fact vaguely unsettling, Russian tradition dictates that the father's name would be used as a second name for his sons. Thus, by tradition, both Orrin and Michael would have the name "George" as a middle name.

Michael "The Bomber" Bolton — We all know of Michael's great love for playing softball, but here are the statistics gleaned from Louis Levin's Scouting Report (which appeared in the 1995 Michael Bolton Foundation Black Tie Gala program). Michael has a "very strong" right-handed throw that gets "runners out easily." He can play 1st, 2nd, and 3rd base equally adroitly, digging bad throws out of the dirt, stopping anything, and turning double plays with his quick arm. His batting average is .676 and Louis remarks that he is "ca-

pable of hitting it out of any ballpark and belting it out of any arena." His softball personality is described as "team leader, very competitive, has a strong desire for perfection." As an additional remark, Louis writes, "Personally, what manager would not be considered lucky to coach and guide the best player in the league!" after which he tells Michael, "You are the M.V.P.!" We couldn't agree more.

MIDNIGHT, A TIME FOR LOVE — This compilation record, released by Intersound Records in 1993, included Michael singing, "Now That I Found You."

Miller Beer — Michael Bolton was "The Voice" for Miller Beer in 1986.

Misprints — Some of Michael's records have been released with obvious misprints on the labels. A few of the most notable misprints are:

"Everybody's Crazy" Single — Side A was misprinted with the copyright information "Columbia Archives 1908".

The Early Years—Michael Bolotin — This RCA cassette was misprinted with the copyright information on side 2 reading "1991, 1876, 1875 BMG Music".

But probably the most personally distressing misprint for Michael appeared on the label of the "Bah, Bah, Bah" single where the name in the songwriting credits appears as "M. Bolotkin."

Michael "The Bomber" Bolton

42

Also on a personal level, we have heard a story about a birthday cake at a party for Michael given by music industry connections where upon the name appearing on the cake was incorrectly spelled, as especially noted by one of Michael's daughters. "They spelled my dad's name wrong," she allegedly told several attendees.

"Missing You Now" — Written by Michael Bolton, Walter Afanasieff, and Diane Warren.
    Appeared on TIME, LOVE & TENDERNESS (Columbia, 1991). Also appeared on GREATEST HITS 1985-1995 (Columbia, 1996).
    Produced by Walter Afanasieff and Michael Bolton.
    Kenny G. plays sax on this cut and Walter Afanasieff plays keyboards, synthesizers, synth bass, drums, and percussion. Teri Hatcher is featured in the video with Michael, which appears on Michael's SOUL & PASSION videotape.

Monogamy — Michael believes every relationship should be monogamous, saying, "There's no other reason to be in a relationship."

Mood Music — Michael has said that he doesn't use music to set the tone romantically, "...I like to make my own music. Having music on while I am making love would distract me because I listen to music critically."

Morris, Colleen — Colleen is the blonde actress appearing in Michael's videos, "How Can We Be Lovers" and "How Am I Supposed To Live Without You." She gained fame as the first "Mento's Girl."

Moten, Wendy — This singer and her band were one of the opening acts for Michael during his 1993 tour.

Mother's Voices — This charity was set up to bring an end to AIDS. Michael appeared at their February 13, 1997 Gala in New York City to perform and receive an honor for his work through The Michael Bolton Foundation.

Mr. Murder — On page 292 of this book, written by Dean Koontz, it mentions Michael Bolton "...singing about love. The song is touching." (See "Hideaway" entry for more information about the Dean Koontz/Michael Bolton connection.)

MTV — This cable music station does not play Michael Bolton videos. The Fan Club has requested that fans write to MTV at 1515 Broadway, New York, NY 10036 to ask that they add Michael's videos to their play lists.

Much Music — A Canadian tv show based in Toronto, Ontario. Michael appeared on this show June 12, 1991 doing a very entertaining interview with Steve Anthony, where upon they traded both roles and personnas. Michael pretended he was Steve and asked question that the real Steve (pretending to be Michael Bolton) answered. Some of the answers were quite humorous.

Mullaney, Jan — This songwriter collaborated with Michael on "Don't Tell Me It's Over" and played keyboards on his EVERYBODY'S CRAZY album.

Mumbling — Michael has stated that he feels he's been mumbling his whole career until he sang opera.

Music Reading — According to Michael, "I still can't read music technically."

"My Girl" — This is the song that Michael sang as the "First Dance" at Joyce and Wayne Logan's wedding in November, 1986.

"My World Is Empty Without You" — Written by B. Holland, L. Dozier, and E. Holland
    Appeared on WORLD'S APART (Polydor, 1980)
    Produced by Eddy Offord

NBA All-Star Game — Michael Bolton sang the National Anthem at this basketball game held February 9.

National Committee For The Prevention Of Child Abuse — Michael has been the National Spokesman for the NCPCA since 1990 and is on the National Board of Directors. In 1991, Michael did public service announcements on behalf of the Committee and received a special honor from former First Lady Barbara Bush for his efforts. (For address information, see listing at the back of this book.)

National Library Association — Michael was a "poster boy" in a NLA campaign to promote reading. The full color poster shows him reading his favorite book (SHIBUMI by Trevanian) with a big smile on his face.

"Never Get Enough Of Your Love" — Written by Michael Bolton, Diane Warren, and Walter Afanasieff.

Appeared on THE ONE THING (Columbia, 1993)
Produced by Walter Afanasieff and Michael Bolton

New Haven, CT — New Haven, a former Indian village named Quinnipiac that is now home to Yale University, is the city where Michael was born and raised. Michael has said, "(New Haven) is really where I want to raise my kids."

New Haven Register — The Register is a Connecticut newspaper that prints frequent Bolton news, keeping up with their "native son."

New Haven's Savoy Agency — This agency was the management group that helped Michael advertise for opening acts in the early 80s. Members of the Savoy Agency showered Michael's car with roses when it passed in front of their building during the October, 1983 Columbus Day Parade. The hiring of RIVAL was as a result of this agency's efforts.

"New Love" — Written by Michael Bolton, Diane Warren, and Desmond Child.
Appeared on TIME, LOVE & TENDERNESS (Columbia, 1991).
Produced by Walter Afanasieff and Michael Bolton.
Walter also plays keyboards, synthesizers, synth bass, drums, and percussion on this track.

New York Music Awards — Michael won his first New York Music Award in 1989 for Best Male R&B Vocalist. In 1990, Michael's SOUL PROVIDER album was nominated for seven awards and he won four of them: Artist of the Year; Best Male Pop Vocalist; Best Male R&B Vocalist; and Best Pop Album. Winning four awards in one year was an unprecedented accomplishment. Michael went on to win Best Male Pop Vocalist again in 1991.

"Night Has Me Callin' For You, The" — Written by Michael Bolotin, Bruce Kulick, and Robert Kulick.
Appeared on BLACKJACK (Polydor, 1979).
Produced by Tom Dow.d

1995 GRAMMY NOMINEES — This album of various Grammy nominees was released by Grammy Recordings/Sony Music in 1995. It includes Michael singing, "Said I Loved You...But I Lied."

1996 European Tour — Michael did 24 concerts in 20 cities throughout Europe in February and March, 1996, as part of his GREATEST HITS 1985-1995 World Tour.

Nirvana — Nirvana was a Manhattan dance club that Michael was featured in during the 80s.

Nomads — The Nomads were a New Haven bar band that Michael sang with at age 11. They later changed their name to Joy and traveled to California, resulting in a record contract. (See the listing for "Joy" for more information.)

Normalcy — When discussing the pressures of fame in an interview with Joan Lunden, Michael said, "A little bit of normalcy, that's all you get."

"Nothin' Like The Real Thing" — Michael Bolton sang this song with Patti LaBelle at Motown's 30th Anniversary on November 25, 1990, as part of a three-song medley celebrating the hits of Marvin Gaye and Tammi Terrell.

Nova, Aldo — A special guest musician on the MICHAEL BOLTON album and Michael sang back-up on his 1986 LP..

"Now That I Found You" — Written by Michael Bolton and Diane Warren. Appeared on TIME, LOVE & TENDERNESS (Columbia, 1991). Produced by Walter Afanasieff and Michael Bolton Walter also plays keyboards, synthesizers, synth bass, drums, and percussion on this track.

"Number 1" — "I knew I had made it as a performer in January of 1990. Donnie Ienner, the president of Columbia Records, called me up and said, 'I just wanted to be the one to tell you . . . you're in next week. You have the number one single in America, congratulations! We're just beginning." Then he hung up the phone. It was really nice that he wanted to tell me, but I was alone in my office studio in New York. I remember just sitting in the chair, digesting it, looking around and thinking, "Wow, what a long road it's been.' " — Michael Bolton

NUMBER 1 HIT MIX — This compilation album, released by Foundation Records in 1994, included Michael's version of "Yesterday."

Numero Uno — Michael appeared as a judge on this Swedish game show on Halloween, 1995.

Numerology — In numerology, Michael's number is three and his personal profile reads in part "...he has the ability to excel in many ways but his claim to fame is his ability to communicate. His ability extends from writing and speaking to singing, if only in the shower." Michael is also young at heart, seeking fun wherever he goes, and he is welcomed by people of all ages. He rightfully claims center stage and thrives on audience appreciation.

An interesting sidenote is that Michael is the third of three children and has three daughters himself.

 "O Holy Night" — Traditional carol in public domain. Appeared on THIS IS THE TIME - THE CHRISTMAS ALBUM (Columbia, 1996). Produced by Walter Afanasieff and Michael Bolton. The Arrangement is by Walter Afanasieff and Mariah Carey

Oakdale Theater — Michael Bolton performed a concert in the Wallingford, Connecticut theater in June of 1988. The show had the distinction of being the last time Michael Bolton performed a concert in a "small" theater (3000 seat house).

O'Donnell, Rosie   Rosie first met Michael Bolton at a Cystic Fibrosis Ski Weekend in the mid-80s and they became good friends. In 1996, Rosie appeared at the Fourth Annual Michael Bolton Foundation Black Tie Gala and performed a comedy routine that had the entire audience laughing long and hard. Several weeks later, on October 22, 1996, Michael returned the favor by appearing on Rosie's talkshow. They good-naturedly needled each other on national television, Rosie teasing Michael about his dislike for getting out of bed early in the morning and Michael returning that some people had nothing better to do but write letters on their computers. He promised a follow-up appearance at a later date.

"Once In A Lifetime" — Written by Michael Bolton, Diane Warren, and Walter Afanasieff. Appeared on the ONLY YOU soundtrack (Columbia, 1994). Produced by Walter Afanasieff. Arranged by Afanasieff and Michael Bolton.

Michael, Diane, and Walter were shown a rough cut of the film while it was in production and this song was the result. Michael sings both lead and background vocals.

1-900-407-BOLTON — This is Michael's Hot Line phone number. (A disclaimer stating that you must be 18 years of age or have parental permission before calling is one of the first things you hear on this hotline.) The current cost of this Hot Line is $1.99 per minute and you can listen to a personal message from Michael, current tour information, softball game news (when pertinent), What's New with Michael, or receive information on The Michael Bolton Foundation or joining Michael's Fan Clubs.

There is also a Michael Bolton trivia contest to play for Bolton-related prizes. A portion of the charge is donated to Michael's Foundation and this phone service is very popular. By April 15, 1994, $10,000 had been generated for the Foundation and was presented by Joyce Logan.

Michael's personal message is updated approximately every two weeks (except when he is busy recording or touring, when it is updated monthly) and there is also a place for you to leave a message for Michael to hear. (However, we haven't had the nerve to do so yet.)

"One More Time" — Written by Tom Snow and Dean Pitchford. Appeared on the SING soundtrack (Columbia, 1989). Produced by Michael Omartian.

Michael's performance of this song, with the cast of Sarafina backing him, plays while the movie credits roll at the end of the film.

THE ONE THING — This album, Michael's seventh Columbia album, was released on November 16, 1993. Producers listed are Michael Bolton, Walter Afanasieff, David Foster, and Robert John "Mutt" Lange. Jeremy Lubbock and David Foster arranged and conducted the orchestra. The album is dedicated to the memory of David Warren. The songs are:

Michael Bolton and Joyce Logan with a BIG Check for the Michael Bolton Foundation

1. *Said I Loved You...But I Lied*
2. *I'm Not Made Of Steel*
3. *The One Thing*
4. *Soul Of My Soul*
5. *Completely*
6. *Lean On Me*
7. *Ain't Got Nothin' If You Ain't Got Love*
8. *A Time For Letting Go*
9. *Never Get Enough Of Your Love*
10. *In The Arms Of Love*

(See individual song listing for writer and producer information.)

THE ONE THING — (CD4 UK Import) This United Kingdom version of THE ONE THING album includes the song, "Voice Of My Heart", which does not appear on the U.S. version. (Note: If you want to try to order a copy of this import, its order number is Columbia 6601772.)

"The One Thing" — Written by Michael Bolton, Diane Warren, and Desmond Child.
    Appeared on THE ONE THING (Columbia, 1993).
    Also appeared on THINKING OF YOU (Sony Productions, 1996).
    Produced and arranged by Walter Afanasieff and Michael Bolton.
    Walter also plays keyboards and synthesizers for this track.

Only You — Michael's song, "Once In A Lifetime" is featured in this 1994 movie starring Marisa Tomei and Robert Downey, Jr. It also appears on the soundtrack album.

Opera Solo — Michael has been known to break into Canio's solo from the opera, "I, Pagliacci" by Leoncavello, during his live shows. (Note: He sings it beautifully, too.) In 1995, Michael sang opera with Luciano Pavarotti at the Pavarotti & Friends Together For The Children Of Bosnia benefit in Modena, Italy. (See Pavarotti, Luciano listing for more information.)

Orchestra New England — Founded in Connecticut in 1975, ONE backed Michael for a concert at Yale University on April 22, 1994. The concert was a benefit performance for ONE and The Michael Bolton Foundation. James Sinclair conducted the orchestra.

Osbourne, Ozzy — Michael opened for Ozzy in the early '80s.

Oxford Society — This world-renowned society is based in London, England. They have invited Michael to speak, but his schedule has not yet permitted him to do so.

Page, Tommy — Michael sang back-up for Tommy Page on the song "Whenever You Close Your Eyes," which Michael co-wrote with Diane Warren. This song appeared on Page's album, FROM THE HEART, released on Sire Records in 1991.

"Paradise" —Written by Michael Bolton and Scott Zito.
    Appeared on MICHAEL BOLTON (Columbia, 1983).
    Produced by Gerry Block and Michael Bolton.
    Scott Zito played rhythm guitar, piano, lead guitar, synthesizer, bass guitar and sang background vocals with Michael for this album cut.

Paramount Theater — Michael performed a concert in Paramount Theater on January 16, 1993 to benefit CityKids, a New York City multi-cultural youth organization.

PARLIAMENT LIGHTS—PLATINUM COLLECTION — Released by RCA Records in 1990, this promotional album featured Michael singing, "(Sitting On) The Dock Of The Bay."

Passion Studio — Located at Michael's home in Connecticut, this studio is where Michael does a great deal of the production work on his albums.

Paternostro, Mark — Mark is responsible for the cover artwork on the Blackjack album, WORLDS APART.

Paul Newman's Hole In The Wall Gang — This organization, founded by Paul Newman in 1988 and located in northeast Connecticut, supports a residential summer camp for children with cancer or life-threatening diseases. They annually accept 800 kids between the ages of seven and fifteen at no charge. On October 14, 1995, the Hole In The Wall Gang co-sponsored a martial arts charity event at Yale University in New Haven with the Michael Bolton Foundation. The event benefitted the summer camp and the Michael Bolton Foundation's "Safe Space" project in Connecticut. See "Kids for Life Benefit" listing for more information.

Pavarotti, Luciano — Pavarotti, the premier tenor in the world, invited Michael to Modena, Italy to sing opera with him at a benefit concert to raise money for the Children of Bosnia Relief Fund. Over $1 million was raised. Michael performed two arias with Pavarotti, "Vesti la Giubba" by Leoncavello and Puccini's "Nessun Dorma." On April 11, 1996, Michael and Pavarotti appeared on the David Letterman show together singing "Nessun Dorma." Michael said he listens to Pavarotti daily for inspiration, saying, "He is the voice of the century to me."

Pebble Mill — Michael appeared on this British television show on December 12, 1995, singing "Can I Touch You...There?" and "A Love So Beautiful." He was also interviewed by the host of this "Tonight Show"-type program.

Pentagram Records — Michael was in the midst of recording sessions with them when this record company folded.

People's Choice Awards — Michael was nominated for Best Male Performer, but lost to Garth Brooks on this awards show telecast March 9, 1993.

"Perfume Women" — The way the fan club refers to women who spray cologne on their letters to Michael.

Pete Rose All-Stars — Played a benefit softball game against the Bolton Bombers in Delaware on September 24, 1994.

Petty, Dini — When Michael appeared on her Canadian talk show, he challenged the World Series winners, the Toronto Blue Jays, to a softball game against the Bombers. Michael also told Dini that he would someday like to act, if the proper role presented itself. When asked if his current level of success enabled him to slow down and relax a bit, Michael said, "I'm too driven to relax in success."

Pictures of his Kids — What Michael says is the first thing he would save if his house were burning. Pictured at left, Michael with Holly, Isa and Taryn.

Pisces — Michael's zodiac sign. Pisceans are intensely sensitive and crave the artistic life, gravitating towards all things beautiful. They have a deeply ingrained personal integrity and are generally humble and modest about their achievements. Being a water sign, Pisces people can often be found near the water, whether it is in the form of an ocean, river, jacuzzi, or pool.

Planet 'Song' — Michael calls Diane Warren "my sister from the planet 'Song'."

Pre-Inaugural Gala — This gala was held in Washington, D.C. on January 19, 1993. Many entertainers performed in honor of President-elect Bill Clinton. Michael sang a rousing rendition of Bill Withers' hit, "Lean On Me." (Note: At all future musical events, the First Lady should be seated between the President and the Vice President. This would avoid the American public noticing that their movements are totally out of synch with each other.)

Press Release — A copy of Michael's press release read at the May 2, 1994 press conference in New York City regarding the outcome of the Isley Brothers lawsuit was sent to all Michael Bolton Fan Club members.

Princess Di — Michael has said that he wanted to meet her, saying that if they were single at the same time, he would find her attractive. Since she was a special guest at Pavarotti's Benefit for Bosnia in Modena, Italy, we're pretty sure Michael was introduced.

Private Michael Bolton Auction — Also referred to as "Spring Cleaning At Michael's," this annual event is sponsored by Fan Emporium, Inc. It traditionally offers hard-to-find or one-of-a-kind Michael Bolton memorabilia including Commemorative Multi-Platinum plaques from Columbia Records for the SOUL PROVIDER, THE ONE THING, and TIME, LOVE & TENDERNESS albums which had previously been hanging in Michael's home and office. The 1996 auction included 150 signed items with "his fingerprints still warm on them" and bearing a certificate of authenticity from Fan Emporium and Michael's office. Some examples of the items offered are: an unsigned, sealed copy of the QUIET STORM SAMPLER CD that Michael made during the Desert Storm war; a signed two-version CD of "(Sittin' On) The Dock of The Bay" (referred to a Lightnin' Bolton Mix); a signed CD of "A Love So Beautiful" LIVE IN THE UK (includes the songs, "To Love Somebody" and two versions of "Can I Touch You...There"); a framed "Everybody's Crazy" poster; and a signed full color photo cover TIMELESS:THE CLASSICS booklet form Sony Music with a background history of Michael and his music. Bids are mailed to Fan Emporium and highest bidder takes home the goods.

Public Speaking — Although Michael Bolton is frequently called upon to make public statements, he takes the time to write his own speeches, rather than relying on a professional speechwriter. Michael always employs the personal touch.

Michael Takes the Podium Again

Publishing — Michael says he has his own music publishing company named after his daughter's initials. Let's see, Holly, Isa, Taryn...

 Q102 — The radio station that promoted (and participated in) one of Michael's 1994 softball games. During the game, they asked trivia questions for prizes and one of the questions was: "What color are Michael Bolton's eyes? Black, red, yellow, or blue?" Oops, the correct choice, hazel, didn't even make the list.

QUIET STORM SAMPLER — This demo CD, released by Columbia in 1991, consisted of selections from the TIME, LOVE & TENDERNESS album and included interview segments.

 Radice, Mark — This songwriter collaborated with Michael on the songs "Call My Name" and "Start Breaking My Heart." He was also one of the keyboard players on Michael's EVERYBODY'S CRAZY album.

Ralston, Matthew — Matthew is the photographer responsible for the TIMELESS: THE CLASSICS album cover photo.

Ray Charles: 50 Years in Music — Ray has always been one of Michael's favorite singers and Michael must have been thrilled when he got to sing "Georgia On My Mind" with him on this TV special. The show was first telecast on October 6, 1991.

RCA Records — Michael signed his first record deal with RCA in 1968. One year later, he was released from his contract. In 1974, he was again signed to RCA, this time for a two-record deal. He received a $10,000 advance and a budget of $40,000 for his first album with them, MICHAEL BOLOTIN. His second RCA album was EVERYDAY OF MY LIFE and then, once again, Michael was a free agent.

"Reach Out, I'll Be There" — Written by B. Holland, L. Dozier, and E. Holland. Appears on TIMELESS: THE CLASSICS (Columbia, 1992). Produced by Walter Afanasieff and Michael Bolton.

The Four Tops sang background vocals on this song. Lead vocals were recorded at Passion Studios, CT.

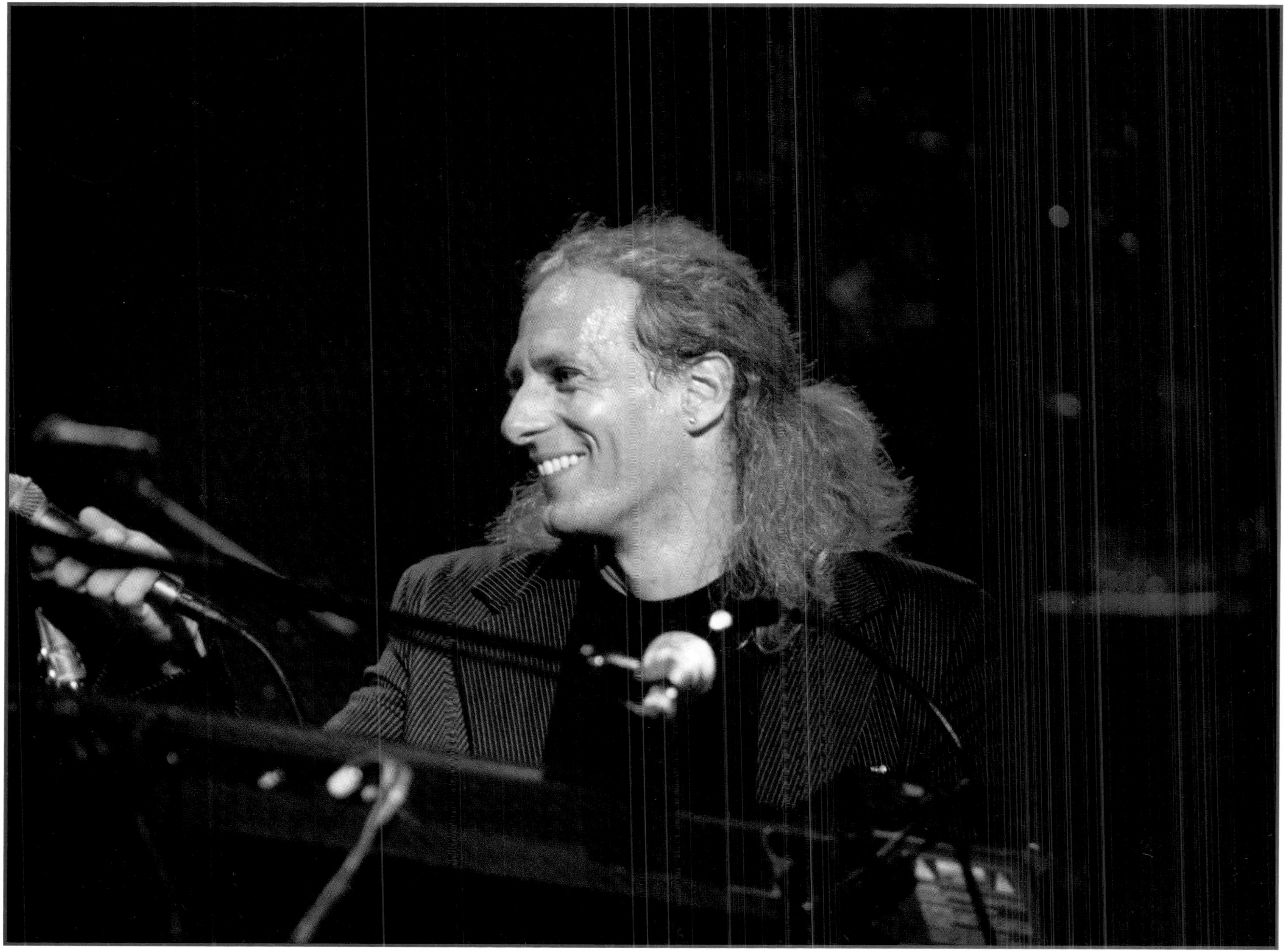

Photc Credit: Wayne Logan

In Concert — Tampa, Florida, 1985

Young Bolton — Tampa, Florida, 1985

The Leather Days, circa 1980's

Bolton and Friends (Bob and Mark) and author Joyce Logan, Columbus Day Parade, 1983.

Sharp Dressed Man

Michael in California in the Early '80s

Mike Reno, Joyce Logan and Michael.

It's Puppy Love for One of Bolton's Youngest Fans

Janet Schupp, Michael and Joyce, 1983

"Talk About Love, Talk About Trust..."

"Walk Away..."

Moody Blue

Moody Blue

"He's Looking At Me..."

"He's Looking At Me..."

In The Spotlight

In The Spotlight

Black Tie Performances

Black Tie Performances

Hometown Hero

Hometown Hero

Dressed Down...

Dressed Up...

"Really Wanna Know" — Written by Michael Bolotin and Bruce Kulick. Appeared on WORLDS APART (Polydor, 1980). Produced by Eddy Offord

Recording Industry Association of America (RIAA) — This association, founded in 1952, evaluates manufacturing and recording standards. They also certify sales figures for authentic Gold Record (sales of 500,000), Platinum Record (sales of one million), and Multi-Platinum Record awards.

Red Cross Gala at Monaco — On August 9, 1996, the Salle des Etoiles in Monaco was the setting for the 48th Anniversary Benefit Gala of the Red Cross. Michael Bolton performed for Prince Rainier and his three children, Prince Albert, Princess Caroline, and Princess Stephanie.

Red Faces — Michael performed "Can I Touch You...There?" and acted as a judge on this Australian "Gong Show" type of game show.

Regis & Kathie Lee — Michael did a promotional appearance on their morning show for TIMELESS: THE CLASSICS. He did a short interview segment during which he said, "The body is the life-support system for the voice."

On September 19, 1995, the day the GREATEST HITS 1985-1995 was released, Michael appeared on their show and announced a bi-coastal album signing he would be doing at HMV Records in New York and Sam Goody's in Los Angeles that day.

Religion — Michael has said that, although he has a strong belief in God, he doesn't believe in religion. "God is not limited to one form of religion...I've always perceived God as an ultimately wise and guiding force, much more as my closest friend. My perception is that I have a very personal relationship with God."

Replay Records — This music store, located in New Haven, Connecticut, frequently carries the older, hard-to-find copies of Michael's music. We found the owners, Doug and Mary, to be very friendly and helpful. If you want to give them a try, they are located in Saw Mill Plaza, West Haven, CT 06516 and their phone number is (203) 934-9999.

REQUIEM FOR THE AMERICAS (Songs from the Lost World) — Michael sings "Let There Be Peace" with Patti D'Arcy on this album released by Enigma Records. REQUIEM FOR THE AMERICAS, about the American Indian, was written by Jonathon Elias.

Reviews, Good — Although most critics seem to enjoy taking pot shots at Michael's voice, hair, band, delivery, etc., there have been a few notable exceptions. The following is a list of some of the publications and approximate dates of their good reviews. Notice that most of them were written in the mid-70, during Michael's hard rock days, and long before Bolton fever struck mainstream America. *Rolling Stone Magazine*—1976; *Riverside Press*—1976; *Berkley Press/Star News*—mid-70s; *Aquarian*—mid-70s; *Match Entertainment Guide*—mid-70s; *L.A. Times*—summer, 1991; *Amsterdam News* (NY)—1994; The Minal News—1994; *Appleton Post/*

After making the announcement live on the Regis & Kathie Lee show, Michael is shown signing albums at HMV Records, 1995.

Crescent—1995; *Baltimore Sun*—1995; *Kalamazoo Gazette*—1996;

Rhythm and Blues — This type of music has been a long-time favorite of Michael's since his teenage years of singing Screamin' Jay Hawkins and Junior Wells in New Haven Clubs.

Ritz, The — Michael headlined a charity performance at the Ritz to benefit Forward Face on March 3, 1993. (See Forward Face entry for more information.)

Rival — Michael gave this local Connecticut band their first job in the early '80s. According to Dennis Mardell, they opened about twelve shows for him.

Roberts, Julia — Before her marriage to Lyle Lovett, Michael had been romantically linked to Julia Roberts by the tabloids. And (surprise!) it wasn't the last bit of creative reporting on this pair. Although one of the weeklies reported that he attended the Lovett wedding, Michael says it just isn't true.

Robotman — Syndicated cartoon which featured one of the strip's main characters appearing (and being cut from) a Michael Bolton video. The cartoons appeared in newspapers during the week of April 26, 1993.

Rock The Vote — Besides lending his face to posters for this campaign, Michael attended their 1997 bash at the Red Sage Restaurant, given by MCI and the RIAA. Michael, urging support for President Clinton, was quoted by the January 21, 1997 edition of *USA Today* as saying, "We think entertainment is tough...That's like playing Whiffle Ball compared to coming to Washington and trying to get something done here. It would be great to see a lot more support and positive energy go towards what the president's trying to do."

Rockefeller Center — This New York City landmark hosts the annual "Lighting of the Christmas Tree," one of the largest, decorated trees in the United States. Michael appeared, and sang "Santa Claus is Coming to Town" while Ektarina Goreeva skated at the 1996 tree lighting ceremony. At the end of the hour-long televised special, "Christmas at Rockefeller Center," Michael flipped the switch on the tree with Yankee Manager Joe Toire.

"Rocky Mountain Way" — Written by J. Walsh, J. Vitale, K. Passarelli, and R. Grace.

Appeared on EVERY DAY OF MY LIFE (RCA, 1976).
Also appears on THE ARTISTRY OF MICHAEL BOLOTIN (RCA RE-RELEASE, 1993).
Produced by Jack Richardson for Nimbus 9 Productions. Michael used to open every performance with this song in the '70s when he was playing on the bar circuit.

Rodriguez, Dennis — Dennis is Michael's tour manager.

Role Model — Michael has said that his role model is Tony Bennett.

Rolling Stone Magazine — Although *Rolling Stone* generally makes a habit out of ignoring Michael Bolton, he has made it onto their hallowed pages several times. The first time was on July 31, 1975 when they did a one paragraph review of MICHAEL BOLOTIN. On April 21, 1988, a half-page advertisement for THE HUNGER appeared and then on May 17, 1990, a picture of Michael with Lenny Kravitz appeared, along with a short note on Michael's collaboration with Bob Dylan. In 1992, Michael made it in three times, the first being in the March 5 issue as part of the *Rolling Stone* 1992 Music Awards.

Michael was #2 on the Best-Dressed Male Artist list and #4 on the Best Male Singer list. His second appearance that year was in the April 16th issue, when a picture of Michael was printed in the "Random Notes" section along with a short piece on the Grammy Awards mini-scandal. His third mention was in their "In The News" column of the October 29, 1992 edition.

Rolls Royce — Michael's dream car is a cream-colored 1955 Rolls Royce Orniche.

Romance Novel — Charles Young interviewed Michael and commented that his live performances resemble "the cover of a women's romance novel." Ah, yes-the stuff of dreams.

Jonathon Ross Presents — VH1 broadcast Jonathon's interview with Michael Bolton in June of 1994. The interview took place on the bench at a Bomber's game. This interview was a lot of fun to watch and it appeared to be a lot of fun to make. Jonathon matched wits with Michael on subjects ranging from Michael's career to his love life, from his disaffection with critics to his special relationship with his fans. While discussing Michael's vocal range, they got into a short discussion on the proper pronunciation of the word "octave" (or "oc Tave," as Jonathon called it) and decided it depended on whether you were a civilized Englishmen or a heathen American. Moments later, a slightly off-color reference found Jonathon's voice breaking and he admitted that he had almost hit the high octave himself on that one.

Rowland, John G. — In early April, 1995, Michael met with the Governor of Connecticut, John G. Rowland, to discuss plans to use an abandoned mall to create a "Safe Space" for women and children. (In the fall of 1995, the "Safe Space" project was realized and includes medical services, child care, and a variety of other services.) During the meeting, Governor Rowland told Michael that he had proposed to his wife at a Michael Bolton concert. Governor Rowland was the Honorary Chairman of the Third Annual Michael Bolton Foundation Celebrity Tennis Classic, Softball Game, and Black Tie Gala in 1995 and he and his wife, Patricia, were special guests at the 1996 Michael Bolton Foundation Black Tie Gala.

Michael Bolton and Governor Rowland "working together" on the Safe Space Project.

Rush, Jennifer — Michael sings a duet of his song, "Same Heart" with Jennifer on her PASSION album, released in 1988 on Epic Records. Jennifer also recorded Michael's song, "Love Get Ready."

Safe Space Opening — 1995

Russell, Leon — Michael opened for him on Russell's 1971 tour and it was his band backing Michael's vocals on the demo tapes which resulted in the contract with RCA Records in 1974.

Russian/Jewish — This is Michael's heritage. His grandparents on his father's side were Russian immigrants.

R.V. (or Remarkable Vitriole) — The way Jonathan Ross described the manner with which critics review Michael Bolton, on his interview show, "Jonathon Ross Presents..." Michael was obviously amused with the description.

Sabatini, Gabriella — Michael had been romantically linked to this Pro Tennis player.

Safe Space — In 1995, The Michael Bolton Foundation worked with Connecticut Governor John G. Rowland to transform an abandoned mall in downtown New Haven into a "Safe Space for New Haven's Youth" and it includes medical services, child care, and other family-related services. Located at 560 Ella Grasso Boulevard, it features a state of the art music studio, a theatre/multi-use room, computer/video labs, and offices. The Foundation received a grant for $650,000 from the State of Connecticut to aid in the renovations.

"Said I Loved You...But I Lied" — Written by Michael Bolton and R.J. Lange.
Appeared on THE ONE THING (Columbia, 1993).

Also appeared on GREATEST HITS 1985-1995 (Columbia, 1995)

Produced by R.J. "Mutt" Lange and Michael Bolton

This song garnered Michael his fourth Grammy nomination, but did not win. It had the distinction of being one of only three songs to hold the top spot for 12 weeks on Billboard's Hot Adult Contemporary Chart. It was the first single released from THE ONE THING album and it's "B" side was "Soul Provider." It was recorded at Out Of Pocket Productions, Ltd. Studios in Surrey, England with Mutt Lange on back-up vocals.

Sally's Pizza — Located at 237 Wooster Street in New Haven, CT, this was the hometown shop whose pizzas so enamored Michael that he has them delivered backstage to his concerts in Connecticut. His favorite pizza toppings are cheese and fresh tomatoes. (Note: If you plan to try out their pizzas yourself, get there early. A line forms before opening time, and the wait could be considerable. We agree with Michael, though, and think it's definitely worth it.)

Sam Goody's Record Store — 3,000 New York City fans showed up to meet Michael at Columbia Records most successful in-store appearance. Later, on September 19, 1995, Sam Goody's Los Angeles store was the second stop on Michael's bi-coastal album signing to promote his GREATEST HITS 1985-1995 album.

Samuel Bull Homestead Designer Showcase — The Samuel Bull House is a fifteen-room pre-Revolutionary building in Woodbury, Connecticut. For this June of 1996 event, internationally renowned and distinguished interior designers transformed the house into a showcase for their talents. A special pre-opening weekend tour was held to benefit the Michael Bolton Foundation and Paul Newman's Hole In The Wall Gang.

Sanborn, Dave — Dave played sax for Michael on the 1975 album, MICHAEL BOLOTIN.

Sangiamo, Nick — Photographer for the EVERYDAY OF MY LIFE album cover.

"Santa Claus Is Coming To Town" — Written by J. Fred Coots and Haven Gillespie.

Appeared on THIS IS THE TIME - THE CHRISTMAS ALBUM (Columbia, 1996).

Produced by Walter Afanasieff and Michael Bolton.

Arranged by Walter Afanasieff and Michael Bolton.

Sante's Manor — This restaurant in Milford, Connecticut, was the site of a dinner-dance hosted by Michael Bolton to benefit THIS CLOSE for Cancer Research. It was held on November 17, 1991, and Chuck Norris and Victoria Jackson appeared.

"Save Me" — Written by Michael Bolton, Walter Afanasieff, and Andrew Goldmark.

Appeared on TIME, LOVE & TENDERNESS (Columbia, 1991).

Produced by Walter Afanasieff and Michael Bolton.

Walter also played keyboards, synthesizers, synth bass, drums and percussion, while A. Mark Russo performed the sax solo.

"Save Our Love" — Written by Michael Bolton and Mark Mangold

Appeared on EVERYBODY'S CRAZY (Columbia, 1985)

Produced by Neil Kernon and Michael Bolton

Saxophone — Michael has been interested in music for most of his life. When he was 7 years old, his parents rented him a sax. He didn't learn to play it, but he would hold it to his mouth and pretend to play, using his voice instead.

Scales, Steve — Steve, Michael's percussionist, was born in Brooklyn, NY and started playing music in 1975. He has previously played with Tina Turner, the Talking Heads, and Bryan Ferry. Steve has also worked as an actor, appearing in the movies SOMETHING WILD and PHILADELPHIA. He currently lives in Hamden, CT.

Schaetzle, Bud — Bud headed the production team for the "This Is Michael Bolton" tv special and video.

Schoemer, Karen — When reviewing a Bolton concert in November, 1991, this New York Times reviewer said, "...his voice never, ever lets up. He emotes 100% of the time. The fantasy he seems to inhabit gratefully never has a chance to dissipate."

Schon, Neal — This former member of the band, Journey, collaborated with Michael on "You're All That I Need."

Schotteman, Cristophe — Michael has reportedly had his hair cut by this Beverly Hills barber (who has also done President Clinton's hair.)

Scrabble — When he's on the road, Michael is a compulsive Scrabble player.

Scribbles — In the Valentine's Day, 1996 edition of USA Today, handwriting expert Michael Watts does a short analysis of a "Love Always, Michael" sample of Michael's "scribbles." Watts said, "When [Bolton] does fall in love, you can be certain that his feelings will be incredibly passionate, highly romantic, and overwhelmingly intense."

"Secret of the Lost Kingdom" — The name of the children's book that Michael has written for Hyperion Books, a division of Disney Books. (For more information, see the listing for Hyperion.)

Seger, Bob — Michael opened for Bob on the 1982-83 THE DISTANCE tour.

Seven — David Foster bid against Andre Agassi (right) for an AKC-registered Golden Retriever puppy at the First Annual Black Tie Gala Celebrity Auction in 1993. Bidding was heavy but he finally won the puppy for a $7,000 bid and promptly named him "Seven." (This is also the number on the back of Michael Bolton's softball jersey.)

"She Did The Same Thing" — Written by Michael Bolton. Appeared on MICHAEL BOLTON (Columbia, 1983). Produced by Gerry Block and Michael.

"She Wants You Back" — Written by Michael Bolotin and Bruce Kulick.
Appeared on WORLDS APART (Polydor, 1980). Produced by Eddy Offord.

Shelter Records — Michael auditioned for Joe Cy at Shelter in 1971. Denny Cordell heard him from the next office and booked him to open on Leon Russell's tour.

Sheridan, Nicollette — This former "Knot's Landing" star has been romantically linked to Michael on and off for several years. She played tennis at the Michael Bolton Foundation's Second Annual Celebrity Tennis Classic and made numerous public appearances with Michael. She is the ex-wife of actor Harry Hamlin.

Sherman, Judy and Mickey — Judy and Mickey are close friends of Michael's. In 1993 they acted as event chairpersons for the First Annual Black Tie Gala to benefit The Michael Bolton Foundation.

Shibumi — Written by Trevanian. This action thriller (published in 1979) is Michael's favorite book. It is the book Michael is holding on his poster for the National Library Association campaign to promote reading.

Shields, Brooke — At one time, Brooke was romantically linked to Michael Bolton. She is now married to his friend, Andre Agassi.

Shopping — Michael said when he's with his daughters, this is their #1 activity.

Showbiz Magazine — The October 6-12, 1991 issue of this magazine features Michael Bolton on the cover.

Showtime At The Apollo — Michael sang "(Sittin' On The) Dock Of The Bay" on this TV special, telecast in October, 1987. Videotapes were released by Video Yesteryear. His second appearance on this show took place on October 6, 1995 and was televised on November 11, 1995.

Showtime Coast to Coast — Michael Bolton appeared on this show, filmed at the Los Angeles China Club and televised in February, 1990.

Signature — We can only imagine how many times a day Michael Bolton is called upon to write his name. Let's see, contracts, letters, memorabilia....etc., etc.

"Silent Night" — Traditional carol in public domain. Appeared on THIS IS THE TIME—THE CHRISTMAS ALBUM (Columbia, 1996). Produced by Walter Afanasieff and Michael Bolton. Arranged by Afanasieff and Dan Shea

"Best Wishes," Michael Bolton

Michael at his childhood home.

"Simply Mad About The Mouse" — In 1991, Walt Disney Classics released this videotape of popular musicians singing classic Disney movie songs. The videos are a blend of live action and animation. Michael personally selected and performed "A Dream Is A Wish Your Heart Makes" from Cinderella. The videotape and soundtrack are still available.

"Since I Fell For You" — Written by B. Johnson.
    Appeared on TIMELESS:THE CLASSICS
      (Columbia, 1992).
    Produced and arranged by David Foster and
      Michael Bolton.
    Orchestra arranged and conducted by Johnny Mandel.

Sing — Michael sings the song "One More Time" over the closing credits of this movie.

"Singin' The Blues" — Written by McCreary
    Appeared on EVERY DAY OF MY LIFE
      (RCA, 1976). Produced by Jack Richardson.

Six Feet — Michael's height.

610 Whalley Avenue — Michael's New Haven address in 1966.

Skiing — One of Michael's favorite sports. It was during a skiing benefit that Michael injured his knee. (See Anterior Cruciate Ligament earlier in this book.)

Sledge, Percy — Percy is the original singer of the hit, "When A Man Loves A Woman" whom Michael inadvertently neglected to mention when accepting his 1992 Grammy for that song. He later sang the song with Michael on the VH1 "Centerstage" special in 1993.

Smaga, Jacqueline — Jacqueline, the former director of "This Close" For Cancer Research, became the Executive Director for The Michael Bolton Foundation in 1993.

SOFT HITS COLLECTION—Collector's Edition — This album, from Brooks Howard Productions, Inc., was done in collaboration with 95 KKLD of Tuscon, Arizona to benefit the AIDS Coalition of Tucson. Among various artists singing their hits, Michael appears singing, "When I'm Back On My Feet Again."

Softball — Michael's favorite game.

Songwriters Hall Of Fame Award — Michael appeared and sang "Yesterday" and "You've Lost That Lovin'

Feeling" with Jeffrey Osborne on this show, June 22, 1989. Michael then received the Hitmaker award on May 31, 1995, presented to him by David Foster.

Sony — The name of Michael's recording company.

"Sooner Or Later" — Written by Michael Bolotin and Bruce Kulick.
>Appeared on WORLDS APART (Polydor, 1980).
>Produced by Eddy Offord.

SOUL & PASSION — This is a 55-minute videotape collection of Michael's music videos. Kenny G. appears in the videos for "Georgia On My Mind" and "Missing You Now." The video of "(Sittin' On) The Dock Of The Bay" features Jonathan Cain, Neal Schon, Randy Jackson, and Mike Baird. (Available in VHS and LaserDisc format.) The videos are:
1. *That's What Love Is All About*
2. *(Sittin' On) The Dock Of The Bay*
3. *Wait On Love*
4. *Soul Provider*
5. *How Am I Supposed To Live Without You*
6. *How Can We Be Lovers*

7. *When I'm Back On My Feet Again*
8. *Georgia On My Mind*
9. *Love Is A Wonderful Thing*
10. *Time, Love & Tenderness*
11. *Missing You*
12. *Steel Bars*

Soul of My Soul — This UK import CD was released by Columbia in 1994. It contained two different versions of "Soul of My Soul," a live version of "Steel Bars" that was recorded at Wembley Arena in 1991, and "The Voice Of My Heart," a song which does not appear on any of Michael's other releases.

"Soul Of My Soul" — Written by Michael Bolton, Diane Warren, and Walter Afanasieff. Appears on THE ONE THING (Columbia, 1993). Produced and arranged by Walter Afanasieff and Michael Bolton.

Michael and Percy Sledge — Center Stage 1993

Walter also plays keyboards and synthesizers for this track. Vann Johnson, Janis Liebhart, and Pat Hawke sing background. Michael calls this song, written for his children, a special inspiration.

SOUL PROVIDER — This album, released in June, 1989, sold over 7,000,000 copies worldwide, produced five Top Ten singles (one of which, "You Wouldn't Know Love," was re

leased simultaneously in 1989 by Michael and Cher), and garnered Michael two Grammy nominations. It won a 1990 NY Music Award for Best Pop Album and remained on the Billboard Top 100 chart for over two years. The album was dedicated to the memory of Rose Levin and special guests included Kenny G., Richard Marx, Terry Brock and Suzie Benson. The album was produced by Peter Bunetta, Rick Chudacoff, Michael Bolton, Susan Hamilton, Michael Omartian, Desmond Child, and Guy Roche. The album tracks are:

1. *Soul Provider*
2. *Georgia On My Mind*
3. *It's Only My Heart*
4. *How Am I Supposed To Live Without You*
5. *How Can We Be Lovers*
6. *You Wouldn't Know Love*
7. *When I'm Back On My Feet Again*
8. *From Now On*
9. *Love Cuts Deep*
10. *Stand Up For Love*

(See individual song listings for writer and producer information.)

"Soul Provider" — Written by Michael Bolton and Andrew Goldmark.
  Appears on SOUL PROVIDER (Columbia, 1989).
  Also appears on GREATEST HITS 1985-1995 (Columbia, 1996).
  Produced by Peter Bunetta and Rick Chudacoff.
  Kenny G. performs a sax solo for this song. Released as a single, it hit #1 on the R&R Adult Contemporary charts and #3 on the Billboard charts. Michael said this song is about wanting "to be there for someone in every way." He received BMI's 1990 Writer and Publisher Awards for this song. The video appears on Michael's SOUL PROVIDER: THE VIDEOS, SOUL & PASSION, and DECADE 1985-1995 videotapes.

Soul Provider: The Videos — This 18-minute, three-video compilation was released by Sony Music Video Enterprises in April, 1990. Michael introduces each video and chats about his career. The three videos are: "How Am I Supposed To Live Without You", "How Can We Be Lovers", and "Soul Provider." This videotape was certified RIAA platinum in the summer, 1990.

Soul Train — Michael appeared on this long-running music show on October 28, 1995, singing "Can I Touch You...There?" and "When A Man Loves A Woman."

Sound Check — Like most bands, Michael's band takes part in an informal sound check in the afternoon before a show. However, unlike many star performers, Michael is given to showing up at these sound checks, also.

Joe Turano and Mugs Cain — Sound Check 1996

"Southern Ballad (If This Means Losing You)" — Written by Michael Bolotin and Bruce Kulick.
  Appeared on BLACKJACK (Polydor, 1979).
  Produced by Tom Dowd.

Spontaneous Laughter — This is what Michael is engaging in for seven takes at the beginning of the "This Is Michael Bolton" TV special and video.

"Stand Up For Love" — Written by Michael Bolton, B. Mann, and C. Weil.

Appears on SOUL PROVIDER (Columbia, 1989)
Produced by Michael Omartian for Rhema Productions, Michael Bolton for MBO Productions, Inc, and Barry Mann

Stanley, Paul — A singer for the rock group, KISS, Paul collaborated with Michael on the song, "Forever," which was recorded by KISS. He also gave a short interview about the collaboration for THE MICHAEL BOLTON STORY radio show.

"Star Gauging" — This item appeared in the June 17, 1993 edition of *USA Today*. They named Michael "the person fans want to read more about" and he got the most votes in their write-in poll.

"Start Breaking My Heart" — Written by Michael Bolton and Mark Radice.
> Appeared on EVERYBODY'S CRAZY
> (Columbia, 1985).
> Produced by Neil Kernon and Michael Bolton.

"Stay" — Written by Michael Bolton and Bruce Kulick.
> Appeared on WORLDS APART (Polydor, 1980).
> Produced by Eddy Offord.

"Steel Bars" — Written by Michael Bolton and Bob Dylan.
> Appears on TIME, LOVE & TENDERNESS
> (Columbia, 1991).
> Also appears on GREATEST HITS 1985-1995
> (Columbia, 1996).
> Produced by Walter Afanasieff and Michael Bolton.
> Walter plays keyboards, synthesizer, Hammond B-3 organ, drums, and percussion for this song. This Michael Bolton/Bob Dylan collaboration was written in two days at Dylan's California home. Michael said it was the quickest song he had written. The video of this song appears on Michael's SOUL & PASSION videotape.

Steel Bars UK (Limited Edition) — This limited edition CD package, released in Great Britain on January 27, 1992, contained two live tracks and photos.

Storm N. Norman — This popular Connecticut deejay did radio commercials for Blackjack at the Keg House in New Haven in 1979. In 1987, he was the first deejay to play Michael's single "That's What Love Is All About" on the air and Joyce Logan hooked his radio show up with Michael for a live half-hour interview. He currently is the voice on Michael's 900 phone line.

Success — According to Michael, "Someone said to me there's a slogan-'Success is not the goal, success is the fuel.'"

Summer, Henry Lee — Michael co-wrote the song "Till Somebody Loves You" with Henry Lee and Diane Warren. Michael also sang back-up for him on this song on the WAY PAST MIDNIGHT album, released on Epic in 1991.

Suspenders — The fashion accessory that Michael sometimes uses that we most admire (along with his infamous "arrow" belt which points due south.)

Sydney Bay, Australia — On February 23, 1994, Michael kicked off his first Australian tour with a concert in Sydney Bay. Michael worked his Australian fans into a frenzy, substituting "Sydney" for "Frisco" while singing "Dock of the Bay."

"Take A Look At My Face" — Written by Michael Bolton and Martin Briley. The song appeared on THE HUNGER (Columbia, 1987). Produced by the late Keith Diamond. Keith also played drums, bass, keyboards, and fairlight for this track.

"Take Me As I Am" — Written by Michael Bolotin.
> Appeared on MICHAEL BOLOTIN (RCA, 1975).
> Also appeared on THE ARTISTRY OF
> MICHAEL BOLOTIN (RCA, 1993).
> Produced by Joe Cy and Michael Bolotin.
> Strings for this song were arranged and conducted by John Abbott.

Taryn — Michael's youngest daughter, Taryn lives with her father in Connecticut. Her birthday is October 3. (On the EVERYBODY'S CRAZY album liner notes, Taryn's name is spelled "Tarryn.")

Teen Stars Photo Album — This rock stars photo magazine included a photo of "newcomer" Michael Bolton signing autographs and talking to fans while touring with Bob Seger. The magazine is dated February, 1984 and shows a Michael with much darker hair.

Television Transcripts — Michael Bolton has frequently appeared on television, both as talk show guest and as segments of various television entertainment news programs. Transcripts of some of the shows can be ordered from the following companies (please contact them for specifics):

For transcripts of CBS or NBC shows: Burrelle's Transcripts, P.O. Box 7, Livingston, New Jersey 07039-0007 and the phone number is 1-800-777-TEXT.

For transcripts of ABC or CNN shows: Journal Graphics, 1535 Grant Street, Denver, Colorado 80203 and the phone number is 1- 800-TALKSHO.

"Tell Me How You Feel" — Written by Michael Bolotin.
    Appeared on MICHAEL BOLOTIN (RCA, 1975).
    Also appeared on MICHAEL BOLOTIN:
      THE EARLY YEARS (RCA, 1991).
    Produced by Joe Cy.
    Recorded December 18, 1974.

Tennis — One of Michael's favorite activities, he has said, "I have this running competition with the people I play against, always keeping score of who won."

Practice, Practice, Practice

"That's What Love Is All About" — Written by Michael Bolton and E. Kaz.
    Appeared on THE HUNGER (Columbia, 1987).
    Also appears on GREATEST HITS 1985-1995
      (Columbia, 1996).

Produced by the late Keith Diamond.

Keith also played drums, bass, keyboards and fairlight for this track, which includes the Group Of 10 for strings and horns. This was the first single released from THE HUNGER and it was the first time Michael hit the Top 20 as a singer. Michael won a 1989 ASCAP Writer/Publisher Award for this song.

On November 10, 1991, Michael recorded a version of this song live from the Wembley Arena for the BBC Radio 1 FM in England. This version, produced by Jeff Griffith, appears as the "B" side of the "Completely" single. The video appears on Michael's SOUL & PASSION videotape.

"These Eyes" — Written by Burton Cummings and Randy Bachman.
    Appeared on EVERY DAY OF MY LIFE
      (RCA, 1976).
    Also appeared on MICHAEL BOLOTIN:
      THE EARLY YEARS (RCA, 1991) and
      THE ARTISTRY OF MICHAEL BOLOTIN
    (RCA, 1993).
    Produced by Jack Richardson for Nimbus 9
      Productions.
    This track was recorded Valentine's Day, 1976.

THINKING OF YOU — This limited edition CD, sold exclusively at WalMart, was released in 1996 by Sony Music Special Products. Songs are:

1. *Time, Love and Tenderness*
2. *(Sittin' On) The Dock of the Bay*
3. *It's Only My Heart*
4. *I'm Not Made of Steel*
5. *How Can We Be Lovers*
6. *Georgia On My Mind*
7. *The One Thing*
8. *Bring It On Home To Me*
(See individual song listings for writer and producer information.)

30 Degrees — This was the approximate temperature of the air when Michael walked out of the water in the "Said I Loved You...But I Lied" video.

This Close for Cancer Research, Inc. — This organization was set up by Joel Brander to raise money for cancer research. Michael Bolton is the national Chairman and performs at the annual fund-raising event.

"This Close" Michael Bolton Laboratory — Located at the New York Medical College in New York City, this lab was dedicated on April 9, 1992.

This Is Michael Bolton — This hour-long NBC primetime special aired October 28, 1992. It was produced and directed by Bud Schaetzle and consisted of: concert clips; baseball footage; candid interviews with Michael; short interviews with Walter Afanasieff, Michael's back-up singers, David Foster, and Kenny G; backstage clips; and some of Michael's videos. An extended version was released on videotape and laser disc.

"This Is The Time" — Written by Michael Bolton and Gary Burr.

> Appeared on THIS IS THE TIME - THE
> CHRISTMAS ALBUM (Columbia, 1996).
> Produced by Keith Thomas for Yellow
> Elephant Music, Inc. and Michael Bolton.
> Arranged by Keith Thomas.

This song, a duet with Wynonna Judd, is the song Michael sang on the 1996 Country Music Awards Show. Nashville String Machine provided strings for this track.

THIS IS THE TIME—The Christmas Album — This album, released by Columbia Records in October, 1996, is the first album released by Michael that is a CDExtra, including a free multimedia portion of the CD. The multi-media portion features an album catalog (which, when a specific album is selected, lists the song titles on the album,

highlights a specific song, and plays a section of the song), a short slide show featuring selected concert scenes, and a video player. There is also a concert video of Michael singing "White Christmas." The graphics are excellent and Michael appears throughout.

The musical portion of the CD was produced by Walter Afanasieff, Michael Bolton, and Johnny Mandel (who also conducts the orchestra on three of the songs.) Cover photography was again done by Timothy White. Michael dedicated the album to "the memory of David Sorin Collyer, my mentor and friend in voice. Your are in my heart always." Michael recorded with a full orchestra and, in a recent Sony Music online info release, said, " I tried to get a sense of what I could do, where I could take certain songs. Fortunately, there are a lot of surprises when you get onto hallowed ground with a 60-piece orchestra. As you start to get into it, the sense of magic and nostalgia becomes overwhelming and you have to let the music take you where it wants to go. I just wanted to do justice to these beautiful arrangements and songs." We believe he did.

> The songs included are:
> 1. *Silent Night*
> 2. *Santa Claus Is Coming To Town*
> 3. *Have Yourself A Merry Little Christmas*
> 4. *Joy To The World*
> 5. *Ave Maria (a duet with Placido Domingo)*
> 6. *The Christmas Song*
> 7. *O Holy Night*
> 8. *White Christmas*
> 9. *This Is The Time (a duet with Wynonna Judd)*
> 10. *Love Is The Power*

(See individual song listings for writer and producer information.)

"This River" — Written by Diane Warren.
Appeared on Michael Bolton Greatest Hits 1985-1995 (Columbia, 1995). Produced by Tommy Sims and Michael Bolton. This song was recorded at Passion Studios, The Dugout, and Cherokee Studios. Micah Wilshire Choir sang back-up.

Thyme, Love & Tenderness Cookbook — This vegetarian cookbook was put together by Tere Jackson and sold through Fan Emporium, Inc.

"Time Is On My Side" — Written by N. Meade.
Appeared on Michael Bolton (RCA, 1975). Also appeared on Michael Bolotin: The Early Years (RCA,1991) and on The Artistry of Michael Bolotin (RCA, 1993). Produced by Joe Cy and Michael Bolotin.

TIME, LOVE & TENDERNESS — Michael released this album April 23, 1991 and it became his third consecutive RIAA-certified platinum album. The album hit #1 on the Billboard Chart in a record 3 weeks and has sold over 10 million copies to date. It won a 1992 American Music Award for Favorite Album in the Pop/Rock category. On the International Album Charts it was #1 in Norway, #2 in England, and #3 in Sweden. The first single off the album, "Love Is A Wonderful Thing," was pre-released and became a radio hit three months before the album was released.

Produced by Walter Afanasieff and Michael Bolton, TIME, LOVE & TENDERNESS also features guest appearances by Kenny G., Patti LaBelle, Desmond Child, and Joe Lynn Turner. The album notes give special thanks to Bobby Brooks. Songs included are:

1. *Love Is A Wonderful Thing*
2. *Time, Love & Tenderness*
3. *Missing You Now*
4. *Forever Isn't Long Enough*
5. *Now That I've Found You*
6. *When A Man Loves A Woman*
7. *We're Not Making Love Anymore*
8. *New Love*
9. *Save Me*
10. *Steel Bars*

(See individual song listings for writer and producer information.)

"Time, Love & Tenderness" — Written by Diane Warren. Appears on TIME, LOVE & TENDERNESS (Columbia, 1991). Also appears on GREATEST HITS 1985-1995 (Columbia, 1996) and THINKING OF YOU (SONY Music Special Productions, 1996). Produced by Walter Afanasieff and Michael Bolton.

Walter also plays keyboards, synthesizers, synth bass, drums, and percussion. Background vocals include Joe Turano. The video for this song appears on Michael's SOUL & PASSION and DECADE 1985-1995 videotapes.

Time, Love & Tenderness World Tour — This tour, kicked off in July, 1991, was the first tour that Michael headlined. He performed with his five piece band and three back-up singers at more than 150 shows in the United States, Canada, and Europe, entertaining over 1.5 million concert-goers. At every show, a local church choir joined Michael on stage to sing "Time, Love & Tenderness" with him.

TIMELESS—THE CLASSICS — Released in 1992 by Columbia Records, this album hit #1 on the Billboard Album chart and has sold over 8 million copies world-wide. The album dedication says, "I believe that a great song can live forever. This album is dedicated to the great writers and the great artists whose in-

spired performances have made these songs the 'classics' they deserve to be." — Michael Bolton

Timeless was produced by David Foster, Walter Afanasieff, and Michael Bolton and includes the songs:

1. *Since I Fell For You*
2. *Reach Out, I'll Be There*
   (The Four Tops sing back-up.)
3. *You Send Me*
4. *Bring It On Home To Me*
5. *Yesterday*
6. *Hold On, I'm Coming*
7. *Knock On Wood*
8. *Drift Away*
9. *To Love Somebody*
10. *Now That I Found You*
11. *White Christmas*

(See individual song listings for writer and producer information.)

Tiny Toons Adventure Spring Break Special — This animated cartoon featured a Michael Bolton look- and sound-alike character performing on stage.

T.J. Martell Foundation For Leukemia, Cancer, And Aids Research — This organization was founded in the mid-70s and is supported by people in the music and entertainment business. They fund research at the T.J. Martell Memorial Laboratory in Mount Sinai Medical Center in New York and at the Neil Bogart Laboratory in the U.S.C. Medical Center in Los Angeles. Michael's songs have appeared on two compilation albums to benefit this Foundation.

"To Love Somebody" — Written by Barry and Robin Gibb. Appears on TIMELESS: THE CLASSICS (Columbia, 1992)
>   Produced and arranged by David Foster and
>   Michael Bolton
>   The orchestra was arranged and conducted by
>   Jeremy Lubbock.

Toad's Place — Michael frequently played this New Haven club, located at 300 York Street, New Haven, in the late 70s. Its owner, Mike Spoerndle, was allegedly the inspiration for the song, "Hometown Hero," which appeared on the MICHAEL BOLTON album and a mention of "Mike Sprindel [sic] of Toad's" appears in the liner notes.

Toad's Place — 1989

The Today Show — This morning news program featured a segment wherein Michael was interviewed in his home studio by Jill Rapaport. At one point, she asks him about the effect he has on women and he gets a coy smile on his face while replying, "I don't know. What effect do I have on women?" When the attractive brunette expresses disbelief over his lack of awareness, he says, "I want to hear it from you."

Top of the Pops — Michael Bolton frequently appears on this popular London-based entertainment show when in England.

Tour Rehearsals — Michael says that although the band rehearses for four-six weeks before a concert tour (to get all the technical things down pat), he likes to take two weeks to ready himself with the band for his tours.

Troccoli, Kathy — This singer opened for Michael on his Time, Love & Tenderness tour.

The Trouble With Angels — This book, written by Debbie Macomber, makes reference to Michael Bolton's "low, sultry voice" on page 188.

Trumbull Shopping Mall, Connecticut — Michael has made personal appearances here, meeting and shaking hands with his fans to benefit the annual Toys For Tots campaign.

Trumbull Shopping Mall to benefit Toys For Tots

Turano, Joe — Joe was born in Milwaukee, Wisconsin and has worked with Rickie Lee Jones, Rod Stewart, and Joe Cocker, among others. He currently plays saxophone and keyboards in Michael's band and also sings backup for Michael. He was featured playing sax in the

61

"Love Is A Wonderful Thing" video. Joe, a self-professed crossword puzzle fanatic and jazz freak, is married to Jeannine, has a small home studio and enjoys the Los Angeles session scene when not touring with Michael. He has said, "Michael Bolton is a genuinely great person. He's made my life richer and I'd like to say thank you."

TV Guide Crossword Puzzle — Michael Bolton was one of the answers to crossword puzzle #231 in the July 3, 1993 issue.

Twain, Shania — Pictured to the right with Michael, country music star and wife of Michael's friend and producer, R.J. "Mutt" Lange, Shania was the beneficiary of some Michael Bolton softball expertise. Michael gave her batting advice at his home in Connecticut before she played in a celebrity softball game in Nashville. Apparently it helped, too. Michael said that after the lesson, "She started killing the ball, just driving it." Shania repaid her debt to Michael by appearing as a special guest performer at the Fourth Annual Michael Bolton Foundation Black Tie Gala.

University of Connecticut — Michael gave the commencement address to the graduating class on May 20, 1995. He also was presented with an honorary Doctorate Degree during the ceremony. In his address to the graduates, Michael quoted from such dignitaries as Thomas Jefferson, Booker T. Washington, Franklin D. Roosevelt, Walt Disney, and Rodney Dangerfield.

University Microfilms International — Copies of various magazine and newspaper articles may be available from this search service. Contact them for more information at: U.M.I. Info Store, 500 Sansome Street, San Francisco, California 94111. Their phone number is 1-800-248-0360, ext. 282 and their Internet address is orders@is1.infostore.com.

U.K. Promo Tour — During his 1992 world tour, Michael also made numerous promotional appearances on radio and television. In England, Michael appeared live on "The Terry Wogan Show."

USA Today — Michael's appearances on the pages of this daily national newspaper are too numerous to count. On June 17, 1993, Michael got the most votes in a "Star Gauging" Write-in Poll for being "the person fans want to read more about" and Michael's fan club, Gold Club, and *Bolton Behind The Scenes* magazine were featured in an article on September 28, 1993. He was the subject of one of their Weekend Magazine articles on February 3, 1996 and they did a short article on a handwriting analysis of his signature on Valentines Day, 1996. (See Scribbles listing for more information.)

US Magazine — Michael has made numerous appearances within the pages of this entertainment/celebrity magazine. In a November, 1994 issue, Michael was voted both Best Male Singer and Worst Male Singer by its readers. In the May, 1995 edition, Michael is prominently mentioned in a Jocasta & Pepper cartoon by Mimi Pond titled, "Who Would You Do?" In September, 1995, a letter written by John Sykes (President of VH1) appeared in the "Letters to the Editor" column saying that he was "surprised and unhappy" that Michael had appeared in the NOT side of their previously published "HOT/NOT" box. He reassured *Us* that Michael was, indeed, very hot on his new VH1 format.

Vanity — This one-time protégé of "the performer formerly known as Prince" had been romantically linked to Michael Bolton. However, 1995 saw Vanity meet and marry L.A. Raiders defensive end Anthony Smith.

Vegetarian — According to his mother, Michael became vegetarian at the age of twelve.

Vegetating — Michael says this is how he relaxes, in the middle of the lake, alone.

Vest — Michael can often be seen wearing one of these, frequently in his favorite color, blue.

Veteran's Memorial Coliseum — Located in New Haven, Connecticut, Michael's home town, this venue was the site of a December 19, 1991 Michael Bolton concert, playing to 10,000 eager fans. The December 20, 1991 edition of the New Haven Register said the show was a crowd pleaser, especially when Michael called out, "This is where I was born" to the crowd. It was also a charity event, with fans donating hundreds of toys to the annual Toys For Tots campaign.

VH1 — This cable station has been very supportive of Michael in the past. They named August 15, 1991, Michael Bolton & Kenny G. Day, showing videos and interview clips all day, they presented "A Conversation with Michael Bolton" as part of their VH One to One series, they showed segments of Michael at the VH1 Ski Weekend Benefit, and they awarded him one of their first VH1 Honors Awards in honor of his charity work.

VH1 Honors — The First Annual VH1 Honors award show was telecast live on June 26, 1994. The awards were a salute to musicians who do outstanding charity work and Michael was one of the first seven honorees. Awards were also presented to Stevie Wonder, Kenny G., Bonnie Raitt, Melissa Etheridge, Garth Brooks, and the artist formerly known as Prince. Film clips of each artist's charity works were shown, followed by a live performance by that artist and the award presentation. Michael's segment featured The Michael Bolton Foundation and he sang, "Said I Loved You...But I Lied" before Kathy Ireland presented him with his award. The show was hosted by Ellen DeGeneres and during breaks in the presentations, she did a couple of comical backstage shots where she "broke" the strings on Melissa Etheridge's guitar and blamed it on Michael. A portion of the shows proceeds were donated to The Michael Bolton Foundation.

VH1 Video For Your Ears — This promotional cassette is a collection of songs released by VH1 in 1992. Michael sang "Missing You Now" and other performers include Amy Grant, James Taylor, and Kenny Loggins.

Victoria's Secret — Their 1996 Holiday Gift Catalog offers the album SONGS OF LOVE. Michael Bolton is one of the featured singers on this collection of "your favorite romantic songs." Michael also attended the February, 1996 Victoria's Secret Valentine Fashion Show in New York City. See the *Entertainment Tonight* listing for more information.

Videosyncrasy — This hour-long special of music and interviews was taped in Canada and aired as "In Synch With Michael Bolton" on Halloween, 1991.

"The Voice" — Michael acquired this nickname because of his 4-octave range. Coincidentally, it is also the name of the movie that Michael will star in about an 18th century opera singer.

Voice Lessons — Michael says he took 4 or 5 lessons to increase his musical range and power and then practiced repeatedly on his own. He also supplemented his income in the '70s and ' 80s by giving lessons in New Haven, Connecticut.

"Voices That Care" — This song, written by David Foster, Peter Cetera, and Linda Thompson Jenner, was done to support American troops in the Middle East. The CD was released by Giant Records in 1991 and names Michael as one of the "Lead Voices" on the song. On January 28, 1991, Michael joined 100 other celebrities on a TV special to demonstrate his support. Included in the songs were "Messages of Care," spoken messages to the troops. Michael also took part in the "Messages" portion, saying "We care, we're expressing that to you, we're with you." The videotape, including documentary footage and the video for the song, was released by Warner Reprise in 1991.

Voting Campaign Posters — Michael donated his time and image to four campaign posters in 1988 attempting to get people to vote. They were:

1. *Decision '88 - Image US Reality*
2. *Connections - A Presidential Past*
3. *Connections - We Want You To Vote*
4. *Your Voice, Your Choice*

"Wait On Love" — Written by Michael Bolton and Jonathan Cain. Appeared on THE HUNGER (Columbia, 1987). Produced by Jonathan Cain for Cain Street Productions. James Ingram sang background vocals on this song and Jonathan Cain played keyboards. The video for this song appears on Michael's SOUL & PASSION videotape.

"Walk Away" — Written by Michael Bolton and Diane Warren.

> Appeared on THE HUNGER (Columbia, 1987).
> Produced by Susan Hamilton.
> The lyrics to this song do not appear on the CD song listings, although the rest of the songs from the album do.

Warner Brothers Publications — Copies of Michael's sheet music are available for purchase through this company. For information, call 1-800-638-0005.

Warner/Chappell Publishing — Michael has a co-publishing deal with them.

Warren, Diane — Diane frequently collaborates with Michael on his songs. Some examples of their writing are: "Walk Away," "How Can We Be Lovers," "It's Only My Heart," and "Missing You Now." Diane was solely responsible for writing Michael's hits "When I'm Back On My Feet Again," "Completely," and "Time, Love, & Tenderness."

Diane Warren has been referred to as Michael's "sister from the Planet Song" and pictures of Diane with Michael appear in his fan club publications quite frequently.

Weber, Ernst, Jr. — In the mid-70s, Ernst made concert posters for Michael's appearances and was responsible for photographing Michael's shows. He was also occasionally called upon to act as the designated auto mechanic, patching up the "broken-down relics" Michael drove.

His autographed copy of WORLDS APART is inscribed, "Ernst, Love and Happiness for you through the madness. Always, Michael."

Weil, Cynthia — This songwriter collaborated with Michael and Barry Mann on "Stand Up For Love."

"Welcome To The World" — Written by Michael Bolotin. Appeared on WORLDS APART (Polydor, 1980). Produced by Eddy Offord.

Wentworth, Alexandra — An actress who had regularly appeared on the Fox comedy show, "In Living Color," Alexandra was also a guest of Jay Leno's one of the nights that Michael made an appearance. Her supermodel impersonations greatly amused him and the camera caught his expressions several times.

"We're Not Making Love Anymore" — Written by Michael Bolton and Diane Warren.

> Appeared on TIME, LOVE & TENDERNESS (Columbia, 1991).
> Also appeared on Patti LaBelle's album, BURNIN'
> Produced by Walter Afanasieff and Michael Bolton

Although it was originally written as a duet, Barbra Streisand first recorded this song solo. Patti LaBelle sings it with Michael on his album and they once performed it live at the Annual All-Star Benefit Concert on behalf of L.A. County Department of Children's Services.

Westport, Connecticut — Michael lives in a spacious 5-bedroom home that he purchased in 1991. It is decorated in shades of cream, white, and fawn, and features a pool, tennis court and indoor gym. Michael also bought the house next door and turned it into his personal recording studio, Bolton Music.

Westville — Westville is the posh New Haven neighborhood where Michael, his wife, and multiple friends lived in a commune-like atmosphere in a colonial mansion during the 70s.

What's Goin' On—Motown's 30th Anniversary — Michael performed with Patti LaBelle on this TV special, aired March 25, 1990.

"When A Man Loves A Woman" — Written by C. Lewis and A. Wright.

> Appeared on TIME, LOVE & TENDERNESS (Columbia, 1991).
> Also appeared on GREATEST HITS 1985-1995 (Columbia, 1996).
> Produced by Walter Afanasieff and Michael Bolton.

This song hit #1 on Billboard's Hot Singles Chart on November 23, 1991. It received a 1992 Grammy nomination, Michael performed it on the Grammy telecast, and it won. Michael said it was his first "number one song with no video." (It seems he was touring Europe at the time and couldn't make a video.) According to Oprah Winfrey, this song is played by savvy advertising people in grocery stores between the hours of noon and 5 p.m. Apparently, hearing Michael's version of this song makes women think fondly of their "man" and they buy more groceries in response.

"When I'm Back On My Feet Again" — Written by Diane Warren. Appeared on SOUL PROVIDER (Columbia, 1989). Also appeared on GREATEST HITS 1985-1995 (Columbia, 1996).

Produced by Michael Bolton with additional production by Walter Afanasieff

This song, which was originally recorded as a demo for another singer, became a hit for Michael and an inspiration for fans around the world. It stayed at #1 on the Billboard Adult Contemporary charts for three weeks. "Walk Away" was the B side of the single. The video for this song appears on Michael's SOUL & PASSION videotape.

White, Timothy — This photographer for Columbia Records is responsible for the TIME, LOVE & TENDERNESS, THE ONE THING, MICHAEL BOLTON GREATEST HITS 1985-1995 and THIS IS THE TIME album cover photos. Apparently, Timothy is the one responsible for those infamous blue eyes. Timothy is also the photographer that took the beautiful photos of Michael at home that appeared in the December, 1996 issue of *In Style* magazine.

Michael Sings "White Christmas"
to some lucky fans, 1995

"White Christmas" — Written by Irving Berlin.
  Appeared on TIMELESS: THE CLASSICS (Columbia, 1992).
  Also appeared on THIS IS THE TIME (Columbia, 1996).
  Produced and arranged by David Foster and Michael Bolton.
  Orchestra arranged/conducted by Johnny Mandel.

White Roses — Michael's favorite flower.

WINDOWS OF MY SOUL — This album, by Michael's guitar player, Chris Camozzi, was released by Higher Octave Records in 1996. This solo album, Chris' first, was billed as "a captivating collection of guitar instrumentals."

Michael and Oprah Winfrey for
"Oprah: Behind the Scenes" 1992

Winfrey, Oprah — Oprah interviewed Michael in his recording studio for her first primetime special, "Oprah: Behind the Scenes" on May 19, 1992. Since then, Michael has appeared on her daytime talk show several times. On November 18, 1992, Michael appeared on a show about obsessive fans, singing several songs and totally overwhelming an unsuspecting fan. Later that year, on Christmas Eve, Michael was abetted by fellow guests Tony Bennett and Liza Minelli in suprising Oprah herself with a special secret appearance to sing "White Christmas" and hold mistletoe over her head.

On November 7, 1994, a backstage visit to Michael was featured as a segment on Oprah's "Dreams Really Do Come True" show. Oprah has become a self-confessed avid fan of Michael and his music, and in December of 1995, she fulfilled a fantasy of hers by singing back-up for Michael on "Can I Touch You...There?" on her show.

"Without Your Love" — Written by Michael Bolotin. Appeared on BLACKJACK (Polydor, 1979). Produced by Tom Dowd.

Women — Michael's all-time favorite animal.

Wonder, Stevie — Michael says he and Stevie have discussed writing songs together and that at one time, Stevie Wonder came into Michael's dressing room and spontaneously began singing, "How Am I Supposed To Live Without You." According to Michael, "I used to think if God chose a voice to represent him, Stevie Wonder would be the guy. I'd never heard range, emotion, and spirit [like that]. Singing along with [his records] made my voice more malleable." Michael has said that if he had to choose one record that most inspired him in his musical career, it would be Stevie's "Fingertips, Part 2."

Wong, Donna — Donna was a guest of Maria Shriver on Maria's "First Person" telecast in June of 1994. Interviewed at her home, a Bolton concert, and a Bombers' softball game, she expressed her feelings and ideas on what it's like to be a Michael Bolton fan. At the ballgame, she tried unsuccessfully to get Michael to autograph a softball for her, but he did sign one for her later.

Woolsey Hall — Located at Yale University, New Haven, Connecticut, this theater serves as the university's performance hall. On April 22, 1994, Michael gave a concert with Orchestra New England (ONE) to benefit The Michael Bolton Foundation and ONE. A post-concert reception was held at Berkeley College, Yale University, giving Michael the opportunity to meet and personally thank his fans for their contributions. (See The "Close Encounters" section of this book for more indepth information about this affair.)

World Series — Michael sang the National Anthem at the fourth game of the World Series on October 20, 1991 between the Oakland A's and the Cincinnati Reds, and at the second game of the World Series between the Toronto Blue Jays and the Philadelphia Phillies in Toronto, Canada, 1993.

World Trade Center — On February 7, 1997, Michael officially kicked off Grammy Month at the World Trade Center where NARIS was scheduled to present Mayor Guiliano with a check for $100,000. Michael performed two songs in the Wintergarden Room at the event.

Front Cover: Worlds Apart

WORLDS APART — This album, Blackjack's second, was released by Polygram in 1980. It was produced by Eddie Offord at a Woodstock, N.Y. studio and the songs included are:
1. *My World Is Empty Without You*
2. *Love Is Hard To Find*
3. *Stay*
4. *Airwaves*
5. *Maybe It's The Power Of Love*
6. *Welcome To The World*
7. *Breakaway*
8. *Really Wanna Know*
9. *Sooner or Later*
10. *She Wants You Back*

(See individual song listings for writer and producer information.)

Xylophone — It is a pretty safe bet that this was one of Michael's first musical instruments (and we are desperate for an "X" entry).

"Ya, ya, ya, ya, ya, ya, ya" — This is what Michael sings to warm-up his voice before concerts.

Yale Safe Space Benefit — On October 14, 1995, Yale was the site of a martial arts demo and competition co-sponsored by Paul Newman's Hole

In The Wall Gang and the Michael Bolton Foundation to benefit the Safe Space fund.

Yale University — Ivy League university which is located in Michael's hometown, New Haven. This was the site of the April 22, 1994 benefit concert by Michael Bolton and Orchestra New England. Almost 2,600 Bolton fans attended the concert.

"Yesterday" — Written by John Lennon and Paul McCartney.
> Appeared on TIMELESS: THE CLASSICS (Columbia, 1992).
> Produced and arranged by David Foster and Michael Bolton.
> Orchestra arranged/conducted by Johnny Mandel.

"You Don't Want Me Bad Enough" — Written by Michael Bolton.
> Appeared on EVERYBODY'S CRAZY (Columbia, 1985).
> Produced by Neil Kernon and Michael Bolton.

"You Make Me Feel Like Loving You" — Written by Michael Bolotin.
> Appeared on EVERY DAY OF MY LIFE (RCA, 1976).
> Produced by Jack Richardson.

"You Mean More To Me" — Written by Michael Bolotin.
> Appeared on EVERY DAY OF MY LIFE (RCA, 1976).
> Also appeared on MICHAEL BOLOTIN— THE EARLY YEARS (RCA, 1991).
> Produced by Jack Richardson.

"You Send Me" — Written by Sam Cooke.
> Appears on TIMELESS: THE CLASSICS (Columbia, 1992).
> Produced and arranged by David Foster and Michael Bolton.
> String arrangement by David Foster.

"You Wouldn't Know Love" — Written by Michael Bolton and Diane Warren.
> Appeared on SOUL PROVIDER (Columbia, 1989).
> Produced by Michael Bolton.

"You're All That I Need" — Written by Michael Bolton, Jonathan Cain, and Neal Schon.

Appears on THE HUNGER (Columbia, 1987).
> Produced by Jonathan Cain for Cain Street Productions.

Jonathan also plays keyboards on this track and his brother, Mugs Cain, took care of percussions and drum programming.

"You're No Better Than A Common Thief" — Written by House.
> Appeared on EVERYDAY OF MY LIFE (RCA, 1976). Produced by Jack Richardson

"You're No Good" — Written by C. Ballard, Jr.
> Appeared on MICHAEL BOLOTIN (RCA, 1975).
> Also appeared on THE ARTISTRY OF MICHAEL BOLOTIN (RCA, 1993).
> Produced by Joe Cy and Michael Bolotin.

"You've Got The Love I Need" — Written by Michael Bolotin.
> Appeared on EVERY DAY OF MY LIFE (RCA, 1976). Produced by Jack Richardson.

"You've Lost That Lovin' Feelin' " — Michael sang this duet with Barry Mann on the "Salute to the American Songwriter" shown on VH1 during December, 1988.

"Your Love" — Written by Michael Bolotin.
Appeared on MICHAEL BOLOTIN (RCA, 1975). Also appeared on MICHAEL BOLOTIN—THE EARLY YEARS (RCA, 1993) and on THE ARTISTRY OF MICHAEL BOLOTIN (RCA, 1993).
> Produced by Joe Cy and Michael Bolotin.

> Wayne Perkins played lead guitar and Dave Sanborn played soprano sax for this track. Background vocals were done by Mary McCreary, Marcy Levy, Lani Groves, and Barbara Massey.

Zealous — An adjective frequently used to describe Michael's fans.

Zero To Hero, From — On Friday, June 20, 1997, ABC broadcst this special featuring Matt Frewer, Bobcat Goldthwaite, Susan Egan and Michael Bolton. Showcasing the new Disney feature film, *Hercules*, this show was written by Michael E. Zack, edited by William Kerr, produced by Michael Meadows, and directed by John Pattyson. Michael Bolton appeared as the bartender, Mikos, in a greek taverna named "The Dig" and also performed "Go The Distance" as himself in the taverna.

Riki Lake and Michael Bolton

Phil Donahue and Michael Bolton

Close Encounters

After leaving that first Michael Bolton concert, the adrenaline flowing inside us could have moved buses. We expected that to happen, it was a normal concert reaction, especially when the concert was so emotionally satisfying. What we did not expect was maintaining that level of excitement for any significant amount of time.

Somehow, a week later, we found ourselves gathering to discuss our reactions. For the first time ever, we wanted to TELL an artist how much his performance had meant to us. After much discussion and many attempts at describing the experience adequately, we wound up sending Michael an almost blank sheet of paper. At the bottom, before signing our names, we wrote simply, "One week later, and we still have no words to tell you what your concert meant to us."

Suddenly, it seemed that Michael was everywhere. VCRs were pre-set to tape his appearances on talk shows and news programs. Videotapes and CDs were purchased, and we gathered as a group for each first viewing/listening experience. "This Is Michael Bolton" was telecast that fall and we avidly watched it together. In fact, it became a weekly "Ladies Night Out" to get to-gether, watch videos, dance and sing with Mr. Bolton, and talk, talk, talk. Obsession came easily and you would have thought we were sixteen again when we were together, much to the chagrin of our families and significant others, who repeatedly said we "should act (our) age."

The following summer, Michael was on tour again and we packed supplies and lawn chairs and drove to our local video store/ticket office, camping out all night for concert tickets. We had chosen our ticket office carefully, making sure there were all-night restrooms nearby, but we couldn't do anything about the insect hordes or the surprise thunderstorm. (We have since discovered that there are ALWAYS unexpected difficulties associated with our Michael Bolton events. It seems that some higher power is saying, "How badly do you want this?" But we generally find that the higher the price we pay in inconvenience, the greater the rewards.) Eleven hours later, we were the proud (if bedraggled) possessors of front row seats to a concert only 3 1/2 hours from our homes.

Weeks later, purely by chance, we discovered that Michael would be playing a ball game the night before our concert. A short scramble ensued for tickets and hotel reservations and our mini-vacation was set. We had faxed an urgent request to the fan club (by now we were, of course, members) for special handling of our Bolton Bombers baseball jerseys and caps so we would have them in time for our first Bombers event. (Normal delivery would have gotten them to us 4 weeks too late. As it turned out, we were the only fans to be wearing official apparel at the game.) They have our undying gratitude for answering our plea with two days to spare.

When the day of the baseball game finally came around, we left work early, loaded up our rented van, and took off in a state of high expectation. Arriving in Syracuse, we drove directly to the stadium, not bothering to stop at our hotel, changing our clothes in the back of the rental without even a hesitation. The weather was beautiful, the stadium accommodating, and then, there was Michael and his team, smiling, waving, and joking with the crowd right there in front of us. Our seats were next to third base (Michael's position), but towards the end of the game we moved over to the first base side and edged down towards the fence, hoping for autographs when Michael left the field. Suddenly the game was over and Michael and his entourage were making their way across the field towards us.

Leaning against the waist-high fencing, we held out sheet music and pictures that we hoped to get signed, and one of our bravest called out, "Michael." He looked up at us, saw our out-stretched pens and said, "I can't, they'll mob me."

Then he noticed our jerseys and paused, a big grin on his face. Grabbing the front of his own shirt, he pointed and gave us the thumbs up. Then he was gone, into the limo, and off the field. We were so thrilled that most of the people had left the stadium by the time we made our way out front. Imagine our excitement when we found the tour bus parked just outside the front doors, waiting for the rest of the Bombers. Unfortunately, several fanatical groupies were waiting, as well, and we hesitated, extremely reluctant to be included in their group. Before we could give in to our reservations, like a gift from heaven, the guys came out. They were very friendly, stopping to talk and sign autographs. Finally, the bus was gone and we made our way to the parking lot to leave. The camaraderie between fans was some-

thing we had never experienced until we were stopped by several people wanting to know where we got our shirts and caps. We gave them the address of the fan club and chatted for a while, then decided we were starving and that perhaps we should check in to our hotel. After a very late dinner, we retired to our rooms to rehash the whole affair until the wee hours of the morning.

Rising late the next day, we opted for brunch and made our way to the hotel restaurant. We had nothing to do until show time later that evening, so we enjoyed a slow, leisurely meal. Our waitress was very friendly and when she brought our check, she asked us if we were going to the State Fair. We told her we were only there for the Michael Bolton concert that night and she off-handedly replied, "Michael Bolton? Oh, that's right. He stayed here last night." We said, "You've got to be kidding!"

"No, really. All the performers stay here when they play the fair. Last year Reba McIntyre and Garth Brooks were here..." but we didn't wait to hear anymore. As one, we bolted for the door to the courtyard to the accompaniment of squeals and "Oh, my God!"'s. Scenes of Beatlemania ensued, with hotel floor plans being studied and analyzed like someone trying to bypass CIA security at the White House. We didn't find anything except numerous large body-guard-looking gentlemen in the hallways and in retrospect, it's all just as well. We would have died from humiliation if anyone (Michael!) had seen us lurking in the hallways, and we certainly would not have had the nerve to approach him, let alone speak. But it was an interesting diversion until it was time to get dressed for the concert.

We did have a few bad moments when the weather turned threatening and tornados were predicted, but at the last minute, the radio announcement came across that the show would be going on anyway and we breathed much easier.

The concert was everything we remembered, but better, seeing it as we were from the very front. Michael played the crowd, and us, extremely well, and we all left absolutely sure that he had made eye-contact with each one of us. (Is there a class performers take so that we can fall into a trance?) Although we scanned the parking lot of the hotel closely for clues to his continued presence, there was no sign of anything odd, and we decided he had left town right after the show. Sleep was difficult, as was the return to reality the next day.

We did have many pictures and memories to see us through, though, and in January of the following year, Michael gave a concert in a city neighboring our hometown. Again, we experienced minor difficulties attending, (14 inches of snow postponed the concert one day) but the show was a bright spot in the bleakness of winter.

In early March, we opened our mailboxes to find engraved invitations from The Michael Bolton Foundation and Orchestra New England to an "Intimate Evening of Music" at Yale University, which alone would have warranted a trip to Connecticut. Our initial interest gave way to unbridled excitement when the invitation also afforded us the opportunity to attend a private, post-concert reception to "meet and greet" Michael Bolton. Our reservations were faxed immediately and we were left with one whole month of uncertainty, guessing and waiting.

Thrilled with the thought that we would soon be attending a social function with Michael Bolton, we suffered long and hard over the possible guest list, meeting scenarios, conversations (Please don't let me sound like a geek!), attire, how to stand out from the crowd without being an obvious outsider, wondering if there would be a receiving line, worrying if Michael would approach us or would we have to approach him, and if so, which one of us got that job? Normally, we are quite adept at social situations, however, this was THE MAN and we had stress with a capital S.

Finally, ready or not, it was "Michael, here we come."

Each of us having home obligations the day before the show, we elected to drive all night, leaving at midnight the day of the concert. Checking into our rooms at 11:00 a.m., we tried to get some sleep, hoping to be fresh and bright-eyed at our meeting, but it was just impossible. Our excitement was too high.

Again, we encountered a small difficulty prior to the show. Against our better judgment, we wound up taking the hotel courtesy van to the concert, and rode the entire way praying to make a hurried and unobtrusive exit from the van outside the hall. Much to our chagrin (and un-

dying embarrassment) the van driver noted that traffic was much too congested to pull over, so he threw the van into park in the middle of the street, got out and came around to help us down, all the while holding up traffic in both directions. Unobtrusive we were not.

The concert was wonderful. The buildings at Yale University (where the concert and reception were held) are breathtaking— ornate wooden molding and heavy stone archways—and the tingles started just as we walked through the doors and only increased when we found ourselves seated five rows from the stage. Directly in front of us was a suspiciously familiar, long-haired blonde, and after staring for a short while in silence, we begin mouthing the word "Brother!" to each other and nodding in his direction. His profile, mannerisms and movements made us believe we were, in essence, sitting with Orrin Bolton. The orchestra was skilled and impressively played several Bolton tunes, the music filling the hall.

And then there was Michael, dressed in a tailored suit, shining and smiling, visibly relaxed and happy to be home. His family was seated in the front rows and he spoke to them several times during the show, which is when we saw the REAL Orrin Bolton. (The man in front of us did have all the lyrics and movements down pat, as well he should. He turned out to be a professional Michael Bolton impersonator.) Michael sang much longer than we expected and when the show was over, we still had our meeting to look forward to.

We walked the block to the reception with many other concert-goers and although the April night was chilly, we couldn't feel the cold. Once inside the heavy doors, we passed through a series of small outer rooms and halls before entering a large, two-room reception area. (The building resembled a castle in many ways.) We joined a diverse crowd of people: record company executives, radio personalities, photographers, members of Michael's family and band, the socially elite, and the common folk, all waiting for Michael's arrival. Uniformed waiters offered large trays of hors d'oevres (crab, shrimp, and vegetable puff pastries) and drinks were made at several bars situated throughout the two rooms. A huge display of fruit and cheese surrounding an ice sculpture dominated one long table in the entry hall. After a short exploration of the two rooms, we posted ourselves near the entry, sipping our drinks and making socially correct small talk with whomever came near.

The wait for Michael's appearance seemed interminable. During a conversation with a Sony executive, we were informed that Michael had retired to private offices to dine before greeting the horde. Finally, a flurry of activity from the photographers towards the main salon gave us our first clue that Michael may have snuck in the back.

Joining the flow of people into the front room, we saw a concentrated group in one corner. Patiently waiting our turn to speak with the man, we listened while the people around us (including our Michael Bolton impersonator) exchanged stories of their previous meetings with Michael. At last, there he was, directly ahead.

He had several people gathered behind him and two very large bodyguards stationed several feet in front of him, leaving space between them for exactly one person to pass through at a time. As each member of our group entered the small enclosure, Michael took them by the hand, smiling, speaking, and giving them the gift of his undivided attention. Each one came away with a special memory to cherish forever. Each one, that is, until our last group member.

As she waited her turn between the bodyguards, Michael was shaking hands and speaking to the woman ahead of her. It was very warm in that corner and Michael looked tired, but he wasn't hurrying any of the conversations, graciously making time for everyone. When at last the way was clear, she stepped through and Michael held his hand out to her. "Hi, I'm Michael," he said.

She took his hand and introduced herself, thinking how very soft his hand was. Someone behind him tapped him on the shoulder and Michael turned his head for a moment to speak to him. She must have been experiencing sensory overload or something, or maybe it was

just that she had met and touched Michael and was totally satisfied, because she let go of his hand and moved on to leave the room. Suddenly, a hand reached out of the crowd next to her and knocked her up against the wall. A voice hissed, "Michael's talking to you!" and she became aware of Michael's voice saying "Hel-looo" behind her. Caught, she looked over her shoulder quickly to see Michael grinning and waving at her.

With an embarrassed smile, she waved a small, nerdy wave and faintly said, "Hi."

"Thank you so much for coming," he said.

"Oh, sure," she wittily replied, and her first meeting with Michael was over. She practically ran out the door to catch her breath and regroup after her experience.

She was joined by the rest of our group, similarly awed, and to this day we're not sure why we left the reception then. It wasn't a conscious thought, just sort of a mutual agreement that we had accomplished our purpose and so we left. Only much later, to our chagrin, did we realize that we have no idea how long Michael stayed or if he actually mingled with the crowd later.

The next morning we explored Michael's hometown of New Haven but those stories would be a book by themselves. Suffice it to say that like "Hotel California," you can go there "anytime you like, but you can never leave." It was only with extreme luck and strange circumstance, that we were finally, with relief and reluctance, able to set out for home. We all eagerly looked forward to summer and a new tour.

Mugs Feels "The Hunger"

Michael Bolton's "Heavy Metal Days"

Michael Bolton Discography

The following is a list of the recordings by Michael Bolton throughout his career.

1968 - "Bah, Bah, Bah" single by Joy (Epic Records)

1975 - MICHAEL BOLOTIN (RCA)

1976 - EVERY DAY OF MY LIFE by Michael Bolotin (RCA)

1979 - BLACKJACK (Polydor)

1980 - WORLDS APART by Blackjack (Polydor)

1983 - MICHAEL BOLTON (Columbia)

1985 - EVERYBODY'S CRAZY by Michael Bolton (Columbia)

1987 - THE HUNGER by Michael Bolton (Columbia)

1989 - SOUL PROVIDER by Michael Bolton (Columbia)

1991 - TIME, LOVE & TENDERNESS by Michael Bolton (Columbia)

1991 - MICHAEL BOLOTIN-THE EARLY YEARS (RCA reissue)

1992 - TIMELESS:THE CLASSICS by Michael Bolton (Columbia)

1992 - BLACKJACK 2-CD re-release (Polydor)

1993 - THE ARTISTRY OF MICHAEL BOLOTIN (RCA reissue)

1993 - THE ONE THING by Michael Bolton (Columbia)

1995 - GREATEST HITS 1985-1995 (Columbia)

1996 - THINKING OF YOU (Sony Music Special Productions)

1996 - THIS IS THE TIME (Columbia)

1997 - HERCULES SOUNDTRACK (Disney)

Michael has also made many guest appearances on other albums, from movie soundtracks to charity benefit recordings to duets and background vocals for other singers. See alphabetical listings and Covering Michael Bolton sections of this book for more information.

Michael Bolton Videography

Michael has also released and/or appeared in the following videos:

1973 - Blume In Love

1983 - Fool's Game

1985 - Everybody's Crazy

1989 - Kenny G. Live

1990 - Soul Provider - The Videos

1990 - How To Get A Record Deal

1991 - Simply Mad About The Mouse

1991 - Voices That Care

1992 - Soul & Passion

1992 - This Is Michael Bolton

1993- Michael Bolton's Winning Softball: Hit Harder, Play Smarter

1993 - For Our Children - The Concert

1993 - VH1 Center Stage Sampler

1994 - Grammy's Greatest Moments

1994 - It's Now Or Never - A Tribute To Elvis

1995 - Decade 1985-1995

1995 - The History of Rock 'n' Roll - The Sounds of Soul

1996 - Luciano Pavarotti & Friends Together for the Children of Bosnia

1996 - The Garth Brooks Video Collection

Michael also appeared on one of the three "Showtime At The Apollo" videos. Check your local video store for ordering information on these videotapes.

Michael's Honors &
Awards

Michael as Humanitarian:

C.O.R.E. Award	1996
Special Service Award, NY Benevolence Council	1995
Gold Plate Award, American Academy of Achievement	1995
ITT Humanitarian Award	1995
Lewis Hine Award-National Child Labor Committee	1994
Hendon Fellow, Berkeley College — Yale University	1994
VH-1 Honors Award	1994

Michael in the Industry:

Hitmaker's Award, Songwriter's Hall of Fame	1995
Academy of Popular Music	1995
American Music Award-Favorite Male Artist:Pop/Rock	1995
American Music Award-Favorite Male Artist:Adult Cont.	1995
American Music Award-Favorite Male Artist:Pop/Rock	1993
American Music Award-Favorite Male Artist:Adult Cont.	1993
American Music Award-Favorite Male Artist:Pop/Rock	1992
American Music Award-Favorite Pop/Rock Album — *Time, Love and Tenderness*	1992
NY Music Award — Best Male Pop Vocalist	1991
Grammy — Best Pop Male Vocalist — *When A Man Loves A Woman*	1991
ASCAP Writer/Producer Award — *How Am I Supposed To Live Without You*	1991
Grammy — Best Pop Male Vocalist — *How Am I Supposed To Live Without You*	1990
NY Music Award — Artist of the Year, Best Male Pop Vocalist, Best Male R&B Vocalist, and Best Pop Album for *Soul Provider*	1990
ASCAP Writer/Producer Award — *That's What Love Is All About* and *I Found Someone*	1989
NY Music Award — Best R&B Vocalist	1989

Michael's BMI Awards:

Million Performance Award — Soul Provider	1989
Pop Award — Soul Provider	1989
3 Million Performance Award — How Am I Supposed to Live Withour You	1990
Pop Award — How Am I Supposed to Live Without You	1983
Pop Award — How Am I Supposed to Live Without You	1990
Writer/Publisher Award — How Am I Supposed to Live Without You	1990
Million Performance Award — How Can We Be Lovers	1991
Pop Award — How Can We Be Lovers	1990
Writer/Publisher Award — How Can We Be Lovers	1991
Million Performance Award — Steel Bars	1992
Pop Award — Steel Bars	1992
Million Performance Award — Love is a Wonderful Thing	1992
Pop Award — Love is a Wonderful Thing	1992
Million Performance Award — Missing You Now	1992
Pop Award — Missing You Now	1992
Million Performance Award — By the Time This Night is Over	1993
Pop Award — By the Time This Night is Over	1993
Million Performance Award — Said I Loved You...But I Lied	1994
Pop Award — Said I Loved You...But I Lied	1994
Pop Award — Ain't Got Nothing if You Ain't Got Love	1995
Pop Award — Once In A Lifetime	1995
Pop Award — Can I Touch You...There?	1996

Michael's Other Distinctions:

Board of Directors, Joe DiMaggio's Childrens Hospital	1995-98
Board of Directors, One to One	1995-Present
Board of Directors, CityKids	1995
Martin Luther King Center for Non-Violence	1995
Honorary Doctor of Fine Arts Degree - University of Connecticut	1995
Connecticut Artist Distinguished Achievement Award	1995
Honorary Chairperson of the National Committee to Prevent Child Abuse	1993
National Chairperson of This Close For Cancer Research	1992

Michael Bolton Shows a Little Attitude!

Covering Michael Bolton

The following songs were written or co-written by Michael Bolton. Many people have done covers of Michael's songs as you can see by the list. The song title is followed by the name of the artist(s) who recorded it and the record company that released it.

Song	Artist
Am I Wrong	Witness (Fiesta)
At Last You're Mine	Cheryl Lynn (CBS Records)
By The Time This Night Is Over	Kenny G/Peabo Bryson (Arista)
Call My Name	Jennifer Rush (CBS/Epic)
	Night Ranger (MCA Records)
Can't Fight The Feeling	(CBS Discos)
Can't Hold On, Can't Let Go	Eric Martin (Capitol Records)
Conspiracy	Paris Black (SBA)
Deeper Than I Wanted To Go	Billy Newton Davis
Desperate Heart	Starship (RCA)
Don't Wanna Let Go	Irene Cara (Electra)
Emergency	Shy (MCA)
Emotional Fire	Cher (Geffen)
Fallin'	Glenn Medeiros (MCA)
Forever	KISS (Polygram)
From Now On	Lee Greenwood (Capitol)
Give Me Love	Irene Cara (Electra)
	Sheryl Lee Ralph (NY Music)
Givin' It All	Thelma Houston (MCA)
Heartbeat	Pointer Sisters (Planet)
Here She Comes Again	Night Ranger (MCA)
How Am I Supposed To Live Without You	Laura Branigan (Atlantic)
You	Shannon Gramma (Hal Leonard)
	Tony Rivera (Sony Discos)
I Almost Believed You	Bill Medley (RCA)
	Millie Jackson (Jive)
I Can't Keep Runnin"	Gregg Allman (Epic)
I Found Someone	Cher (Geffen)
I Need You In My Life	Bill Medley (RCA)
I Think About You	New Frontier (Mika/Polydor)
It's Been Hard Enough Getting Over You	Cher (Geffen)
	Laura Branigan (Atlantic)

Song	**Artist**
Just The Thought Of Losing You	Kenny Rogers (RCA)
	Conway Twitty (MCA)
Living Without Your Love	Joe Cocker (Capital)
	Eric Carmen (Geffen)
	Jocelyn Brown (Warner)
Lock Me Up	Irene Cara (Electra)
	Weather Girls (Columbia)
Love Get Ready	Jennifer Rush (CBS)
No Doubt About It	Six Was Nine (Virgin)
Now That It's Over	Irene Cara (Electra)
	Jennifer Rush (CBS)
Please Come Home	Bill Medley (RCA)
Same Heart (Duet w/Michael)	Jennifer Rush (CBS)
So Lost Without Your Love	Nicole (ONA)
Soul Provider	Peabo Bryson (Columbia)
Starting Over	Cher (Geffen)
Still In Love With You	Cher (Geffen)
Still Thinking Of You	Larry Graham (Warner Bros)
	Rachel Sweet (Rhino Records)
	Carl Anderson (CBS)
	Rex Smith (CBS)
	Bob Gulley (Rogue)
Take Another Look At Your Heart	Bonnie Tyler (CBS)
Talkin' 'Bout My Baby	Patti Austin (Warner)
There's Always Love	Patti LaBelle (Epic)
Till Somebody Loves You	Henry Lee Summer (Epic)
Tonight Is The Night	Various Artists (T.K. Records)
Try Gettin' Over You	Gary Morris (Warner Bros.)
	Seiko (CBS)
Walk Away	"Little" Louie Vega w/Marc Anthony (Atlantic)
	Lacy J. Dalton (MCA)
We're Not Making Love Anymore	Barbra Streisand (Columbia)
	Patti LaBelle (MCA)
Whenever You Close Your Eyes	Tommy Page (Sire/Warner)
Where Can You Run	Barbara Weathers (Reprise/Warner Bros.)
Where You Are	Donna Washington (Capitol)
Working Girl	Cher (Geffen)
You Wouldn't Know Love	Cher (Geffen)

Michael in Print

Below is a partial listing of articles, magazines, and reference listings that have featured Michael Bolton. There are many more but these are a few of our favorites. For a more complete listing, see THE MICHAEL BOLTON COLLECTOR'S JOURNAL put out by Fan Emporium, Inc. (The address can be found in the listing at the back of this book).

Magazine Articles

The following is an alphabetical listing of some of the most notable, most interesting, or most trivial magazine appearances that Michael has made to date.

AQUARIAN - "Michael Bolton: He's young, He's hot, He's talented, and He's Gonna Be Big" by Charlie Frick (Article and photo, August, 1975).

BILLBOARD - To date, Michael has appeared on their pages more than 25 times (20 photos).

CASHBOX - A full page ad for the BLACKJACK album appeared on July 7, 1979.

CIRCUS - "Michael Bolton: Everybody's Crazy." This article included a very brief biography and a photo on June 30, 1979.

COSMOPOLITAN - "Michael Bolton Tuned In To OUR Emotions" This was a paragraph and a photo in the June, 1993 issue.

ENTERTAINMENT WEEKLY - This magazine likes to illustrate their newsbits on Michael with caricatures.

FAMILY CIRCLE - Michael was mentioned in the article, "Circle This - Singing For Their Supper" on September 1, 1993. A photo was also included.

FIRST FOR WOMEN - Michael has appeared on these pages a total of three times, two of them with his mom, Helen Bolotin.

IT'S HIP! - "The Write Stuff! Michael Bolton" This article and photo appeared in the August, 1989 issue.

MCCALL'S - "Michael Bolton-Why He's So Hungry For Love" This was a fairly in-depth article and includes two photos. It appeared in the August, 1993 issue.

MONITOR MAGAZINE - This was Michael's first cover story.

NEWSWEEK - Michael had appeared in *Newsweek* four times as of the Winter/Spring '93 Commemorative Issue.

PERFORMANCE MAGAZINE - They gave their 1990 Tour Package of the Year award to the Kenny G./Michael Bolton tour.

PEOPLE - By October 23, 1995 Michael had appeared in this magazine 15 times; they had run 14 photos. The December 7, 1992 issue included Michael on the cover and a complete article inside.

PLAYBOY - In the April, 1992 issue, a photo and mention of Michael was made in the article, "Top Performers - 1992 *Playboy* Music Poll Winners."

PLAYGIRL - In September, 1990, *Playgirl* printed what we already knew. Michael Bolton was named one of "The 10 SEXIEST Men of 1990." The layout included a paragraph and photo. Note: Sorry, ladies, back issues are NOT available.

SEVENTEEN - Although Michael is a bit more mature than the heart throbs you might expect to find in this magazine, he had made four appearances here by June, 1994.

SINGLES MAGAZINE - Michael appeared on the cover of this magazine in October, 1994. The article, "Michael Bolton - Performer, Athlete, Philanthropist" detailed a concert and softball game and included a short interview.

TIME - Michael had appeared on the pages of this news magazine three times as of May 3, 1993.

US - Michael graced the cover of this entertainment magazine in February, 1993 and the accompanying article, "Michael Bolton," written by Laura Morice, included several photos.

WOMAN'S OWN - Alan Jackson's article on Michael was called, "I'll Never Cut My Lucky Hair" and appeared on May 17, 1993.

YM - Michael was named the Best Male Recording Artist in the *YM* Reader Entertainment Poll printed in the November, 1991 issue.

Foreign Magazines

As you can imagine, Michael has also been featured in many different publications worldwide. Here is a listing of just a few (with the countries in which they appear).

AFTENPOSTEN - Norway
ALLAS VECKOTIDNING - Sweden
ASAHI SHIMBUN - Japan
AUF EINEN BLICK - Germany
BONGGA DYARYO - Philippines

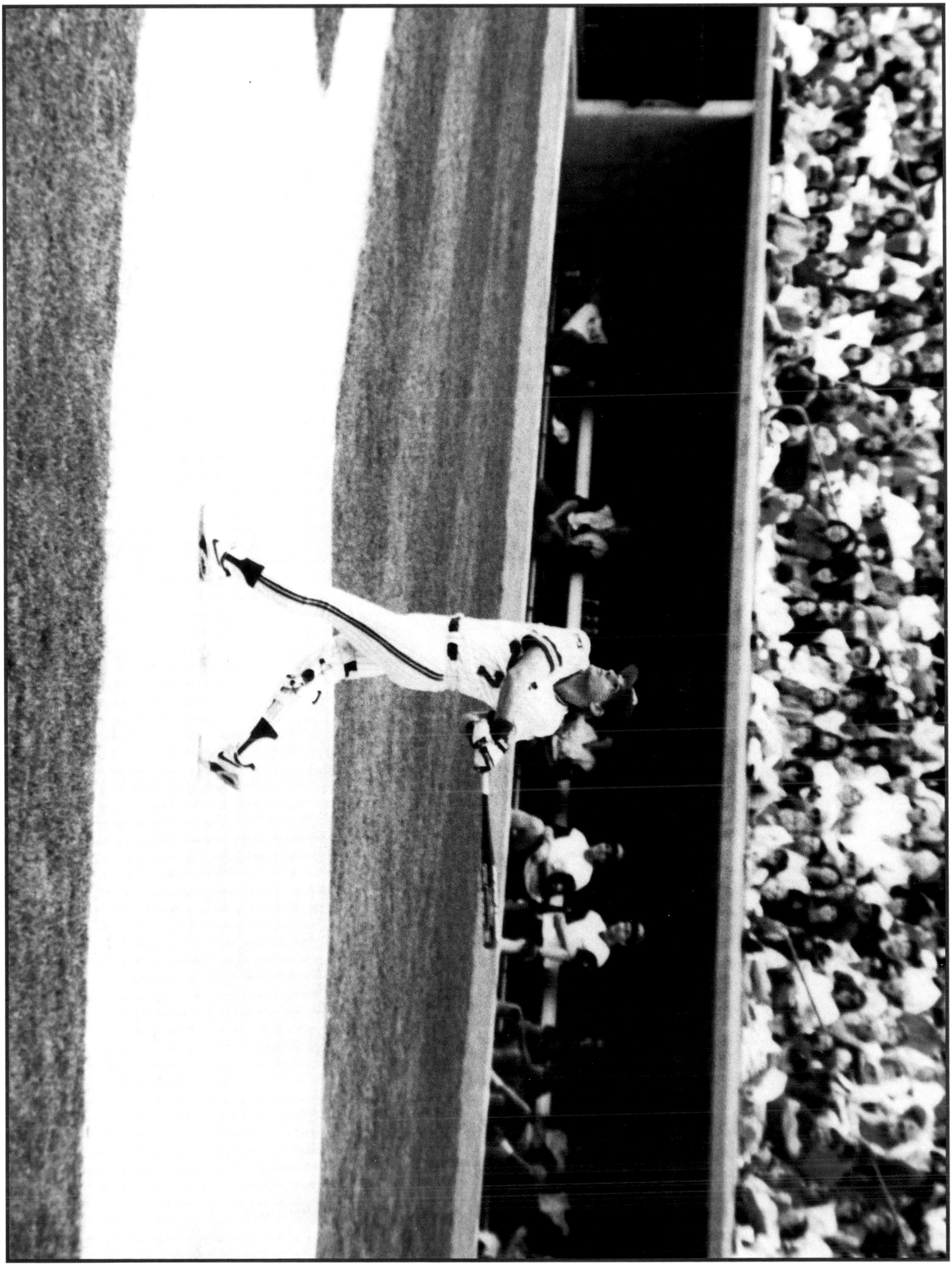

Photo Credit: Layne Seeloff

Serious About The Game!

Serious About The Game!

Having Fun At The Game

Having Fun At The Game

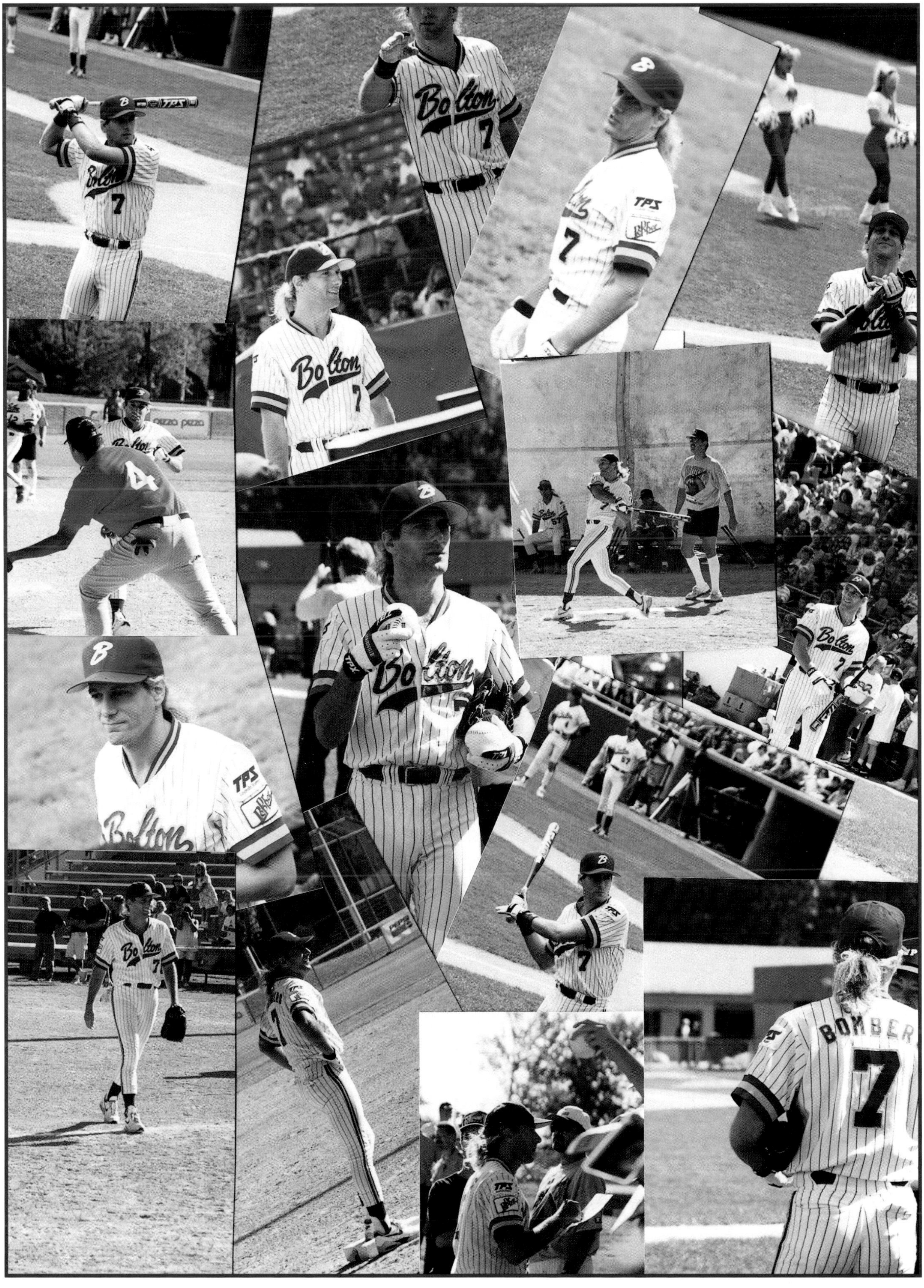

Photo Credit: Margaret Eaton

Clete Boyle, Pat Kelly, George Foster and Michael

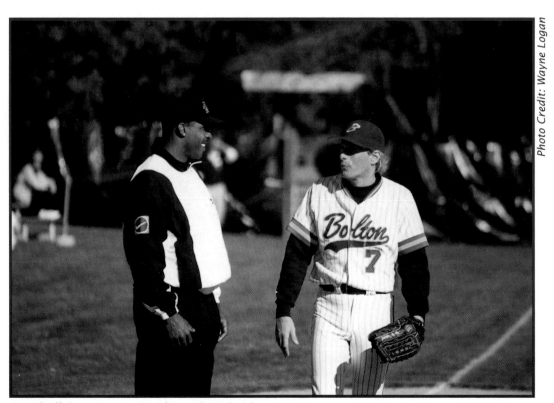

Baseball Star Barry Bonds and Michael

*Michael Enjoys Some Time On The Tennis Court and
with Andre Agassi*

Michael and Agassi Meet The Masses

Michael and Vitas Gerulaitis

Michael Shares A Humorous Moment With Ray Charles

Michael, Demi Moore and Bruce Willis at City Kids, 1995

A Solitary Moment

Chris Camozzi and Michael Bolton on the 1996
European Tour

Michael and Diana Ross

Al Jarreau and Michael Bolton

Safe Space Press Conference

Michael, Chuck Norris and Victoria Jackson

BRISBANE TV WEEK - Australia
CLASS - Jamaica
DAILY EXPRESS - England
DIE WOCHE - Austria
GOOD NEWS - Switzerland
M3 (MOVIE MUSIC MONTHLY) - Singapore
MALAY MAIL - Malaysia
POPCORN - Spain
ROTTERDAMS NIEUWSBLAD - Netherlands
RTE - Ireland
SOUNDS - UK

Reference Materials

Michael has been included in many music reference books. The following is a partial listing, so next time you're in the library, look him up.

ROLLING STONE ENCYCLOPEDIA OF ROCK
ROCK ON- ILLUSTRATED ENCYCLOPEDIA OF ROCK N ROLL VOL. 3
INTERNATIONAL ENCYCLOPEDIA OF HARD ROCK & HEAVY METAL 1983
CONTEMPORARY MUSICIANS VOL. 4
SINGER-SONGWRITERS 1994
ULTIMATE ENCYCLOPEDIA OF ROCK 1993
ROCK MOVERS & SHAKERS: TURNING POINTS - PIVOTAL MOMENTS IN THE LIVES
BILLBOARD BOOK OF NUMBER ONE HITS - 3RD EDITION
CURRENT BIOGRAPHY YEARBOOK 1993
HARMONY ILLUSTRATED ENCYCLOPEDIA OF ROCK 7TH EDITION
FABER COMPANION TO 20TH CENTURY POPULAR MUSIC 1995

Shopping for Michael Bolton

Nancy Finlan with some of her Michael Bolton Collection.

The following companies have offered Michael Bolton photos and, in some cases, memorabilia for fans.

Fan Emporium-P.O. Box 679, Branford CT 06405.

Photoworld-Order Department, P.O. Box 20747, Houston, TX 77225. They have a fairly large selection of Michael Bolton photos.

Shooting Stars Celebrity Photo Agency-P.O. Box 1597, Lucerne Valley, CA 92356-1597. Shooting Stars offers hundreds of color photos and will supply the date and event of the photos if requested.

Sound City 2000 Inc.-P.O. Box 22149, Portland, OR 97269-2149. Sound City has Michael Bolton import CD's available.

American Hits-P.O. Box 365, Bellmawr, NJ 08099. They have Michael Bolton singles on vinyl, cassette and CD. They also offer some videos.

Warner Brothers Publications-265 Secaucus, NJ 07096-2037. You can get sheet music from them.

Hal Leonard/Music Dispatch-P.O. Box 13819, Milwaukee, WI 53213. Sheet music is available here.

Replay Records-Saw Mill Plaza, West Haven, CT 06516. They offer albums, cassettes and CDs.

Addresses & Fan Club Info

Fan Emporium, Inc.

<u>Home Office</u>
P.O. Box 679
Branford, CT 06405
Phone — 1-800-810-9004
Fax — 1-203-483-2845

<u>Atlanta, Georgia Office</u>
P.O. Box 43231
Atlanta, GA 30336
Phone — (770)969-6453
Fax — (770)306-2096

<u>London, England Office</u>
37 Store Street
London, England WC1 E7BS

<u>Tokyo, Japan Office</u>
P.O. Box 5445
2-3-3 Otemachi
Chiyoda-ku, Tokyo
T 100-31, Japan
Phone — 011-81-488614480
Fax — 011-81-488614610

The Michael Bolton Foundation
P.O. Box 936
Branford, CT 06405

This Close For Cancer Research
Research Square
P.O. Box 3725
New Haven CT 06525

The Board of Directors of Fan Emporium, Inc.

National Committee For Prevention of Child Abuse
32 South Michigan Avenue
Suite 1600
Chicago, IL 60604

Michael Bolton Fan Club
Michael Bolton Gold Club
P.O. Box 679
Branford, CT 06450

Artist Relations Office
P.O. Box 247
Pinellas Park, FL 34664-0247

Bolton Photos

P.O. Box 746
Mechanicsville, VA 23111-0746
(Send photocopies — your pictures can't be returned. Include written permission for photos to be printed in fan club materials.)

Bolton Collector's Journal

P.O. Box 746
Mechanicsville, VA 23111-0746
(Send copies of articles and original publication with the name, date and page number the article appeared on.)

Michael Bolton PenPal Exchange

P.O. Box 6849
Warwick, RI 02886

Bolton Behind The Scenes

P.O. Box 679
Branford, CT 06450
(For *Letters to the Editor* and *Mailbag*, address that way to this address.)

International Creative Management, Inc.

40 West 57th Street
New York, NY 10019

BOLTON ABROAD

This newsletter is produced by Fan Emporium's Judine McGinley and Anna Mason. A useful tool for those who require the simplest and easiest way to keep in touch with what Michael Bolton is doing, this was originally designed for foreign fans as a way to keep them in the "information loop." *Bolton Abroad* provides items of interest directly from those who work for and with Michael. Issues can be ordered directly from the Artist Relations Office. (See listing, previous page.)

PHONE NUMBERS

Gold Club: 1-800-879-8244
Bolton Behind The Scenes: 1-800-879-8244
Bolton Hot Line: 1-900-407-BOLTON
 ($1.99 per minute)
To call in Canada: 1-900-451-4343 ($2.95 per minute)
To call in the U.K.: 0891-299-770 ($0.39 per minute—cheap rate and $0.49 per minute other times)
To call in Italy: 001-300-525-1004 (Rate information not available)
To call in Germany: 456-624-1004 (Rate information not available)
Other Countries: 001-150-525-1004 (International rates apply)

E-MAIL ADDRESSES

Fan Emporium (via America OnLine)—
FNEMPORIUM

Via Internet —FNEMPORIUM@AOL.COM
(The fan club has instituted a NewsFlash Mailing List at the above addresses. If you would like to be added to the list, send your e-mail address to them. Be sure to include your name and a list of all the clubs to which you belong. They would also like to know if you subscribe to *Bolton Behind the Scenes*.)

For Newsletter items only —
FENEWSLTR@AOL.COM

Sony Music Online —
HTTP://WWW.SONY.COM

For Music Screeners —
HTTP://WWW.SONY.COM/
MUSIC/SCREENERS

Seven Points for Fan Club Members

Often, Michael's fans write to the Fan Club asking how they can help Michael. The Fan Club came up with a list of seven activities that can help Michael a great deal. They are:

1. Write your favorite TV shows or magazines and request to see Michael featured. If you are a fan club member, don't mention it; individual requests are viewed better.

2. Call your local radio station and request Michael's songs. Remember to vary the time of day that you do call. Too many calls, at the same time of day for the same artist are not as likely to be honored. Again, if you are a fan club member, don't mention it so that it doesn't appear to be an organized effort.

3. Send contributions of photos you've taken of Michael and comments you may have on club services to the newsletters. Help other fans enjoy your Michael Bolton experiences.

4. If you see an article in a newspaper or magazine that mentions or is about Michael, send it to the fan club. They are maintaining an archive of media articles on him.

5. The Media Information Service (MIS) will help with your questions about how to contact magazines, TV shows, etc. If you have a question or would just like to receive mailings from MIS, send 2 self-addressed stamped envelopes to MIS, PO Box 746, Mechanicsville VA 23111-0746.

6. Keep the fan club informed when you move. Make sure the latest newsletter and mailings make it to your door.

7. If your letter to the fan club needs a reply, please include a self addressed stamped envelope; otherwise, they will not be able to respond.

The Average Michael Bolton Fan

One of the *USA Today*'s cover stories on September 8, 1993 was an article on the Michael Bolton Fan Club. In that story and its attendant side-bars, they described the average Michael Bolton Fan as 31 to 45 years of age, living in a mid- to large- sized city, and holding at least a high school diploma (although twice as many Bolton fans hold college degrees as the national average for women). More than a year later, Joe Erschel of *USA Today* described Michael's fans as "...lovelorn old ladies in stretch pants who are absolutely tone deaf and nearsighted." We have met and corresponded with many Michael Bolton fans and we can tell you beyond all doubt that the average Michael Bolton fan is:

Margaret Bonney — This fifty-seven year old mother of two lives in South Australia with her understanding and supportive husband. Margaret always enjoyed Michael's music but in March, 1994, Margaret attended her first Michael Bolton concert and has been firmly "hooked" ever since. She has said that her fondness for Michael Bolton has opened a new world for her, that she had never before been a fan club member or had a penpal, and that she is enjoying herself immensely.

Margaret Bonney and Pauline Frost

Nancy Finlan — Nancy first joined the Michael Bolton fan club at the tender age of thirteen. Now sixteen, living in Levittown, NY with her parents, she is fortunate to have a doting dad who is willing to drive her to events in nearby Connecticut. Acting in tandem with an older Bolton buddy, Nancy has been a volunteer hostess for the Michael Bolton Foundation at five events. She has attended six concerts and regularly attends as many Bolton public appearances as possible. As busy as she is, Nancy corresponds with three dozen penpals.

Nancy Finaln and Friends

Jim Finlan — This forty-seven year-old technical writer is married, and the father of one son and two daughters (including Nancy). Jim lists his hobbies as photography and acting as Commissioner of Girl's Softball, but certainly a good deal of time and effort is spent chauffering and chaperoning his daughter at Michael Bolton events. When asked about his attendance at these events, Jim said, "See Nancy's list."

Pauline Frost- Pauline (pictured on the preceding page) also lives in South Australia and is, in fact, a friend of Margaret Bonney's. Pauline has been a fan of Michael's since 1992 when she bought the TIME, LOVE & TENDERNESS CD because she liked the cover. Playing it repeatedly, she discovered that as much as she liked the photo, she LOVED the voice. Pauline is fifty-four years old, married, with two grown sons and four grandchildren. She attended Michael's 1994 concert and was very disappointed when the 1996 Australian tour was canceled as she had her tickets already in hand. She's hoping it was more postponement than cancellation.

Cathy Kincaid — Cathy, now thirty years old, first heard Michael Bolton on the radio while attending college at Kent State University and has been a fan ever since. Although she has a dislike for trying to navigate her wheelchair through crowds, Cathy makes exceptions for Bolton events. And with good reason. At one memorable concert event, Michael handed her his guitar pick and had her escorted backstage, chatting comfortably and posing for a picture. She says, "Michael Bolton...talked to me, not seeming to pay attention to my wheelchair. I'm usually quite shy and uncomfortable meeting someone, this was not the case at all meeting Mr. Bolton. He was so kind to me that it was very easy to talk to him. Two months later I sat in the front row in Pittsburg. Mr. Bolton saw me and...talked for a few minutes as he was on the stage. What was really amazing was the fact that he called me by name...considering the amount of people Michael Bolton meets in a two month period."

Cathy Kincaid and Michael Bolton

Alison Knapman- Alison (pictured at right) has been a Bolton fan since 1989. Living in Surrey, England, she has seen several Michael Bolton concerts at Wembley Arena since her first in 1993. In her post-concert excitement, Alison generally waits at the stage door for a last glimpse of Michael

and has been lucky enough on several occasions to be the recipient of handwaves, smiles, and on one memorable night, conversation. After handing Michael a small gift, "...he said, 'Thank you very much,' with infinite sincerity. As he read the card attached to the gift, Michael spoke my name. A dream came true that night, something I'll never forget." Single, thirty-five years old, Alison enjoys tennis and would love to see Michael in a match. But unless he makes Wimbledon soon, she will have to settle for photos.

Jan Lowry — Jan, forty-nine, a loyal Canadian fan living in Saskatchewan with her musical husband, son, and daughter, freely admits to being a music appreciator, not an active participant. She has been a fan since 1992 when, vacationing in Hawaii, she saw a Michael Bolton impersonator. Enjoying the music immensely, she went

straight for the real thing at her local record store, buying TIME, LOVE & TENDERNESS. Succumbing easily and completely, she owned his complete collection by the end of that week. Jan has seen Michael in concert and playing softball. Besides Michael Bolton, she enjoys raquetball, golf, travel, and computers. "Surfing the Net" for Bolton information, she has "met" and corresponds with many other fans.

Maria Ines Revuelta — Maria (pictured left) is a divorced forty year old mother of two, living in Cordoba, Argentina. Maria loves walking, bike riding, reading, writing, listening to Michael Bolton, her son and daughter, their two dogs, three cats, two tortoises, and two hamsters. Maria was at an especially rough part in her life when she first heard "When A Man Loves A Woman" on the radio. She immediately fell in love with *The Voice* even though she had no idea what the words were. "I heard Michael's voice for the first time in 1991-my roughest time period. He made me want to hear music again." Receiving *Time, Love & Tenderness* as a gift, she bought a "BIG Spanish/American Dictionary" and set about translating the songs. She said the first song took about two months, but that as time went on, it got easier. She joined the fan club, put her name on the penpal list, and continued to learn and practice her new language with her friends. "I think Michael changed my life in many ways. The one thing I hope is, someday, in a near future, to be able to meet him and say thanks personally." Maria has never seen him live but has repeatedly requested a South American stop from Michael's management.

Suzanne St. Pierre — Suzanne, (pictured right), an Admissions Assistant at a Massachusetts' hospital, is a divorced thirty-seven year old mother of four. Besides Mr. Michael Bolton, her passion is dancing—both learning the latest steps and choreographing. Suzanne is the brave fan that attended her first

Michael Bolton Foundation event alone. (See "The Price You Pay" for more information.) She has also attended four concerts, five softball games, two tennis matches, and one toy drive in the Trumball Mall.

Sherril Hickman — Sherril (pictured in a family photo below), is a forty-three year old production worker at a local toy factory. Married for twenty-four years, she is the mother of two boys. She enjoys bird-watching, softball, knitting, crocheting, sewing, ceramics, and reading. Despite her many interests, Sherril says, "No matter what kind of song that Michael sings, I stop what I'm doing to listen to him. He sends chills up and down my spine, what a voice!! He has also been known to bring a tear to my eyes when he sings his love songs." Due to scheduling problems, Sherril has not yet attended a live Michael Bolton event, but hopes to soon.

Cheryl Hill — Cheryl (pictured right), is a thirty-three year old legal secretary from Wilson, NY. She and her eleven year old daughter, Brandi, enjoy spending time together listening to Michael Bolton,

but it is her six year old son, Andy (a miniature entertainer and novice Elvis-impersonator), who really "gets down" when his favorite Bolton songs come on the radio. Although she has been a fan of his music since 1990, Cheryl saw her first Michael Bolton concert in 1994, attending with her sweetheart of a husband, Carl. Cheryl hopes to attend many more Bolton-related events in the future.

The Price You Pay

As adults, we are all aware that anything you want has a price that must be paid. Living in today's world, we usually assign this cost a monetary value. Although the financial costs of being a Michael Bolton fan cannot be ignored (ticket prices, travel costs, phone expenses, babysitters, t-shirts, memorabilia, records, cassettes, CDs, etc.), the personal and emotional costs are something not often bargained for ahead of time.

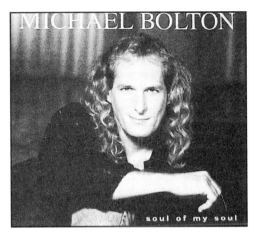

Since we have always found unexpected tolls tied to our appreciation of Michael Bolton, it was always one of the first things we asked other fans about. "Have you experienced any unusual or difficult moments relating to Michael Bolton adventures?" The answers were sometimes amusing, sometimes inspiring, sometimes almost frightening, but always, there was a story to be told.

Every Michael Bolton event can be divided into three categories: preparation for, travel to, and attendance at. For further ease, we have subdivided these categories into smaller, more specific groupings.

The following is an account of the various prices that have been paid by Bolton fans. Perhaps you have had similar difficulties. If not, be prepared, be warned. This could happen to you.

PREPARATION FOR A MICHAEL BOLTON EVENT

1. Notification of impending event:

Sometimes it's as easy as calling the fan club hotline, picking up the Sunday newspaper, or listening to the radio while driving to work. But at other times, when the concert schedule has been announced and your nearest city isn't on it yet or when the Sunday softball game is first announced on the Wednesday before, identifying an upcoming event can get complicated. One woman we spoke to was in the habit of alternating daily phone calls between the venue and the local ticket agent in an effort to avoid overly irritating her sources while attempting to get information on an upcoming Bolton concert. "By week two," she laughed, "the ladies at the venue were getting a bit abrupt when they recognized my voice on the phone." Such persistence generally pays off, she claims. Since concerts aren't announced until contracts are finalized, last-minute shows are often added to tours. Employing her method, she has time to get tickets, and rarely has sat outside the first ten rows.

Another woman spoke about the unreliability of some venues' arrangements. "I had been given an on-sale date for tickets to a softball game for a Wednesday morning, and planned to be first in line. Since the stadium was using assigned seating, I needed to be sure I could get good seats. Purely by chance, I called the stadium box office on Monday to find out what rules they had for ticket lines, only to have the woman at the other end of the phone casually announce that although tickets wouldn't go on sale through the ticket agent until Wednesday, THEY had been selling tickets to the game since Saturday, TWO WHOLE DAYS BEFORE MY PHONE CALL. A somewhat frenzied drive to the stadium with my brother-in-law and nephew ensued. Luckily, almost no one else had any knowledge of this strange ticketing arrangement either, so an hour and a half later, I held four prime tickets in my hand."

2. Getting tickets:

The actual procurement of tickets is an interesting experience, to say the least. Probably the most common payment form for good tickets is whether or not you are willing to brave the wilds camping out at your box office.

The wilds may actually be right smack in the center of a thriving city, but be assured, wilds it is. We heard a story from two of our penpals about camping out in a city in Australia, only to have to answer questions from passerbys all night and take pot shots from any Bolton

Basher that wanted to speak his say. Not a very pleasant experience, we imagine, but one they felt was worth it once they at last held the tickets in their hands.

Camping out for tickets in the true wilderness is another story entirely. If your concert is being held in the country or on a hillside, you had better be prepared to contend with palpable darkness, cold, insects, wild animals, an almost assured lack of restrooms, and any danger that your active imagination can come up with on its own. One consolation for those of us in the Northeast: daylight comes early on long summer days. Of course, then you generally have a lack of shade. (And it is immediately apparent to all who show up in the daylight hours that, yes, you did spend the night in that parking lot).

For a Canadian concert that we wanted to get tickets to, we decided to bypass the camp-out and simply order them over the phone. The entire evening before the tickets went on sale, we were on the phone with various ticket agents, both Canadian and U.S., in an effort to pick the very best and quickest. Imagine our distress the following morning when, having reached our chosen agent in due course, we were told that the concert we wanted tickets to was not appearing on their computer screen. We immediately hung up and called our second choice, only to meet with the frustrating, irritating buzz of a busy signal. We called back our original agent and were told that all agents were busy and our call would be taken by the next available agent. Then, again we were told that our concert did not appear. Again, we hung up. Frenzied, we attempted a third agent. Yes, they had tickets, but not very good ones. Their computer said tickets had been on sale for a week. Frustrated beyond belief, and cursing the ineptitude of computers and their operators alike, we at last gave up.

We believed that was the absolute worst that could happen, but our British penpal wrote us a letter detailing her experience with ticket purchase by mail. It appears that tickets were only available by mail and she duly got her order and check out without delay, asking for the best seats possible. Just imagine her distress when she opened the envelope from the venue, expecting tickets, only to find her check wrapped inside an apologetic note. It seems that whomever opened her order deemed the available seats not quite good enough, and decided to return her check. When she called, the box office advised her to re-submit her request, but she was terribly afraid it would be in vain. Luckily, (remember, the more you suffer, the greater the reward) Michael booked an additional night at her choice venue and her check arrived just in time to get her first row seats. Suddenly, the anguish of the check's return was gone.

Another cause of great stress in the quest for good tickets is that often, you do not have first hand knowledge of the venue where you are attempting to get the best seats. Is third row off to the side better than tenth row center? If you have never been in the concert hall before, you have no way of knowing. Gold Club seating has added a whole new dimension to this quandary.

Since the venue is only obligated to hold two hundred seats in the first twenty rows, sometimes you can get better seats by being first at your local ticket vendor as opposed to first at the venue itself. It's all pick and choose, with little fore-knowledge to base your choice on; this can leave you with only second guessing as to whether or not you did the right thing.

Finally, your tickets in hand, all you have left to do is hire the babysitter, find the right outfit, make arrangements at work, get your hair done, and get to the show. This leads us directly to the next toll booth.

TRAVELING TO A MICHAEL BOLTON EVENT

1. Weather:

If you are attending an outdoor function, weather will be a concern. But it is one you prepare for as best you can. If it's hot, you wear less clothes; cold, you put on a sweater. You always pray for clear skies and gentle breezes.

Surprisingly, most of the problems with weather are found at indoor venues. We met one woman who had driven three hours, one of them in a monsoon-like rainstorm, with no rest area in sight, to attend a Bolton concert. Safely in her seat, she appeared to have suffered no lasting effects; we're sure it was a harrowing experience nonetheless. Another fan told us about shaking in her motel room, listening to the wind howl and windows shake while tornado warnings flashed across the TV screen three hours before concert time. We once had to contend with a blizzard that postponed the concert one night, necessitating a slippery ride on slick roads through a narrow tunnel of snowdrifts, to the show the next evening. The most nerve-wracking part of that experience, however, had to be chewing our nails in front of our radios the day of the scheduled show, listening to announcements of road closings, school closings, accident reports, waiting for news on the status of the show. It was a close call. None of us wanted to be the one to say, "I'm not going," but none of us were looking forward to the two-hour drive either. If our memories are correct, the show was to begin at 8:00. The concert was finally canceled after 5 p.m. Much longer and we would have been on the road.

2. Obstacles:

Weather is not the only obstacle you may have to contend with. We've heard tales of close encounters with raccoons, skunks, deer lying in the middle of the road and once, even an armadillo adventure. Tandem-trailer trucks can also be an exhilarating experience, especially when speeding tickets and increased auto insurance rates are the only way to avoid them.

Then there are the man-made obstacles—construction sites, road crews and detours. Detours in unknown areas are even more fun, especially when you follow the detour sign only to arrive at a road barricade saying "No Vehicles Beyond This Point." That's when you discover that a public employee with a strange sense of humor misplaced the detour sign you passed two miles back. This actually happened to acquaintances of ours who, at one time, despaired of ever finding their way out of New Haven, Connecticut.

Traveling to unfamiliar areas holds other surprises as well. We once pulled into a softball game parking lot only to find that the Bronco next to us, bearing out of state plates, was full of women in various stages of undress, attempting to inconspicuously change out of their traveling clothes. We held up jackets over windows to shield them from other, possibly male, eyes and struck up a conversation when at last they appeared fully clothed. When questioned about their inability to find a more suitable changing room, say a fast-food restroom, they related a previous attempt at doing just that. It seems that harried mothers with anxious children frown on using the bathroom as a changing room. Plus, the logistics of manipulating a tote bag and purse, while attempting to disrobe and don fresh clothing in the confines of one of those stalls was impossible.

We've also found that even people can add to your travel time. A few examples are customs inspectors, policemen, toll booth operators and waitresses. It sometimes seems that everyone you come in contact with, on any given Bolton adventure, has a Michael Bolton story to relate. A customs officer, after discovering that our sole purpose in entering his country was to attend a Bolton Bombers charity game, relaxed his stern demeanor enough to tell us that the field was two blocks from his home. We're quite sure our conversation (questions about the field from us and joking about having Michael as a houseguest from him) was carried on at the expense of waiting drivers in line behind us.

A routine stop at a roadside DWI check can turn into a ten-minute conversation with a policeman who has just moonlighted as security at a Bolton concert. A Michael Bolton t-shirt is practically guaranteed to start a conversation with just about any waitress in the world. They all want to tell you what they love about him, what their favorite song is, and when and where they last saw him perform. (We have no problem with this as long as they bring our food first. Usually, by the time we get there, we need after-Michael sustenance much more than conversation.) But, whether they love him or dislike him, one thing is guaranteed — Michael Bolton is a wonderful conversation starter.

ATTENDANCE AT YOUR BOLTON FUNCTION

1. Concerts:

Apart from the fact that there are ALWAYS far more women than available restrooms at Michael's shows, concerts are actually pretty stress-free. For those of us who are attending, that is. Being our usually chatty selves, we have struck up conversations with several different members from local security teams guarding the stage at Bolton concerts. Their almost unanimous reaction when first faced by the teeming thousands is terror. "Some of these women are scary," one scarred veteran of Bolton concerts told us. "They have only one thought in mind, to get closer to Michael Bolton, and they don't care who they have to go over to get there."

"You have to be careful how you handle them," his partner chimed in. Because they're women, we wondered? "No, because they have nails," he laughed.

2. Bombers' Games:

Some possible costs to be paid at Michael's charity softball games are sunburn, windburn, leg cramps and sore bottoms from uncomfortable seating and, if you're lucky enough to be sitting close to the field, an encompassing layer of dust kicked up by the onfield activity. The raucous quality of loud speaker systems, coupled with the ridiculous sound effects some announcers are prone to use, are additional factors.

Less often, but still too often, there is the reliability of the presenting organization. We once attended an out-of-town game in which the times were printed incorrectly on the tickets. Our tickets said the gates would open at 11 a.m. and the game to start at 1:00. In reality, the gates didn't open until 1:00, with the game beginning two hours later.

You also must blindly hope that the volunteers working the game for their charity are familiar with the usual operations of the stadium. Does the keyholder know that not only must he unlock the gates, but that the turn-stiles must also be unlocked, and preferably before the gates are opened to the masses? Are there ample parking attendants to ensure that handicapped parking spaces remain handicapped accessible throughout the game and do not get lot-bound by late arrivals? We've heard frightening tales about both of these coming true.

3. Black Tie Events:

Gone are the fairly normal stresses of the previous events, now YOU will be on display. Imagine that you have successfully navigated the murky waters of preparation for and travel to your event. There you are in your hotel room, showered, powdered, perfumed, coifed and sitting on your bed donning a pair of sheer, silky, black pantyhose. Halfway up your leg, one beautifully manicured fingernail slices through the nylon and a six-inch run results. No problem, you are prepared. Two pair of pantyhose later, you discover that the "good" hose you specially selected for your magical evening are a bust and you're left with only your old reliable day stockings to see you through. This sad tale was related to us by a co-attendee after several glasses of champagne before dinner.

At the last Michael Bolton Foundation Black Tie Gala we attended, we noticed an attractive young woman standing alone, smiling at everyone who came near, looking like she really wanted someone to talk to. Naturally, we made conversation. She gave us a whole new perspective on the price one may pay.

When tickets were first offered for the Foundation Weekend, she immediately ordered tickets to the softball game and tennis match and attempted to order a ticket to the Gala. At that time, she was told that there were no more tickets available. Sadly disappointed, she asked that her name be put on the waiting list in case of cancellations.

"But you made it," we said. "When did you find out a ticket was available?"

"Last Monday," she replied. We were in awe. Not only had she prepared for that Black Tie event in less than a week, she had also traveled nine hours on a bus,

walked to and from the softball stadium TWICE (once just to see how long it would take her) in an unknown city and made her way to the tennis match and back. What was even more awe-inspiring to us was that she had done all of these things totally, completely alone. The courage she displayed simply walking into that formal affair was unimaginable to us. We had driven through twenty miles of dense fog, traveled all night with no sleep, and fought a losing battle with the resulting dark circles and puffy bags under our eyes, but at least we had each other. We shared our excitement, worries and insecurities, soothing and nurturing one another. To have faced it alone was incomprehensible.

This leads to the last hidden price many Michael Bolton fans experience.

We have been told many times, by many women, that they have no one to share their appreciation of Michael Bolton with. Some women tell us that their husbands or boyfriends have no patience with their interest, some have few contacts outside their homes, and many live in areas where Bolton news and information is hard to come by. In some areas of the world, Bolton fans rely on pen pals, videos and magazines to feed their desire for first-hand knowledge of Michael Bolton events.

Almost unanimously, they express a feeling of isolation from "what's happening" and an inability to understand why Bolton Bashers seem to think its their given right to relate exactly what they think is wrong with anyone who appreciates Michael Bolton.

If you recognize yourself in any of these statements, please take note...there is comfort in numbers. Contact the fan club, select a name from the pen pal list and write that first letter. Michael's fans are caring, friendly people and soon, you'll have new friends who share your interest in Michael Bolton, the man, the music, the experience.

Although this list is long and varied, ranging from the mildly annoying to the seriously threatening, most of the fans we spoke to agreed that the more intense the price, the greater the reward. The old adage, "If you have to work for it, it will mean more" appears to be very true after all.

The Michael Bolton Foundation

Michael Bolton Foundation Black Tie Gala — 1996

The Michael Bolton Foundation was established in 1993 to provide aid for women and children at risk to the effects of poverty and emotional, physical, and sexual abuse. The Foundation's Board of Trustees consists of:

Michael Bolton - President
Louis Levin - Secretary
David L. Feinstein - Treasurer
Jacquelyn Smaga - Executive Director
Andrena Kumnick - Executive Assistant
Robert Epstein - Advisory Council
Marshall Gibson - Advisory Council
James Greenfield - Advisory Council
Mickey Sherman - Advisory Council

The Foundation appears to divide its efforts into three major categories: crisis relief and family services; education and job training; and medical research. Since 1993, more than twenty projects have been instituted by the Foundation and range from the creation of a national bus poster campaign targeted at child abuse to the renovation of an abandoned mall into a "Safe Space For New Haven's Youth," designed to build self-esteem and leadership skills while providing job training and awareness of social issues.

Although a variety of fund-raisers are held in conjunction with the individual projects, The Michael Bolton Foundation hosts one major fund-raising event a year, The Annual Celebrity Tennis Classic, Softball Game, and Black Tie Gala. Hundreds of volunteers donate their time, money, services, and products to make this event the shining success it has proven to be to date. Celebrities, sports figures, politicians, and business people work side by side to ensure that every year is better than the year before.

On behalf of the Foundation, a letter from Michael Bolton appeared on the opening page of the 1995 Weekend Event Program which read, in part, "It is my intention to continue as long as there is need; to assist however and wherever we can. ...Thanks to you, for all you have done, and are doing, to keep us going."

Recipients of grants from the Foundation since 1993 include:

Neighborhood Music School, New Haven, Connecticut.

Kids In Crisis - Greenwich Youth Center, Greenwich, Connecticut.

Stamford Exchange Club Center for Child Abuse, Stamford, Connecticut.

Boys Choir of Harlem, Harlem, NY.

Rogers School Community Center Organization, Stamford, Connecticut.

The CityKids Foundation, New York, NY.

Little Sister of the Assumption Health Service, East Harlem, NY.

National Committee to Prevent Child Abuse, Chicago, Illinois.

Lifehaven Shelter/Yale Child Study Center, New Haven, Connecticut.

Family Campus Initiative, New Haven, Connecticut.

Newhallville Day Care Center, New Haven, Connecticut.

Pediatric Aids Foundation, Santa Monica, California.

The Crenshaw High School Elite Choir, Los Angeles, California.

Congress of Racial Equality (CORE), New York, NY.

Children of the Night, Van Nuys, California.

United Negro College Fund, Fairfax, Virginia.

Cities in Schools, Alexandria, Virginia.

Adopt A Special Kid (AASK), Oakland, California.

Joe DiMaggio's Children's Hospital, Hollywood, Florida.

Harlem School of the Arts, Inc., New York, NY.

The Martin Luther King, Jr. Center for Nonviolent Social Change, Inc., Atlanta, Georgia.

The list keeps growing. Michael Bolton and the Michael Bolton Foundation have made a commitment to do whatever they can to make sure the future is brighter than the present. And Michael has often urged his fans to get involved in whatever way they can so they, too, can enjoy the rewards of helping their fellow man. As Michael has said, the reward is when "you know you're making a difference with your success and your life."

THE MICHAEL BOLTON FOUNDATION MISSION STATEMENT

The mission of the Michael Bolton Foundation is dedicated to two basic areas:

1. The Assistance of Children and Women "At Risk"
2. Through education and effective programs, create social awareness to broaden horizons and expand opportunities for youth across socioeconomic and multicultural lines.

1. Children and Women "At Risk"
Child Development and the Prevention and Intervention of Abuse. To attempt to lessen children's and women's vulnerability to the damaging effects of poverty and emotional, physical and sexual abuse.

GOALS:
• Execution of vehicles for increasing awareness and public education of the issues to families and children.

• Identification of methods for detection, prevention and mediation of their effects.

• Development of innovative therapeutic "safe" centers for protection and healing of victims.

2. **Through education and effective programs, provide opportunities for youth across socioeconomic and multicultural lines.**

To improve the availability and access to resources which foster personal development. Programs should promote positive values and creativity by focusing on self-esteem, empowerment, leadership skills, education, environmental awareness, drugs, crime, abuse, AIDS, health and global issues.

GEOGRAPHIC FOCUS: Nationwide

GOALS:

• To deepen and empower children's engagement in their own education and future at all levels.

• To develop educational support through scholarships, workshops, incentives, internships, and other appropriate avenues.

• To collaborate with the corporate/business community, state and local government, social service agencies, schools and private/public associations in developing outreach programs and employment opportunities which will have a long-term effect on the goals of the Foundation.

Joyce Logan, answering the mail.

Joyce Logan & Michael

95

Live and Silent Auction

*Jack Williams and an AKC puppy up for auction
at the Michael Bolton Foundation Black Tie Gala, 1996*

Having had the pleasure of attending the Foundation Black Tie Galas, we found the Live and Silent Auctions to be a highly entertaining portion of the evening. Below you will find a very small sampling of the items up for auction.

ANDRE AGASSI MEMORA-BILIA — If it's connected to Andre and tennis, he signed it, including a 1994 US Open T-shirt, a tennis racquet, pictures, etc. Value for these items: PRICELESS.

SUPERBOWL XXVIII FOOTBALL — Autographed by Superbowl MVP Emmitt Smith, running back for the Dallas Cowboys. What would be a nice souvenir to take home to the "other" special guy in your life? Value: PRICELESS.

LONDON VACATION — Airfare to London, a place to stay, tickets to Wimbledon, and as if that weren't enough...lunch with Chris Evert while you're there! Value, as you may have guessed: PRICELESS.

GUITAR AUTOGRAPHED BY JAMES TAYLOR — What more can we say? Value: PRICELESS (We have to agree!).

COME SEE THE OPRAH SHOW — Oprah will fly you and three of your guests to Chicago, give you four tickets to her show, and follow it up with a backstage tour. Value: PRICELESS.

DINNER FOR EIGHT — They're not talking macaroni and cheese here, how about a gourmet meal prepared by a Belgian Master Chef! His name is Alain V. DeCoster, and he wants to come to your home and do it all! Value: $250.00 (Sounds like a deal to us).

SPEND THE DAY AT NOELLE'S SPA — Pampering ladies is their business, pure and simple. They even throw in a garden lunch. Value: $300.00.

GUCCI FASHIONS — Italian leather handbag and a fine silk scarf. Value: $1,000.00.

"UNTITLED" — Created especially for Michael's Foundation, this original painting is by Roxanna Alexander. Value: $300.00.

GROTTO BAY BEACH IN BERMUDA — Three days and nights on the pink sand beaches at this wonderful hotel, airfare included. Value: $900.00.

FOOTBALL HELMET — Autographed by the Miami Dolphin's quarterback, Dan Marino. Value: PRICELESS.

LUCIANO PAVAROTTI — CD autographed by this opera legend. Value: $200.00.

"FRASIER" SCRIPT — Autographed by the entire cast. Value: $150.00.

PHOTO OF JOE DIMAGGIO — Action photograph of Joe sliding into base. Value: $700.00.

HEALTHY BASKET — A collection of foods from Westport's very own Organic Market. Value: $50.00.

CHINESE BOWL — Eggshell porcelain bowl. Value: $1,000.00.

SURVIVAL TRAINING — One year of self defense training, done in private and group lessons. Value: $1,500.00.

BABY, WE'RE GONNA MAKE YOU A STAR — You'll do a walk-on in a Lifetime Network original movie and meet all the stars. Value: $1,000.00.

RIDE A NUCLEAR SUBMARINE — Ten couples will be guests at the Foxwood's Resort and taken to the U.S. Navy Base in Groton, Connecticut where they will board a nuclear sub for the day, then back to the resort for dinner and a show. Value: $6,500.00.

AKC REGISTERED PUPPY — Take it from us, these adorable AKC registered puppies create quite a bidding war when they are brought on stage. Value: $750.00 (However, we've seen them go for thousands and thousands of dollars).

DOGGIE DO SALON — This New York City salon will really pamper your male pooch for one day. When "Studly" is ready to go, he'll be showered with gifts...a Harley Davidson biker jacket, a faux Chanel sweater, a beautiful collar adorned with jewels and, of course, a baseball cap complete with chin strap and visor. Value: $190.00.

HOT BIKER "BITCH" — Now it's Ms. Doggie's turn. Same as above only she gets a pink motorcycle jacket and a pink neon ballcap with bandanna. Value: $190.00.

AUTOGRAPHED GUITAR — This little number is signed by Jon Bon Jovi and Ritchie Sambora! Value: PRICE-LESS.

RODNEY'S TIE — Nervous Rodney, always adjusting his tie. Now you can own one! Value: PRICELESS.

RON HOWARD'S SCRIPT — A script from the movie FAR AND AWAY signed by Ron. Value: PRICELESS.

PAUL NEWMAN'S OWN - Paul's jacket from his newest movie, NOBODY'S FOOL, complete with his autograph. Value: PRICELESS.

MICHAEL BOLTON PLAQUE - This platinum album award is autographed by Michael just for you! Value: PRICELESS.

TEACHER MICHAEL - Let Michael teach you the tricks as well as the passion needed to play softball. You will receive a copy of his instructional video and a Louisville Slugger bat — both autographed by Michael, of course. Value: PRICELESS.

"Windows of My Soul" — Chris Camozzi

Introduction of The Bombers

The following is the 1996 line-up for the Bolton Bombers. For the sake of uniformity, we will introduce the Bomber's in order of position played.

Pitcher - #57 - Louis "Flip 'em Again" Levin

Louis, Michael's personal manager, is 5'10" tall and weighs in at 168 pounds. His birthday is June 14 (making him a Gemini) and he is currently living in New York City. Having managed Michael for more than ten years, Louis has also worked with such diverse groups as Aerosmith, Cameo, and George Clinton.

Catcher - #11 - "Booming" Bucky Ford

This Nashville, Tennessee resident is 6'4" and 260 lbs. A marketing representative for Community Health Resources, Bucky has appeared as a Bomber for three years. During that time, he has played various positions including first base, catcher, and outfield. Bucky ended the 1996 softball season with a .728 batting average. His birthday is March 20.

First Base - #15 - Gary "Big Stick" Whitefield

Gary, a manager at K-Mart in his hometown of Birmingham, Alabama, was born on July 31. At 6'4" and 260 lbs., he makes a formidable softball player, ending the 1996 season with a .755 batting average, 220 RBI's, and 94 home runs.

Second Base - #14 - "Killer" Kim Turner

Kim, Assistant to Louis Levin, has the enviable position of being the only woman on the team. At 5'4", 125 lbs., Kim has a history as a four-time All American in field hockey. In 1987, she helped the University of Maryland "Terps" take the NCAA Division 1 National Championship. Statistician for the Bombers, she has played Short Stop as well as second base. Currently living in New York City, Kim's birthday is August 18.

Short Stop - #2 - "Slugger" Mugs Cain
As drummer with Michael Bolton's band for more than five years, Mugs has built up a lot of upper body strength. It shows, too, in that he leads the bombers with a .767 batting average. This Palmdale, California resident weighs in at 5'10", 150 lbs. and was born on October 7.

Third Base - #7 Michael "The Bomber" Bolton
Michael, born February 26, lists his occupation as "Singer/Songwriter." We would add "Humanitarian, Author, Actor, Softball Afficiando, and Full-Time Dad." Michael is 6' tall and weighs 175 lbs. Living in Westport, Connecticut, with his three daughters, Michael is the founder and rock-solid base of the Bolton Bombers.

Right Field - #12 - Phil "New Ball" Higgins
Phil, at 6'1" and 200 lbs., has played competitive softball for more than 20 years. A former member of the 1984 Men's Major ASA National Championship team, he was a four time USA All-American and a five time All Pro. Currently living in Milwaukee, Wisconsin, Phil is employed off-season in the Recycling Industry. His birthday is March 1.

Center Field - #69 - Bobby "The Stinger" Olah
Bobby is the newest Bomber, leading the team with 115 home runs in only two years. At 6'4" and 220 lbs., Bobby's softball talent was obvious even at the age of 16 when he hit a homer in the Daily News All-Star Game at Yankee Stadium. Born May 21, Bobby lives in Bridgeport, Connecticut where he is employed in Flooring Installation.

Center - #16 - Dennis "The Menace" Rodriguez
Dennis, Michael's tour manager for the last 7 years, has been in the music business for more than 20 years. An original member of the Bomber's, he is presently living in San Diego, California. Dennis is 5'10" tall and weighs 165 lbs. His birthday is November 24.

Left Field - #9 - Richie "The Ripper" Vaughn
At 6'2", 210 lbs., Ritchie is employed off-season with the MIS-Nashville Metro Police in his hometown of Nashville, Tennessee. A four year veteran of the Bombers, Richie is one of the featured players in Michael's *Winning Softball: Hit Harder, Play Smarter* home video.

Outfield - #21 - Mike "The Missile" Bolen
His official stats list him as Designated Hitter/OutFielder. Off-season, Mike is a Supervisor with the M&M Mars Company in Cleveland, Tennessee with a life-long love of softball. He is a 12-time All-American slow pitch softball player, has played on nine world championship teams, and has led the nation in homeruns and batting average. Born April 14, Mike is 6'2" tall and weighs 240 lbs.

Although this is a complete list of the current Bolton Bombers line-up, many other people have appeared at special functions and in previous years. Please see the alphabetical listing for Bolton Bombers for more information.

SOFTBALL 101

Let's face it, ladies...love the man, love his passions. And one of Michael's passions is softball, specifically slow-pitch softball. So even if you don't LOVE it, you probably should at least understand it (or sound like you do). Here's a quick course in Softball 101.

Michael and the Bombers play a mean game of Slow-Pitch Softball. There are seven basic differences between "Slow-Pitch" softball and baseball, even though the game looks pretty much the same.

1. Although both games are played with a leather-covered ball, softball employs a ball with a 12-inch circumference instead of the considerably smaller 9" baseball.

2. The infield of a baseball game is delineated by four bases at a distance of 90 feet from each other. Softball is much cozier, with a mere 60 feet between bases.

3. A softball team is allowed ten players, baseball teams use nine.

4. Baseball is pitched overhand, softball is pitched underhand, and "Slow Pitch" softball is pitched underhand with a distinct arc (called a "Lob") of at least six feet which crosses homeplate on it's downward flight.

5. Softball has a "No Bunting" rule that does not appear in baseball.

6. Softball does not allow stealing bases; many baseball games are won with stolen bases.

7. In softball, there is no "leading off" allowed; you must stay on base until the pitch has crossed the plate.

And there you have it—the basics of softball. Now if you really want to sound impressive, we've compiled some "fun facts" so that you can impress any softball lovers in your life.

Wayne Logan — Photographer Extraordinaire!

1. The game originated in Chicago, Illinois in 1887. It was started as a form of indoor baseball and was originally played with an easy-to-hit sixteen-inch ball.

2. In the early 1990's, approximately 40 million Americans (adults and children) played some form of competitive or recreational softball in the U.S. That fact makes it one of the largest team sports in the country.

3. Softball has a Connecticut connection besides Michael Bolton in the form of Joan Joyce, the famed Connecticut pitcher who is credited with pitching more than 130 No-Hitter games throughout the late 1960's and early 1970's, leading her teams to amateur championships.

4. And don't forget to mention the ever-entertaining Eddie Feigner. Eddie and his four-man team, known as "The King and His Court," travel all over the country combining softball skills and slapstick comedy. Eddie is reported to have pitched more than 900 no-hit games and is credited with an amazing 230 perfect games, allowing no hits, no runs, and no walks. Quite an impressive statistic.

And there you have it—a rudimentary education in softball. For a much more in-depth explanation, we suggest you study Michael's video, Michael Bolton's *Winning Softball: Hit Harder, Play Smarter.*

Michael Bolton and "That Girl"

Just a Short Hop From Father to Son

by Michael Bolton
as told to Mr. Jeff Zaslow
(Copyrighted INSIDE SPORTS, Reprinted with Permission)

In some ways, I feel like I was born into the New York Yankees. When I was growing up in New Haven, Conn. in the '50s, everyone knew the Yankees would win the pennant every year. They were the ultimate dominant team, so you just had to love them--and I felt like I was part of it all. My heroes were Mickey Mantle, Roger Maris, Yogi Berra, and Tony Kubek. With free agency today, we'll never see teams like that again.

My dad was a jock. He loved the Yankees--a love he passed on to me--and he played baseball, basketball, and football. He was a very macho character, but he was never afraid to be affectionate. He was the sort of guy who'd keep kissing your face in front of your friends until you were incredibly embarrassed. Then he'd say, "OK, go on, get out of here! And don't forget to get your glove and meet me at 3 o'clock, because we're going to practice."

I was an athletic kid, and my dad worked with me constantly: throwing, hitting, running. I was always fast around the bases--at age 14, I ran a 22--yard dash, without starting blocks, in 22 seconds. I used to make bets with kids about how fast I could run. I never played sports in high school, though, because I never went to high school. I formed my first band at 14 and got a record deal at 16, so I dropped out of school. From then on, the only time I went to school was to play at mixers.

However, once I made it as a singer I still had the urge to play ball. At first my band and I played in pickup games, but then we got more serious and formed a softball team, Bolton's Bombers.

We'd challenge radio stations in towns where I'd be giving concerts. After a while, we noticed opposing teams were getting awfully tough--these stations had all these muscular giants in their lineups. We'd ask, "So when is that guy on the air?" They were playing us with a bunch of ringers.

So naturally we had to toughen up our team with stronger players. They didn't have to know music, as long as they could hit. On my last tour we won 51 games. Joe DiMaggio came to a game last year and he marveled at one of our hottest players. Joe smiled at me and asked, "Ah, Mike, what instrument does he play?"

Actually, not all the Bombers are ringers. My drummer plays second base. (I just hope he doesn't hurt his fingers.) My manager also manages the team and pitches. He's been smacked by plenty of line drives; I worry he'll get hit in the head, start thinking funny, and make decisions that ruin my singing career.

I used to play third base, but I was getting pounded with short hops. The velocity in a serious softball game can be dangerous. I feared I'd get my jaw shattered and have to cancel an entire concert tour, so I moved myself to first base.

Last year the Bombers played the Field of Dreams Game at UCLA against Barry Bonds, Frank Thomas, Ken Griffey, Jr., Ozzie Smith, and other big-leaguers. It was slow-pitch softball with a 300-foot fence, which was to our advantage. Still, those guys thought they'd kill us. Before the game, Barry said to me, "I'll catch anything you hit." I said, "You're going to need a ladder."

Well, in the 2nd inning, I hit a homer over his head. When I rounded second base, I couldn't resist giving Barry some stuff. That was a kick. And the Bombers won 29-17.

I'm pleased that many of today's baseball stars like my music. Orel Hershiser once came backstage at a concert and told me that after his rotator cuff surgery he feared he'd never pitch again, but every day in therapy he'd play my song, "Back On My Feet Again." He said the song got him through. I was very moved by that.

The greatest thrill for me, though, has been meeting and playing against my childhood heroes. DiMaggio has become a dear friend. He's not just a legend; he's a class act. In my home studio, along with all the autographed balls and bats I collect, I'm proud to hang a Joe DiMaggio Children's Hospital jersey.

I feel privileged that I got to meet Mickey Mantle before he died. He said, "I hear you wear No. 7 when you play softball." Of course I wear Mantle's number--when I was a kid and No. 7 came to the plate, anything could happen.

My dad has been dead for 13 years now. He was always my biggest supporter, and when I won my first Grammy I wished he could have been there to see it. But even more, I wish he could be with me when I'm spending time with guys like DiMaggio.

Clete Boyer came to one of our games, and he and I tossed the ball around. At that moment, I desperately wished that my father could see me playing ball with one of our heroes. I know he'd have been so proud when Clete asked me, "Where'd you get that arm?"

I got that arm playing catch with my dad.

Michael Bolton &
Bolton Bomber's Trivia

Just one of a thousand charity games, 1995.

1. Michael's favorite baseball teams are the *San Francisco Giants* and the *New York Yankees.*

2. Michael plays the "Hot Corner" (3rd Base) or 1st Base.

3. Michael's jersey is #7 (which was also the jersey number of Mickey Mantle, Michael's baseball hero.)

4. Before Michael's team was called the Bolton Bombers, they were named the Bolton Badboys.

5. Michael has a large collection of baseball caps.

6. Michael's softball nickname is "The Bomber."

7. Michael sang the National Anthem at the 1993 World Series.

8. The Bolton Bombers are sponsored by Louisville Slugger.

9. Michael Bolton hits and throws right-handed.

10. Michael has a .676 career batting average.

11. Michael has said that in order to hit with power he "gets mad" at the ball.

12. Michael's biggest softball thrill was hitting a Grand Slam! He hit the ball over the fence (290 yards) with bases loaded, scoring four runs.

1. Who sang background vocals for Michael on "That's What Love Is All About"?
2. What kind of guitar did Michael use on THE HUNGER album?
3. Which current member of Michael's band has a brother who was in the rock band, *Journey*? Give yourself one extra point if you can name the brother.
4. To whom does Michael plead, "Girl, I surrender, I'm over my head, say it's forever"?
5. What was the name of the band Michael was singing with when he signed his first record deal?
6. What was Michael's first single?
7. On what album did Richard Marx sing back-up for Michael?
8. Who sang "From Now On" with Michael on SOUL PROVIDER?
9. Who is the album SOUL PROVIDER dedicated to?
10. Who is THE ONE THING album dedicated to?
11. What is the name of Michael's home studio?
12. What Joe Walsh song did Michael open his shows with in the 70s and 80s?
13. Who is Michael's youngest daughter?
14. Where was Michael born?
15. In what Disney production was Michael featured?
16. What year was TIMELESS: THE CLASSICS released?
17. What are Michael's parents names?
18. Of what performers does Michael do impersonations?
      a.
      b.
      c.
19. What is unusual about the picture of Jerry Mele in the 1994 Tour Book?
20. What two positions does Michael play with the Bombers?
21. What member of the Bolton Bombers once played for the NY Mets?
22. What opera solo did Michael perform and claim to have written during his 1994 tour?
23. What color is Michael's knee brace?
24. What is the brand name of Michael's bat, as well as his other uniform accessories?
25. Who wrote "Vesti la Giubba"?

BONUS: Name any 10 of the Bolton Bombers!

(See Answers on page 123)

Basic Black

Cryptogram Quotes

Michael in Concert

1. "J attd djwt J'pt ettx qzqedjxc qm blfdt cpstts."

2. "G drl wzbij pei bitwlghz perp nihnti deh rji egjib ph ajgpgcwi swlga rji cwrtgqgib."

3. "Sdn iykdry l iup giay l kloye lturlg cluputo pd oyp dnp."

4. "Perp'l irlm thj mhw ph lrm...Mhw bhz'p erfi ph nqrm owgprj dgpe F.F. Ygzo."

5. "C ucfl ez epuf ez exl mzild C ille zd exl ozps mxld C'i eopklucda."

6. "Ei lcdonu dcfrod en dg cspcih bnna rgtyr lgupcuk..."

7. "...G ahzjgbic sdjiqt r qgti-jpnnhcl jdjlis thc 'Lei Whgai.'"

8. "Edp Fpyecpg mse jp whes gs jbod exsbfcp wh godssc."

(See Answers on page 123)

Fill in the Lyrics

Test your knowledge of Michael's music and fill in the missing lyrics of these well-known Bolton songs:

1. Nothing heals a broken heart like...
2. Can't wait till I'm alone with you to...
3. ...to give all my love to you.
4. ...can't keep his mind on nothin' else.
5. The fire, the thunder,...
6. Every touch is feeling so much like...
7. ...the very deepest part of you.
8. I'm bound forever...
9. Ridin' the good times is easy,...
10. Talk about love, talk about trust,...
11. ...the price I'm gonna pay for dreamin'.
12. Baby, how can we make love if...
13. If it fell in your hands from the heavens above...
14. And I'm not gonna crawl again,...
15. ...I'm gonna love you like there's no tomorrow.
16. ...like the dawn through the night.
17. You think..., that don't mean that I can.
18. ...in a world that's black and white.
19. ...heart of my heart.
20. When your golden road has reached the end...
21. And you'll be safe and warm...

FOR EXPERTS ONLY

1. ...are safe in the dark.
2. I'm a slave to...
3. Love of my life...
4. If you ever need my love...

(See Answers on page 124)

Match the Nickname

"MONTY"   MICHAEL BOLTON
"BOOBY"   PHIL HIGGINS
"MUGS"   JAMES DANIELS
"THE MOZ"   RICHIE VAUGHN
"THE JUDGE"   FEINSTEIN, WEINSTEIN, EPSTEIN
"COACH"   BUCKY FORD
"MONNY"   DAVE REITZAS
"RIBS"   MARGARET CONE
"THE INNER CIRCLE"   JOHNNY DODD
"HOW'S MY HAIR"   BOBBY OLAH
"THE STINGER"   TRUMAN CROSS SLINGLUFF
                                        MONTFORT, JR.
"THE RIPPER"   TOMMY CAIN
"GET BACK ON THE BUS"   CHRIS CAMOZZI
"BIG STICK"   DAVE CARROLL
"NEW BALL"   RICHARD FRIEDLANDER
"BIG DADDY"   GARY WHITEFIELD
"THE KID"   LOUIS LEVIN

(See Answers on page 124)

THE M.V.P.

108

Coded Songs

Here is a list of Michael's songs that have been put into a simple code. One set of letters has been substituted for the correct set. Look for clues with titles that might betray themselves by their unique spelling or setup. Once you've identified a song, it will help you decode the rest of the list. Good luck!

1. WLLX'J UTCY
2. SYTGZ LW JZLHY
3. ZSY HOUSZ STJ CY VTXXOHU WLG FLB
4. JZTF
5. KSYH T CTH XLNYJ T KLCTH
6. QGOHU OZ LH SLCY ZL CY
7. AHLVA LH KLLE
8. OH ZSY TGCJ LW XLNY
9. UOHT
10. ZSTZ'J KSTZ XLNY OJ TXX TQLBZ
11. KSYH O'C QTVA LH CF WYYZ TUTOH
12. O IGLCOJY FLB
13. JZTHE BI WLG XLNY
14. VTXX CF HTCY
15. TOG KTNYJ

(See Answers on page 125)

Match the "Jobs"

Below is a list of people who share a connection with Michael. Match the names with their respective "JOBS".

1. JOEL BRANDER	HARPO INC.
2. ANDRENA KUMNICK	LEVIN MANAGEMENT
3. JOAN LUNDEN	CBS THIS MORNING
4. JILL TIGER	UNITED NEGRO COLLEGE
5. JOE DIMAGGIO	BOLTON BOMBERS
6. DIANE WARREN	AMERICAN AIRLINES
7. WALTER AFANASIEFF	COLUMBIA RECORDS
8. JOYCE LOGAN	ORCHESTRA NEW ENGLAND
9. JIM KOPLIK	HARLEM SCHOOL OF THE ARTS
10. JAMES SINCLAIR	WALLYWORLD MUSIC
11. DARRYL S. DURHAM	FAN EMPORIUM, INC
12. JACK WILLIAMS	MICHAEL BOLTON FOUNDATION
13. DON IENNER	THIS CLOSE
14. MARK MCEWEN	REALSONGS
15. DAVE CARROLL	CHILDREN'S HOSPITAL, FLA.
16. FRANCES W. PRESTON	I.C.M.
17. OPRAH WINFREY	BMI PRESIDENT
18. JOHNNY PODELL	NAT'L CHILD LABOR COMMISION
19. WILLIAM H. GRAY, JR.	METROPOLITAN ENTERTAINMENT
20. JEFFREY NEWMAN	GOOD MORNING AMERICA

(See Answers on page 125)

Michael and friends at the Michael Bolton Foundation Black Tie Gala

Numbers

The answers to the following questions are all numbers. See how many you know:

1. How many things does Michael ask to be told in "How Am I Supposed To Live Without You"?
2. What is the number on Michael's softball jersey?
3. How many Grammys has Michael won?
4. What year did Michael get his first Grammy?
5. Not including Michael, how many people are in his band?
6. What was the final score in the Bolton Bombers vs. Michael Jordan's Airforce game?
7. What is the car Michael drives in the *Missing You* video?
8. How many children did Michael mention by name in the dedication to *Soul of My Soul*?
9. How many songs are on the Blackjack compilation CD?

10. How many albums did Michael make that are currently out of print?
11. How many times did George Bolotin use the word "big" when referring to Michael's future?
12. How many days did it take Michael to write *Steel Bars* with Bob Dylan?
13. How many octaves is Michael's vocal range?
14. How many bedrooms are there in Michael's Connecticut home?
15. How many members were there in Blackjack?
16. How many years older than Michael is his sister Sandra?
17. How many videos are on Soul & Passion?
18. What day is Michael's birthday?
19. How many opening takes are shown at the beginning of *This Is Michael Bolton*?
20. What is Michael's lucky number?
21. What was the license plate number on Michael's maroon tour bus in September, 1994?
22. How many people call Michael "boss" while on tour?
23. What number did Jay Leno say Michael and Pavarotti looked like, standing side by side?
24. What position does Michael play on the Bolton Bombers?
25. With how many record companies has Michael signed?

(See Answers on page 126)

Song Beginnings

We all think we know all of Michael's songs all the way through. We sing along with the radio and take pride in knowing more than the chorus. Below is a list of the beginnings to some of Michael's songs. See if you can tell what songs these are the beginnings of:

1. I never knew someone who made me feel so good before...
2. You are the candle, love's the flame...
3. I could hardly believe it...
4. There was a time we thought our dream was over...
5. The tickin' of the clock...
6. Gonna break these chains around me...
7. You're knockin' on my door...
8. Here we are, just goin' through the motions...
9. Tonight I feel like a prisoner...
10. We may be strangers...
11. So now you're back...
12. You and I sailed away to a place...
13. You always said I'd never know how much I loved you...
14. Nowhere to run I know...
15. I can still remember when all I had was time...
16. Under the endless sky...
17. Now she's gone from my life...
18. It's over now...
19. In the night I hear you speak...
20. Sittin' here, just starin' at your picture...
21. You can live your life on the edge of your seat...
22. Talk about love, talk about trust...
23. Shadows fall...
24. Birds fly, they don't think twice...
25. As I'm looking back in time...
26. I was standin' in the moonlight...
26. I've been down...

"Tell me how long, can we go on this way?"

28. So you say that you can't go on...
29. So alive, when you're near...
30. Baby, we've been in and out of love so many times...
31. I said a lot of things...
32. There's always something new about you...
33. I see your face and I feel your heartache...
34. I talk to you but it's not the same as touchin' you...
35. Don't you know...
36. I've been thinkin' about the night we held each other so close...

(See Answers on page 126)

Significant Years

Below are listed some milestones in Michael's career and/or personal life. See if you can match the event with the year it occurred:

Michael opens for Bob Seger, 1983.

1.	Release of "Bah Bah Bah"	1975
2.	Married Maureen	1982
3.	Formed BLACKJACK	1965
4.	Louis became Manager	1994
5.	Toured with Kenny G.	1953
6.	First Grammy Award	1983
7.	Formed Michael Bolton Foundation	1971
8.	Received Doctorate	1987
9.	Michael was born	1968
10.	Started playing guitar	1978
11.	First #1 Hit	1995
12.	First Video	1990
13.	Death of Father	1981
14.	Gold Club was formed	1995
15.	Wrote with Bob Dylan	1973
16.	Performed with Pavarotti	1991
17.	First time producing for Cher	1960
18.	First movie appearance	1991
19.	Toured with Bob Seger	1988
20.	Appeared on *Saturday Night Live*	1991
21.	Participated in Glasnost	1990
22.	Mom rented Michael a saxophone	1983
23.	Auditioned for Shelter Records	1993
24.	Bought his Westport home	1990

(See Answers on page 127)

Michael Bolton and Diane Warren, 1987, Glasnost

*Front Cover
Soul Provider—
The Videos*

1. What member of the Bolton Management is playing baseball with Michael and the kids in the "Completely" video?
2. What color guitar is the guitar solo in the "How Can We Be Lovers" video played on?
3. What current band member is featured in the "Love Is A Wonderful Thing" video?
4. What color is the couch Michael is sitting on in the "How Am I Supposed To Live Without You" video?
5. What kind of pants is Michael wearing in the "Fool's Game" video?
6. Decked out in black and red leather, what does Michael wear on his feet in the "Everybody's Crazy" video?
7. What color is Michael's shirt in the "Soul Provider" video?
8. Where was the "Said I Loved You...But I Lied" video filmed?
9. Who was the girl in the "Missing You" video?
10. What was the color scheme of the bedroom in the "That's What Love Is All About" video?
11. Who plays drums in the video "Dock Of The Bay"?
12. What does Michael say at the end of the "Time, Love & Tenderness" video?
13. What color is the handle of the umbrella that floats upside-down in the "Can I Touch You...There?" video?
14. Which daughter appears in the "Steel Bars" video?
15. Who puts Michael up against the wall in the "Completely" video?

(See Answers on page 127)

Who Are They?

How much do you know about the people surrounding Michael? Test yourself by naming the following people:

1. Michael's business manager?
2. Michael's personal manager?
3. Michael's security co-ordinator?
4. Michael's musical director?
5. Michael's fan club president?
6. Michael's mom?
7. Executive Director of The Michael Bolton Foundation?
8. Frequent female co-writer?
9. Michael's personal softball trainer?
10. Michael's tour manager?
11. Bolton Bomber's pitcher?
12. Staff Photographer for Bolton Behind The Scenes?
13. Head of Michael's Artist Relations office?
14. The voice on Michael's 900 number?
15. Michael's personal assistant for the 1994 Tour?
16. Technical assistant to Michael (aka TOUR JESTER)?
17. Michael's production manager?
18. Front of the House mixer on the 1994 Tour?

(See Answers on page 128)

Mom Helen gets a big hug from Michael.

Which Came First?

For each question below, circle the answer that you believe would have come first chronologically as it relates to Michael's life. Then check your answers against ours.

1. **George's Boys or Joy?**
2. **Holly, Isa, or Taryn?**
3. **Columbia contract or RCA contract?**
4. **"MICHAEL BOLTON" or "EVERYBODY'S CRAZY"?**
5. **Joey Melotti or Chris Camozzi?**
6. **Divine Light Mission or vegetarianism?**
7. **Orrin or Sandra Bolotin?**
8. **BOLTON BEHIND THE SCENES or THE BOLTON BEAT?**
9. **VH1 Honors Award or The Lewis Hines Award?**
10. **The birth of the Mickey Mouse Club or Michael Bolton?**
11. **The release of "When I'm Back On My Feet Again" or the release of "Steel Bars"?**
12. **"White Christmas" or Michael Bolton?**
13. **Blackjack or disco?**
14. **SOUL & PASSION video or SOUL PROVIDER:THE VIDEOS?**
15. **THIS CLOSE for Cancer Research or The Michael Bolton Foundation?**
16. **Michael Bolton Day in Connecticut or the Homecoming Concert at the New Haven Coliseum?**
17. **SOUL PROVIDER or Soul Train?**

(See Answers on page 128)

Syracuse, New York — New York State Fair, 1995

116

Name Games

Michael Bolton has a magic that makes us all feel like we're sixteen again, so here's your chance to let loose and really act like a teenager. Remember the games you'd play with your boyfriend's name to see how compatible you were? Try it with Michael's to see if he is truly meant to be your "Soul Provider."

DIRECTIONS — In this game, each of the five vowels is assigned a base number. Next, add up the number of times each vowel appears in Michael's name and write the numbers in the proper columns. Then add up the number of times each vowel appears in your name and put those numbers in their respective columns. Last, add the columns down to get final numbers. Then compare the number of matching finals with the prediction key below to rate your chances with Michael.

Michael Playing Games

EXAMPLE
A E I O U
1 2 3 4 5
1 1 1 2 0   MICHAEL BOLTON
+1 2 1 1 1   JANE DOE PUBLIC
3 5 5 7 6

YOUR GAME
A E I O U
1 2 3 4 5
1 1 1 2 0   MICHAEL BOLTON
+_____   YOUR NAME HERE

(Jane has two matches with Michael. How many did you have?)

SCORING:
- **0 Matches** : Sorry, "You Wouldn't Know Love"
- **1 Match** : You better "Wait On Love"
- **2 Matches** : "How Can We Be Lovers" is your theme.
- **3 Matches** : You will need "Time, Love & Tenderness" to make it work.
- **4 Matches** : "Hot Love" becomes a distinct possibility.
- **5 Matches** : "Completely" one with Michael Bolton.

The Name Game: Short Game

Write your name and Michael's name out as shown below. Then cross out any letters the two names have in common. (Don't worry if one or the other of you completely obliterates the other.) Then, touching each remaining UNcrossed letter in turn, repeat the following chant: Friendship, Love, Courtship, Marriage. If our memories are correct, whatever word you touch your last uncrossed letter on, is the best that you can hope for from any relationship together.

EXAMPLE:

M ~~I~~ C H ~~A E L~~ ~~B O L T O N~~

                                                     &   Courtship

J ~~A N E~~ D ~~O E~~ P U ~~B L I C~~

YOUR GAME:

M I C H A E L   B O L T O N

&

(Your Name Here)

Jim Finlan with daughter, Nancy.

Michael Bolton's Requirements for Love

Frequently, when giving interviews, Michael gives snippets of information regarding what kind of woman he is looking for. We've waded through scores of interviews looking for those clues so that you can see how you measure up and what you may need to work on. Here, then, is what Michael Bolton wants:

bright

loves sports

good communicator

sense of humor

warm

best friend

intelligent

monogamous

long, flowing hair

ready to commit

willing to express herself

someone very secure

sweet

honest

loving

not very needy

movie buff

strong

makes him laugh

soft-spoken

knows her mind

gets along with
his daughters

And I'm worth it!

OK, here's Michael in his own words telling you exactly what he wants and what you'll get. "A soft-spoken, pretty lady always brings out the romantic in me." So basically, he's pretty easy to please. One warning, though. Michael doesn't like "women who talk too loud and swear like a man." He says, "I don't like women who want to look and sound masculine. Men are men and women are women—Thank God."

A Love Affair Through the Music

"Ain't got nothin' if you ain't got love."

Michael Bolton's songs provide the perfect mood music for a love affair, no matter what stage your love affair is in. What we have discovered is that the TITLES of Michael's songs can tell the story of the ultimate love affair, from beginning to end (with a happy ending, of course). Not quite sure if you believe it? Try reading the following list as a story. With a little imagination and the simple addition of a few I's, you's, and prepositions, it tells the whole story. Check it out:

Looking for Love
1. Ain't Got Nothing If You Ain't Got Love
2. Love Is Hard To Find
3. Save Me
4. Dreamin' Dreams

Initial Encounters
1. Take Me As I Am
2. It's Just A Feeling
3. Fallin'
4. Tell Me How You Feel
5. You've Got the Love I Need
6. Now That I've Found You

The Courtship
1. You Make Me Feel Like Lovin' You
2. Love Me Tonight
3. Can I Touch You...There?
4. Hot Love
5. By The Time This Night Is Over
6. You're All That I Need
7. Never Get Enough Of Your Love

The Union
1. Once In A Lifetime
2. I Promise You
3. Soul Provider
4. Forever
5. A Love So Beautiful
6. You Mean More To Me
7. Love Is A Wonderful Thing

Difficult Adjustments
1. How Can We Be Lovers
2. Save Our Love
3. Fighting For My Life

4. Can't Hold On, Can't Let Go
5. Don't Tell Me It's Over
6. Stay
7. Steel Bars
8. Start Breaking My Heart
9. Give Me A Reason
10. We're Not Making Love Anymore

Breakup

1. A Time For Letting Go
2. You Don't Want Me Bad Enough
3. Fighting For My Life
4. Can't Hold On, Can't Let Go
5. Missing You Now
6. Without Your Love
7. The Night Has Me Calling For You
8. Love Cuts Deep
9. Heart Of Stone

Bitterness

1. I'm Not Made Of Steel
2. I Almost Believed You
3. You Wouldn't Know Love
4. Said I Loved You...But I Lied
5. Sooner Or Later
6. It's All Comin' Back To Ya
7. I'm Aware Of Your Love
8. That's What Love Is All About

Reunion

1. Call My Name
2. From Now On
3. Soul Of My Soul
4. Forever Isn't Long Enough
5. Paradise
6. Ain't Got Nothin' If You Ain't Got Love

121

Michael's Pastimes

Over the years Michael has shared with his fans some of his favorite pastimes. Here is a sampling of his hobbies. See how your visuals compare to ours:

Music — We've all seen Michael singing in videos and in concert. Want a new visual? Imagine Michael belting out your favorite song in the shower.

Skiing — Here you have two choices, Michael soaring down the mountainside, hair flowing out behind him, knees bent, arms flexed, or hot toddies by the fire in the lodge.

Tennis — The serious Michael crouched low, brow furrowed in concentration, ready for the next shot. We like Michael (pictured right) the clown, standing at ease, all smiles, calling out "That's yours, right at you", while his partner tries desperately to cover the court.

Softball — The name of the game is win, but the uniform ain't bad either. Check out the photo section.

Reading — Michael reading his new children's book to a group of preschool children.

Movies — Although Michael has admitted to being a movie buff, we like to believe it is study for his own leading role. Picture the "agony" of having to do, oh, 20 or 30 takes of that darn love scene with Michael.

Karate — Imagine the determination, the control, the positions, movement, soft, loose, flowing clothes...

Bowling — You keeping score while Michael strides to the line, bends, thrusts his arm back and forth, smoothly releasing his ball.

Charity Event — Our idea for a charity fund-raiser is Michael in an Armani tux and diamond up for bid, and you have unlimited funds.

Traveling — When Michael travels for pleasure, he travels light. You don't need much in the way of wardrobe for those hot tropical islands.

Opera — True picture, Michael moving us to tears with the clarity and the beauty of his aria. Scene change, imagine him in one of those costumes.

Impersonations — Here's an impersonation we want him to add to his repertoire: Michael strutting the stage in only black satin pants, white wrist cuffs and a bow tie (sorry Rodney).

Basketball — Four words, white men can't jump. But, some of them look pretty good in those muscle shirts.

Billiards — Where would you like to be standing when Michael is lying half the length of the billiards table attempting to make a difficult corner shot.

Scrabble — Michael with an incredulous expression on his face, reaching for his dictionary, after seeing you score 400 points in one play of the game.

The above are Michael's known pastimes, but following are a couple we like to imagine.

Slow Dancing — Engulfed in his arms and moving at his will.

Kissing — You should be able to handle this one on your own. We're not sharing!

ANSWERS TO GENERAL TRIVIA

1. Michael Bolton
2. ESP
3. Mugs Cain, Jonathan Cain
4. Gina
5. Joy
6. Bah, Bah, Bah
7. SOUL PROVIDER
8. Suzie Benson
9. The memory of Rose Levin
10. The memory of David Warren
11. Passion Studio
12. Rocky Mountain Way
13. Taryn
14. New Haven, CT
15. Simply Mad About The Mouse
16. 1993
17. George and Helen Bolotin
18. a. Rodney Dangerfield
    b. Joe Pesci
    c. Bob Dylan
19. It's a dog
20. 1st or 3rd base
21. Bobby "The Stinger" Olah
22. Canio's solo from Leoncavallo's "I, Pagliacci"
23. It coordinates with the uniform he is wearing.
24. Louisville Slugger
25. Leoncavallo

Bonus: See alphabetical listing for *Bolton Bombers*.

CRYPTOGRAM QUOTES ANSWERS

1. "I feel like I've been mumbling my whole career" (on singing opera with Pavarotti).
2. "I was under the delusion that people who are hired to critique music are qualified" (on music critics).
3. "You become a bit like a caged animal waiting to get out" (about waiting to go on stage).
4. "That's easy for you to say...You don't have to play guitar with B.B. King." (in answer to B.B. King after he told Michael to calm down).
5. "I love to talk to the women I meet on the road when I'm traveling."
6. "My father taught me to always keep going forward..."
7. "...I consider myself a life-support system for 'The Voice.'"
8. "The Beatles got me into so much trouble in school."

ANSWERS TO LYRICS

1. Time, love and tenderness ("Time, Love & Tenderness")
2. Show you how I'm missing you now. ("Missing You Now")
3. Forever isn't long enough ("Forever Isn't Long Enough")
4. When a man loves a woman ("When A Man Loves A Woman")
5. We lived to love each other ("We're Not Making Love")
6. The very first touch ("New Love")
7. Need to reach ("Can I Touch You...There?")
8. 'till the end of time ("Steel Bars")
9. The hard times can tear you apart ("That's What Love Is...")
10. Talk about forever, baby, when you talk about us ("Soul Provider")
11. And I don't want to know ("How Am I Supposed To Live...")
12. We can't make amends ("How Can We Be Lovers")
13. You wouldn't know love ("You Wouldn't Know Love")
14. I will learn to stand tall again ("When I'm Back On My Feet Again")
15. From now on ("From Now On")
16. You came to me ("Said I Loved You...But I Lied")
17. I can carry the world on my shoulders ("I'm Not Made Of Steel")
18. And your love is like a rainbow ("The One Thing")
19. Soul of my Soul ("Soul Of My Soul")
20. You find a way to start again ("A Time For Letting Go")
21. Here in the arms of love ("In The Arms Of Love")

EXPERT

1. Secrets ("Wait On Love")
2. Every word that you said ("Gina")
3. How do I let you go ("Walk Away")
4. Call my name ("Call My Name")

MATCH THE NICKNAME ANSWERS

MICHAEL "HOW'S MY HAIR" BOLTON

JOHNNY "THE KID" DODD

LOUIS "THE JUDGE" LEVIN

BOBBY "THE STINGER" OLAH

PHIL "NEW BALL" HIGGINS

TRUMAN "MONTY" MONTFORT, JR.

JAMES "BOOBY" DANIELS

TOMMY "MUGS" CAIN

RICHIE "THE RIPPER" VAUGHN

CHRIS "THE MOZ" CAMOZZI

BUCKY "GET BACK ON THE BUS" FORD

DAVE "THE COACH" CARROLL

DAVE "BIG DADDY" REITZAS

RICHARD "RIBS" FRIEDLANDER

MARGARET "MONNY" CONE

GARY "BIG STICK" WHITEFIELD

FEINSTEIN, WEINSTEIN, AND EPSTEIN ARE THE INNER CIRCLE

124

ANSWERS TO MICHAEL'S SONGS

1. FOOL'S GAME

2. HEART OF STONE

3. THE NIGHT HAS ME CALLING FOR YOU

4. STAY

5. WHEN A MAN LOVES A WOMAN

6. BRING IT ON HOME TO ME

7. KNOCK ON WOOD

8. IN THE ARMS OF LOVE

9. GINA

10. THAT'S WHAT LOVE IS ALL ABOUT

11. WHEN I'M BACK ON MY FEET AGAIN

12. I PROMISE YOU

13. STAND UP FOR LOVE

14. CALL MY NAME

15. AIR WAVES

16. WALK AWAY

MATCH THE "JOBS" ANSWERS

1. THIS CLOSE

2. MICHAEL BOLTON FOUNDATION

3. GOOD MORNING AMERICA

4. LEVIN MANAGEMENT

5. CHILDREN'S HOSPITAL, FLA.

6. REALSONGS

7. WALLYWORLD MUSIC

8. FAN EMPORIUM, INC.

9. METROPOLITAN ENTERTAINMENT

10. ORCHESTRA NEW ENGLAND

11. HARLEM SCHOOL OF THE ARTS

12. AMERICAN AIRLINES

13. COLUMBIA RECORDS

14. CBS THIS MORNING

15. BOLTON BOMBERS

16. BMI PRESIDENT

17. HARPO, INC.

18. I.C.M.

19. UNITED NEGRO COLLEGE

20. NAT'L CHILD LABOR COMMISION

ANSWERS TO NUMBERS

1. 4
2. 7
3. 2
4. 1990
5. 9
6. 7-1, Bombers
7. Mercedes 500SL
8. 10; Isa, Holly, Taryn, Christina, Isabella, Andre, Aaron, Jessica, Taylor, and Max G.
9. 20
10. 6
11. 3
12. 2
13. 4
15. 4
16. 2
17. 12
18. 26
19. 7
20. He's NOT telling!
21. HF 13027
22. About 50
23. 10
24. 1st or 3rd
25. 5

ANSWERS TO SONG BEGINNINGS

1. HOT LOVE
2. SAID I LOVED YOU...BUT I LIED
3. HOW AM I SUPPOSED TO LIVE
4. THAT'S WHAT LOVE IS ALL
5. FOREVER ISN'T LONG ENOUGH
6. WHEN I'M BACK ON MY FEET
7. LOVE CUTS DEEP
8. WE'RE NOT MAKING LOVE
9. SAVE ME
10. SOUL OF MY SOUL
11. YOU WOULDN'T KNOW LOVE
12. CALL MY NAME
13. FROM NOW ON
14. GINA
15. NOW THAT I FOUND YOU
16. I'M NOT MADE OF STEEL
17. WAIT ON LOVE
18. WALK AWAY
19. STEEL BARS
20. DON'T MAKE ME WAIT FOR LOVE
21. AIN'T GOT NOTHIN' IF YOU AIN'T GOT LOVE
22. SOUL PROVIDER
23. THE HUNGER
24. LOVE IS A WONDERFUL THING
25. THE ONE THING
26. FOREVER EYES
27. IT'S ONLY MY HEART
28. TIME, LOVE & TENDERNESS
29. NEVER GET ENOUGH OF YOUR LOVE
30. STAND UP FOR LOVE
31. TAKE A LOOK AT MY FACE
32. NEW LOVE
33. IN THE ARMS OF LOVE
34. MISSING YOU NOW
35. I FOUND SOMEONE
36. YOU'RE ALL THAT I NEED

SIGNIFICANT YEARS
ANSWERS

1. 1968
2. 1975
3. 1978
4. 1982
5. 1990
6. 1990
7. 1993
8. 1995
9. 1953
10. 1965
11. 1990
12. 1983
13. 1981
14. 1994
15. 1991
16. 1995
17. 1988
18. 1973
19. 1983
20. 1991
21. 1987
22. 1960
23. 1971
24. 1991

ANSWERS TO VIDEO TRIVIA

1. Louis Levin
2. Hot Pink
3. Joe Turano
4. Green
5. Tight Leather
6. White sneakers
7. White or grey, with extra points if you said both. Michael wears two different shirts in the same video.
8. Paige, Arizona
9. Teri Hatcher, a.k.a. Lois Lane
10. White on white
11. Mugs
12. "That's a good warm-up. Now we're gonna do it and we're gonna sing in key this time."
13. Yellow
14. Holly
15. Paula Barbieri

ANSWERS TO WHO ARE THEY?

1. David Feinstein
2. Louis Levin
3. Jerry Mele
4. Joey Melotti
5. Joyce Logan
6. Helen
7. Jacqueline Smaga
8. Diane Warren
9. Dave Carroll
10. Dennis Rodriguez
11. Louis Levin
12. Wayne Logan
13. Judine McGinley
14. Storm N. Norman
15. Melanie Wicker
16. James "Booby" Daniels
17. Geoff Perren
18. Truman Cross Slingluff Montfort, Jr.

ANSWERS TO WHICH CAME FIRST

1. George's Boys
2. Isa
3. RCA
4. Michael Bolton
5. Joey Melotti
6. Vegetarianism
7. Orrin
8. The Bolton Beat
9. Lewis Hines Award
10. The birth of Michael Bolton
11. "When I'm Back On My Feet Again"
12. "White Christmas"
13. Disco
14. Soul Provider: The Videos
15. This Close
16. Michael Bolton Day in Connecticut
17. Soul Train

One Enchanted Evening

All the best fairy tales have not only a Prince, but a beautiful Princess, either of whom must overcome monumental difficulties before basking in the presence of their beloved. Like those storybook heroines, we, too, experienced a few difficulties on our way to the Ball.

When we first received our invitation to the *Second Annual Celebrity Tennis, Softball, and Black Tie Gala* for The Michael Bolton Foundation, we were delighted to find that we were not only offered tickets to the tennis matches and softball games, but the gala, as well. The fax line hummed with the speed of our reply.

When the tickets arrived and we learned the name of the hotel the gala would be held in, we called right away to make reservations to stay there. We did not want to show up in a hotel shuttle van for this event.

"The only rooms we have left are on the Security Floor," the hotel clerk told us. "Would that be all right?"

All right? That would be wonderful! Although we remained calm on the phone, we danced and giggled around the kitchen as soon as the receiver hit the hook. Who knew who else might be staying on the Security Floor! And our amenities included an exclusive courtyard buffet and cocktails, mineral water in the bathrooms, the daily paper delivered to our door, plush robes and various other small details. Quite a difference from the Mom and Pop motels we had been staying in for our other Bolton adventures.

So once the tickets and the hotel had been procured, the only thing left to worry about was our clothes. Well, not exactly. Since we had no idea exactly who (or how well-connected) our dinner companions would be, we spent one entire evening sitting around in hysterical laughter, imagining all the small embarrassments and indignities we may be subjected to. You know, things like: a little bit of green stuff caught between your teeth when smiling at The Man, toilet tissue stuck to our shoes, falling, spilling things, sliding our dinner off our plates while attempting to cut it in a lady-like manner, choking, sneezing — the possibilities for personal humiliation seemed endless.

And as to the clothes, well, what was proper for an afternoon tennis match and a Black Tie Gala? Our next call was to the Society Editor of our nearest city newspaper. Evening wear was purchased, outfits put together, and at last we were ready.

Once more, we departed in the middle of the night and once more, our driver had to run an obstacle course to get us to our goal. The first hour of the trip was undertaken in a very heavy fog, and we had barely made it through the fog when a huge semi started fading over into our lane just as we got next to it. We moved onto the shoulder, speeding up to get by it and scared ourselves silly. A revolving red light came on immediately behind us. With our hearts racing in our chests, we pulled over to accept the speeding ticket the uniformed State Trooper wrote out for us. The rest of the journey passed without incident.

After a few small wrong turns in Connecticut, we finally pulled up under the large canopy in front of our hotel, right next to all the limos. A uniformed doorman opened our car doors and helped us out, as a bellhop loaded our luggage onto a cart. The parking attendant took our car away as we were being led through the revolving doors into the lobby by the doorman.

Did we say lobby? Well, this one was not anything like the hotel lobbies we had seen in movies. Immediately inside the doors was the usual small, gracious sitting area with sofas and armchairs strategically placed for conversational ease, but beyond that was a huge, four story atrium, complete with trees, gardens, ponds, a small waterfall, stone walkways, and scattered throughout were arched bridges connecting the walkways. At one end of the garden was a gazebo housing the piano bar and at the other end was another gazebo forming the base of the garden cafe. The hotel desk and various shops lined the outside perimeter.

Walking through that door was like Dorothy opening her door on the land of Oz. Once inside, it became a different world. EVERYONE was pleasant and respectful, from the desk clerk to the bellhops to the shop clerks. Although our room was not ready yet, we were provided with a temporary room to freshen up in before the tennis match.

After phoning down for our car, we took the elevator back to the lobby, stopping at the special Michael Bolton Foundation desk for directions to the tennis match.

While we were chatting with the people there, Chris Evert strolled by on her way to the limo that would take her to the match.

The directions we received were simple and clear, and minutes later we were at the tennis club. The matches were being played on two indoor courts. A quick perusal of the program told us which court Michael would be playing on and we took seats in the stands beside it. Across the room, on the other side of the courts, were tables and chairs for the players and various other guests. We spent the afternoon watching Rosie Casals, Chris Evert, Barry Bonds, Franco Harris, Nicollette Sheridan, and Michael Bolton joke around, mug for the cameras, and play some really good tennis. At the end of the matches, we were given complimentary tickets to the Bombers softball game that afternoon (which had been postponed from the day before because of rain) but we had to get back to the hotel and prepare ourselves for the gala.

Once we were finally back in our own room, we took a few minutes to sit and savor our anticipation. But soon, too excited to sit for long, we were showering, powdering, curling, polishing, dressing, and primping for our long-awaited dinner with Michael. Ready at last, we took one long, final look in the mirror and nervously went down to the reception area.

Entering the wide, long hallway that would take us to the Silent Auction display area, we joined the crowd of tuxedoed men and gowned women already gathered there. Beautiful flower arrangements lined the hall and a large glittering Pegasus had been sculpted in ice and placed near the grand piano that Joey Melotti was sitting at, accompanying the lively conversations with music. We checked in at the Foundation desk and received our table assignment, then picked up glasses of sparkling champagne and joined the people circling the auction displays.

There were all sorts of items to be auctioned, from beaded handbags to gift baskets (for him, her, and the dog), from autographed rock guitars to sports memorabilia. We were most impressed with the signed Peter Max painting, the Andre Agassi memorabilia, and the autographed Michael Bolton softball paraphernalia (We had not yet received notice that we had won an autographed softball bat from a contest we had entered a month before) .

The first time we circled the displays we were looking at the items in them; the second time we circled we looked at the people standing at them. We smiled and said hello to several members of Michael's band, his management, and his brother. After we made small talk with one of the women from the Foundation, we stood quietly chatting among ourselves and turned to find a tv camera aimed right at us.

At last we had exhausted our supply of polite social chatter and were ready to take our seats at our table. The dining room doors were still closed however, so we found the door that would open to our table area, and lounged against the wall next to it, sipping from our glasses. A few feet further along the same wall, Chris Camozzi (Michael's guitar player) and his party had gathered to talk. Suddenly, the hallway lights blinked twice and a small crowd of people came around the corner towards us, lead by several very large security guards. In the center of the group was Michael, accompanied by Nicollette Sheridan. As Michael stopped to talk to Chris, a guard took position right in front of us, moving the people gathering there away. Hands out in front of him, he moved towards the crowd saying, "You'll have to move back. I'm sorry, you just have to move back." We were momentarily afraid he meant us, too, but he looked right at us, smiled, nodded, and turned back to the throng, moving them back and clearing the aisle. We don't know if he thought we were with Chris or if he just had seen us so often recently that he thought we were someone he should know; we didn't care. We got to stay there and Michael had to pass right by us to get in the dining room.

We waited for him to make his way to us and then, there he was. When he saw us, he got a look of recognition on his face and smiled widely, saying, "Hi." He paused for a moment and made a move like he would have taken our hands but they were full of champagne glasses and evening bags, so he thought better of it. We returned his smile and his greeting and seconds later he was led on down the hall to the entrance.

We imagine Nicollette asking him who we were and him replying, "I can't remember their names..." but freely admit that this is wishful thinking. We do know, however, that the people in our immediate vicinity were looking at us as though they were trying to figure out who we were.

Together, we moved into the dining room to take our places at the table. The tables were round, seating ten, and each one had a centerpiece of flowers and candles. Crystal and silver sparkled in the glow and the tablecloth was heavy against our legs.

A young couple was also seated at our table and we struck up a conversation with them. She hadn't even known about the gala, her boyfriend had seen it in the paper and got tickets to surprise her. We agreed he was a sweetheart beyond comparison and told them a few of our Bolton adventures. "Oh, so you're kind of...groupies," he said after a slight hesitation.

She immediately turned and smacked him against the shoulder. "Do they look like groupies to you?" she demanded. He stutteringly began apologizing all over himself, but we laughingly assured him that, yes, that was EXACTLY what we were as far as Michael Bolton was concerned.

Waiters appeared with our salad course and the house lights went even lower. Large screens in each corner of the room came alive with a mini-documentary on "The Michael Bolton Foundation" and its works. Throughout the rest of the meal (a cooked vegetable plate, pasta primavera, and a wonderful molded chocolate, ice cream, and raspberry dessert) we were entertained by singers, a choir, and comedians. The auction began while we were finishing dessert and having coffee; it was thrilling.

Bidding started slowly but halfway through the auction, donators started increasing their gifts (one donation of two airline tickets soon became FOUR airline tickets to any place in the world) and bids increased like crazy. When the puppy was finally put up for auction, it went for over $20,000! (It was a chocolate lab and very cute.) It was exciting just watching the action and the crowds response.

When the auction ended, Michael's band took the stage and went off into a mini-concert that showcased each member's talents. Finally, Michael strolled through the tables, weaving his magic and singing his way to the stage. As hard as it is to believe, some of the people had left before that point and we were able to move into a better viewing vantage point at an empty table closer to the stage. When the last note ended, we made our way

out into the hallway with the rest of the crowd. The women were presented with Revlon gift bags as they left so everyone went home with something.

We went as far as the piano bar at the gazebo just outside the auction hallway. Ordering drinks and sinking down into the comfortable chairs, we watched until the crowd of people leaving the gala became a trickle. It was then that we noticed that one of our group had left without her purse and she had to go back for it.

Her feet were aching in her new heels, so she tried to talk one of the others in our group into going back for her, but it was a no go. She began the long trek down the hallway once more. Halfway down, she saw Nicollette with several other women walking towards her, talking quietly. They didn't look up and she passed by them without saying a word. About 10 feet behind them, however, was Michael, walking totally alone, abandoned even by his security staff. He looked up, saw her and smiled. As he continued walking towards her, he said, "Hi, I'm glad you could come. Did you have a good time?"

"I had a wonderful time," she breathed, her feet suddenly walking on air.

"Good. See you again," he said, and they passed by, continuing on their respective ways. She retrieved her bag and made her way back to the group, glorying in the fact that she had had Michael all to herself for that endless 30 seconds. Giddy and flushed, she sank down into her seat, hugging herself (and her experience) closely.

"We just saw Michael," we said. "He waved when he went by."

"I know, I spoke to him on his way out," she attempted to say calmly. We stared at her in amazement as she told us what had transpired in the hallway. She smiled widely when she repeated his last words.

We had had an evening we would always remember and a happy ending that surpassed our dreams. And yes, we were quite sure he would be seeing us again!

"I love playing baseball and I love my life, but where my music has taken me now, and having the kind of audience I have now, is such a blessing that all I want is more of the same."

—Michael Bolton
on *Jonathon Ross Presents*

133

Index

N

O

P

Q

R

S

T

Acknowledgments

To Tyler, for providing much needed comic relief, and Paul, for his support, understanding, and easy acceptance of every research outing and brainstorming marathon, all our love and a deep and heartfelt thank-you.

To Phil, all our love and deepest thanks for his love, patience, and endless taping throughout the craziness. Thank you to Phillip for "our Ashley," to Sarah and her friends at school for finding this all so cool, and to Ruth for her unyielding sensitive support that made every step of the way possible.

A huge thank you to Wayne Logan for allowing us to go through his files of wonderful photos and for putting up with the crazy late hours. And to two dear unsung heroes, Cosette and Roy Logan, who work endless hours each day sorting through and organizing the thousands of letters the are received each week for Michael. Thank you's galore to Judine McGinley, Vicki Lovett, Janet Schupp and Kathy Benoit for their undying loyalty and friendship.

Special thanks to "Andretti" and "Olivier" who were always there with us, Stacy "O.J." Shannon for her heroic hurtles, Cheryl "Missy" Hill for reading every word over and over until it was right, and Doug and Mary at Replay Records who helped without asking why. And to Matthew, who endured the late nights and the fast-food dinners with almost no complaint, our love, gratitude, and the promise of a home-cooked meal.

And to you, the Michael Bolton fan that is reading this...you are who this book was written for.
Thank you for being there in spirit for all of us!